Coming of Age
in the
Middle East

Coming of Age
in the
Middle East

Trevor Mostyn

KPI

LONDON AND NEW YORK

First published in 1987 by KPI Limited
11 New Fetter Lane, London EC4P 4EE, England

Distributed by
Routledge & Kegan Paul Ltd
11 New Fetter Lane, London, EC4P 4EE, England,

Routledge & Kegan Paul Inc
29 West 35th Street, New York, N.Y. 10001, USA

Set in Bembo by Columns of Reading
and printed in Great Britain by
St. Edmundsbury Press, Bury St. Edmunds, Suffolk

ISBN 0-7103-0208-8

To Ann Mary Fielding,
the novelist who inspired me to write

When I was a child, I spake as a child . . . ;
but when I became a man, I put away childish things.
For now we see through a glass, darkly.

(I Corinthians 13:11-12)

Contents

Preface

I wish to offer my warmest thanks to Peter Hopkins who inspired me to write this book over lunch in a Riyadh hotel, and to Carol Gardiner who edited it not only with meticulous care and personal concern but also with a great feeling for the story and a great acumen for the issues involved. I am extremely grateful to Albert Hourani for reading the proofs.

This book does not aim to make any political statement. A simple record of my travels in the Middle East over a period of twenty years, it is intended faithfully to reflect the region as a catalyst to the development of my own life from carefree youth to maturity and marriage. It is not intended to praise or condemn any country although it will, I hope, reflect the love and respect that two decades of familiarity have bred in me for the Middle East and for so many of its peoples. As an Orientalist, I have attempted to describe these countries as I would describe England, my own country. Many of my closest friends, within this book and without, are Arab or Iranian and those who understand that friendship involves criticism and even healthy banter will, I know, forgive me for treating the region with honesty rather than flattery. What I have written is influenced by a certain feeling of 'belonging' to the Middle East and by a sadness over the breakdown of values that its sudden exposure to the West has sometimes led to.

1

Last pasha at the
Golden Hotel

I flew into Cairo, a penniless student, on a bustling summer's night in 1969. Egypt's year-long war of attrition with Israel had turned the city into a place of gloom. There was an attempt at almost total blackout at night. Shops, hotels and public buildings were protected by anti-shrapnel brick walls which were clumsy obstacles to the boisterous crowds gabbling their ways through the rush-hour streets at dusk. My flight from Tobruk in Libya had left me with about £10. The rest of my Edinburgh University grant had been spent on my journey.

Just off Sulaiman Pasha Square is Sulaiman Pasha Street, now Talaat Harb Street. I saw a crooked sign in yellow above an anti-shrapnel wall with the simple words 'Golden Hotel' written. Like all the buildings in central Cairo it was Rococo with crumbling, blackened stucco. Cairo was still a Victorian city, laid out in symmetrical squares and boulevards. It reflected the wish of the Khedive Ismail to make Cairo a copy of Paris after he had visited the International Exhibition there in 1867.

Ismail was the descendant of Mohammed Ali, the Albanian Ottoman officer who was to create a new Egypt and a dynasty which ended with King Farouk and Colonel Nasser's revolution of 1952. He had taken one look at Haussman's Paris and decided to turn Cairo into a replica of it in two years to impress the crowned heads of Europe invited to attend the hedonistic celebrations to inaugurate the opening of the Suez Canal in 1869. Ismail was, in particular, obsessed with the beauty of the Empress Eugénie, the wife of Napoleon III, and had a palace, the Gezira Palace in Zamalek, built for her by German architects. He also built an exquisite wooden opera house beside the Ezbekiya

Gardens which were laid out by the Parisian landscape gardener Barillet-Deschamps. The opera house was supposed to be an exact copy of Milan's La Scala and Verdi was commissioned to write *Aïda* to be performed in it for the canal's inauguration, but the score did not arrive in time and *Rigoletto* was performed instead.

Ismail's dreams were in vain, for his spending led to Egypt's bankruptcy and his own abdication which was followed by British rule under Lord Cromer. Nor was his infatuation with Eugénie, a 'notorious virgin', reciprocated. When Louis-Napoleon had asked the way to her bedroom in Paris she had promptly replied, 'By the chapel, sire,' and to bed her he had been obliged to marry her and make her his empress. The Khedive's relationship with the pious woman clearly remained platonic.

I was attracted by the simple name of the hotel and went behind the wall and inside. A tall Nubian *bawwab* or door-keeper, in striped and dirty *gelebiah* and with a beautiful, visionary face, leant against the heavy, metal-studded wooden door. At the top of the steps was a decayed wooden lift of the Belle Epoque. I went into the office on the left and saw the shiny bald head of an old man with big ears, bowed over a desk.

He glanced up from his paperwork and smiled a mischievous, winking smile. He wore a suit, tie and collar, all extremely grubby. I asked him for a room. He replied in an impeccable Oxford accent and with a paternal smile, 'I'm sure we can arrange something for you.' The cost of the room with shower was £E2.50 (about £1.50). His name was Fares Seraphim and he has remained a close friend to this day. He had studied at Keble College, Oxford, and umpired the college cricket team. His family, an old Coptic one, had owned extensive lands around Minya in Lower Egypt as well as most of the buildings of which the Golden Hotel was one. 'Nasser', he explained, with a philosophical smile, 'expropriated us of nearly all our estates but thanks to bureaucratic bungling they forgot this building. I don't want to make a profit. Running this hotel is my hobby. I want this to be a happy family.' In the Golden Hotel I was to find myself the only non-Arab. Almost all the guests were Palestinians. Some were members of Al-Fateh. By the end of the year several had been killed on raids into Israel, then still officially known on maps as 'Occupied Palestine'.

Mohammed the *bawwab* and another Mohammed, the cleaning man, who had a squint eye, took me to my room. It was a dingy, smelly room and a naked light bulb dimly lit up the stained yellow walls. Cockroaches scampered around the floor of the shower. In those days I was used to much worse and I was delighted with the hotel's cosiness. A mouse appeared in my room so I began leaving a piece of cheese by my door each day. The mouse recognised the concordat and collected its daily cheese but never annoyed me by running around the room or jumping on my bed.

During the first weeks of that baking summer I spent much of my time with two English friends from the School of Oriental and African Studies in London. We were naive about Egypt. The Cairenes were friendly but the general atmosphere under Nasser was that of East European gloom. You could barely buy a razor blade in the shops and although I never saw the poverty I had seen in India the policy seemed to be one of bringing everyone down to an equal level of tolerable poverty. The poverty that came in the 1970s seemed more terrible. The gorgeous weddings at the Hilton that became common in Sadat's era, and reminiscent of the corrupt period under King Farouk, were unheard-of under Nasser. The rich were keeping a very low profile.

Proud of our Arabic, we made errors that cost us much pain. My friends had long hair and wherever we went people shouted, smiling, 'Saida.' Taking the word to mean 'woman' – another oft-used phrase for us had been *Khunfus* ('Beatle') – we became furious each time. One day a youth shouted 'Saida' when we were walking with an Egyptian friend and the taller of my friends ran up to the offending youth, grabbed him by the collar and told him to go to hell. The youth looked utterly astonished and slipped away, casting us furtive looks. Our Egyptian friend laughed and asked us why we had treated him like this.

'We hate being called "Saida",' we replied. 'He's calling us "Women".'

'Women?' said our friend. 'He's saying you are "welcome".'

We each stood rooted to the spot with shame. For weeks we had misunderstood the word and memories of this repeated incident flashed through our minds. We ran through the streets in search of the youth but never found him.

Cairo in those days was a city at war. It reflected the memories of my parents' generation. You could barely see your way through the streets at night. There were no street lights. Car lights were painted blue and curtains had to be drawn across windows at all times. There were nightly raids over the factories at Helwan and Egyptian families would merrily gather at their balconies to watch the anti-aircraft tracers and listen to roaring Israeli jets.

Everyone had enough to eat if they were willing to queue early at the co-operative butchers' and bakers'. The rich, under constant threat of sequestration, no longer vaunted their wealth. They tended, indeed, to boast old clothing to hide it, a far, far cry from the later years under Sadat when the wealthy came blithely out of the woodwork. Each week in Cairo there was one non-meat day. There were two kinds of food, food for the poor (mostly *foul*, the staple Egyptian black beans) and food for the rich, Western dishes at Western prices.

Pathetic soldiers, sons of *fellahin* from the banks of the Nile, were to be seen everywhere in their baggy uniforms. By and large they were shunned for having failed their country in the disastrous defeat of the June 1967 war. To the foreigner, and there were few of us in Cairo in those days, it seemed that every second man was in the secret police. Yet there was little that was secret about them. Sitting in Groppi's Italian pastry shop with my Palestinian friends, I would only have to open my mouth for men in shabby suits to crane their necks towards us, pulling at their earlobes. But with Palestinians I could say virtually what I liked. The Palestinians were the blue-eyed children of the war and no Englishman would be arrested in their company.

Yet the word *jasus* – spy – was on everybody's lips. Sitting on the balcony of the Golden Hotel with the Palestinians one day I noted that one of them refused to speak to me and eventually walked away. I asked the others why.

'He thinks you're a spy,' they said.

'Why?' I asked.

'Because you've studied Arabic for a year and it's still so bad.'

It was a Catch-22 situation. Had my Arabic been excellent the suspicious would have suspected me of being a spy for perfecting it.

The gentleness of the Egyptians is something that always strikes the foreigner. Night after night we listened to Nasser's impassioned speeches about the Zionist enemy and yet this anger was never reflected in the people of the street. Jews were never persecuted for being Jews. I had found more anti-Semitism in Libya, which had been and always would be totally out of the show. Yet in Egypt the wounded were seen daily trailing into the city from troop-trains which brought them back from the horrors of their slow suicide in bunkers along the banks of the Canal.

Beneath the austere pattern of the everyday, Cairo's glittering social life went on. At parties I would meet the well-spoken officers back from the Canal. Some were contemptuous of the war effort and devoid of patriotism. They scoffed at the war and talked about America. Their indifference was one of the chronic causes of Egypt's abysmal defeat. Technically they were forbidden to associate with foreigners but one met them at elite intellectual parties given by lecturers at the American University. Yet despite their cynicism they were fighting alongside their men. One – on 48-hour leave from the Canal front – told me: 'You know, it's a terrible thing, this kind of war. You go to the front and start killing the enemy across the water and you see your friends dying all around you. Yet nothing is ever gained, not even your First World War hillock to be lost again on the following day.'

But if the Egyptians, even in those days, were already weary of war, Cairo's hundreds of thousands of Palestinians were becoming more determined every day. Funerals of Al-Fateh officers would fill the whole of Sulaiman Pasha Street. The hysterical crowds would move through the street shouting for war as the long brown coffin swayed over their heads. Egyptians and foreigners would disappear into the buildings to escape the roaring crowds, a prelude to the massive take-over of Amman by Palestinian guerrillas one year later. Throughout Cairo was the poster of a commando with a machine-gun and beneath it the words: 'We are fighting today to create the new Palestine of tomorrow, a unified and democratic non-sectarian Palestine in which Muslim, Christian and Jew worship, work and enjoy equal rights. This is no Utopian dream or false promise, for the Palestinians have always lived in peace, Muslims, Christians and Jews in the Holy Land.'

My sympathies had from childhood been moulded by the British news films of Dachau and Auschwitz which followed the Pathe News, and I was essentially pro-Israeli. But the Palestinians in Cairo always spoke of a war against Zionism, never against the Jews. When I spoke of Palestine to one Palestinian girl she simply said, 'It's our land. We want to go home.'

Some years later in Saudi Arabia I met a Palestinian in Riyadh who told me a story which reminded me of those days in Cairo when the Palestinians were still filled with hope. After two years working as a public relations man with a Saudi company he had managed to gain a permit to visit his parents in the Israel-occupied Gaza Strip.

'I found my family after all those years huddled together in a basement flat,' he told me. 'One day I visited the West Bank and walked over the hills to our family farm which had been taken by the Israelis in the 1967 War. I approached the farm door and knocked. The door was opened by a young pale-skinned girl.

'I explained why I had come. I explained that I didn't wish to trouble her. I simply wanted to look once again at the farm that was ours and remember my childhood. The smile went from the girl's face and she began weeping. She told me that she was a Turkish Jew and that she, too, was a refugee. "Until you came," she said, "I believed that we had the right to be here. But now I see that we are both refugees." I looked at the girl and realised how much we two, Jews and Arabs, shared in common. We had both been dispossessed, we had both been persecuted, and for both the persecution had forced us to succeed everywhere in the diaspora in order to survive.'

The Palestinians in Cairo, as they were later to become in Jordan and then in Lebanon, were truly a people in exile. Well educated and financially interdependent, they helped each other in a way that was, ironically, like the Jews. Indeed, they jokingly referred to themselves as the 'new Jews of the Middle East'. The sufferings they were to endure over the next two decades bore out this comment well.

They sometimes echoed the Palestinian phrase '*La route de Tel Aviv passe par Amman.*' Their first war was against the compromising leaders of the Arab world, their second against Israel itself. One told me that the Qur'an allowed the sacrifice of a quarter of the Ummah (Nation) for the sake of the whole Ummah. This would justify the fact that of every ten commandos that entered Israel, only five ever returned. They all admired Arafat and regarded him not Nasser as the strong man of the Middle East. 'Arafat wants war with Israel. If Nasser had the chance he would make peace and to hell with Palestinians.'

In spite of increasing Israeli air raids during this war of attrition, Cairo remained a strangely peaceful city. The cinemas showed films of Britain's resistance to the Blitzkrieg to sharpen war awareness. When, in the Battle of Britain, the BBC newscaster announced, 'Yesterday the RAF shot down twenty planes. We returned with the loss of only two,' the Egyptian audience roared with laughter. They had never been fooled by the incessant propaganda of the Egyptian media.

When I spoke with a journalist on Egypt's official newspaper, *Al-Ahram*, he assured me that it would be unfeasible to publish the true facts. 'If we told the truth Cairo University would be out on the streets in thousands, as happened shortly after the June (1967) War, demanding a stronger leadership and reforms in the army. On the other hand if we exaggerate real victories too much they would be out in the streets shouting: "If we're so strong, then why don't we defeat Israel now?" Our reporters often come back from the Canal with wonderful stories they simply can't publish.'

Once I met some American students in the street and invited them back for coffee. They were studying in Athens; some were also Jewish. As we entered Salah's room, crowded with Palestinians and filled with smoke, I introduced my friends, explaining in advance that some were Jewish. I've never seen such a welcome. Everyone got up and made places, tea was brought. 'Our cousins, our brothers,' said the Palestinians with complete sincerity. The Americans were astonished, not so much because they expected hostility, as they were too ignorant to know much about the Arab-Israeli conflict. One, indeed, a gentile, said quietly after a conversation in which the Palestinians had talked Palestine with me for over an hour, 'Just one small question, please, could you explain the difference between an Israeli and a Palestinian?' But the Jews among them clearly did not expect these lavish attempts at fraternisation.

One day I was with the Palestinians in the Hilton. There was a delightful Arab woman with us. She turned to me and said, frivolously, 'I'm a Jew.' 'Yes, an Egyptian Jew,' said one of the Palestinians with pride. She was their trophy, their token Jewess. Despite the theatre I began to realise in those far-off days that the average Palestinians, even, indeed, the radical and guerrilla fighters, were not remotely anti-Jewish. You only had to slip up with the misnomer 'anti-Semite' for a Palestinian to stress earnestly, 'How can we be anti-Semite when we are Semites ourselves, and the Jews are our brothers?'

Today in Egypt all that is Islamic and, in particular, the most extreme symbol of Islamic identity, the Ikhwan or Muslim Brethren, is ubiquitous. In those wartime, socialist days, long before the Third World had despaired of competing with the West and before hard cash from the Gulf had brought the Mosque clearly into the limelight, Islamic feelings were subdued. Nasser gave the people hope through rhetoric and through his own charisma. He gave them bread and spoke of the approaching day when Egypt would produce everything from a pin to a tank. But underlying all this fundamentalists were active underground, and when he realised that he was unable to win them he crushed them and hanged their leaders.

I met a girl called Leila at the American University. Leila and I walked one day through the howling streets of winter's dusk to the railway-line beside Ataba Square. We held hands and spoke in French. Leila stood clearly waiting for me to kiss her but I panicked and missed the moment and in missing the moment I knew that I had brought an abrupt end to our unspoken and undeclared romance. Pretty, bourgeois Leila was to have represented my attempt to escape the shabby poverty of my student life, a life filled with the talk of war and of the deaths of Palestinian friends, and move quietly to the drawing-room gentility of another Cairo.

Leila belonged to a world far removed from that of the

Palestinians with their revolutionary despair and their whores
and their whisky in broken cups. She belonged to that
thoughtless, cynical caste of Egyptian women who spent most of
their day dressing up and making up for the evening party. She
had once kept me waiting for an hour and a half with her girl-
friends in the drawing-room of her student hostel. 'She'll be
down in a minute,' they reassured me at half-hour intervals. It
was a test but I was too shy to complain or leave. An Egyptian
or a Palestinian would have shouted the house down. At the
railway-line Leila had turned, close to me, smiling, challenging.
We were alone. In my inner mind I was passionately embracing
her but I did nothing. My moment was lost. We walked back to
the University where I said good-bye inadequately and she
turned from me coolly and walked away to hail a taxi.

I returned, weakly, to the Golden Hotel where I revealed my
sad tale to the Palestinians. They laughed sympathetically. Issa said,
'We must find Trevor a woman. He hasn't had one for five months.'

One evening I was discussing the 'cause' with them in
Salah's tiny room when Jihad, a big, jolly Palestinian, half
guerrilla, half businessman, got up to leave. A madame was to
bring a girl to his flat in Adly Street in half an hour. As he
reached the door he turned to me and asked me kindly whether I
would like a girl, too. 'Don't worry, it's on the house,' he
assured me. My Nordic celibacy had evidently been discussed
among them. Salah filled my glass with whisky and with some
trepidation I agreed to this blind tryst. Jihad told me to come to
his flat after one hour and left.

I drank my whisky in one gulp and the glass was refilled.

'Jihad gets nice girls,' said Abd-Ullah.

'Tonight it's a young one,' said Issa.

The conversation moved back to Palestine and to a recent
skirmish on the Canal when the Israelis had killed tens of
Egyptian soldiers on the opposite bank. I had drunk a great deal
of whisky when Salah suggested it was time I left for my rendez-
vous. I was very drunk and could barely stand. I was nervous
and I was thinking of sweet, innocent Leila and the missed kiss
by the railway-line. When I reached the door the twenty
Palestinians raised their glasses to wish me well as if I were a
fida'i on a guerrilla sortie.

I stumbled down Sulaiman Pasha Street in the gloamings, through the seething crowds of pretty Cairene women, old Nubians in white *gelebiahs*, peanut sellers with their smoking braziers, pashas in Savile Row suits and red fezzes. I turned left into Adly Street and went up in the old, oak-panelled lift to Jihad's flat.

He opened the door to me, beaming – a fat, happy, clever man full of warmth and potential cruelty. His drawing-room was pseudo-elegant 'Louis-Farouk', with grotesque gilded chairs and a huge, gilt-framed print of *The Haywain*. I sat nervously in a copious sofa and he poured me a large tumbler of whisky.

An exquisitely pretty girl with long black hair and wearing a white silk negligée appeared dreamily at the bedroom door. 'Nadia, this is Trevor. Trevor's a good friend.' She smiled with genuine warmth, the carefree warmth of an actress rather than that of a prostitute. She was unmannered, charming. Her regular encounters with Jihad had clearly led to a real friendship.

'I've got her sister coming for you,' said Jihad, 'but you're welcome to have Nadia while you're waiting.' He led me to the bedroom where pink sheets were scattered about an enormous brass bedstead. Nadia took my arm with sisterly affection and said, 'OK?' I felt moved by her and deeply, emotionally amorous. 'Don't worry, I'm paying,' said Jihad. Yet, physically so moved, I was mentally repelled by the sheer decadence of the atmosphere. Slaking one's lust for money was one thing. Sharing a prostitute was, somehow, another and I said no, I would wait for the girl Jihad had chosen for me. Nadia shrugged and sat down. Jihad poured me another whisky.

We sat, the three of us, drinking. I talked politely to Nadia about her family. Then there was a knock at the door. Jihad opened. An angry middle-aged woman came in followed by a slim, sulky 17-year-old. They nodded at me abstractedly. I began to feel that I was in the audience of a play in which I might, at any moment, be asked to participate. More tumblers of whisky were poured. The woman was complaining to Jihad in such fast and angry Arabic that I couldn't understand and Jihad was nodding with sympathy. Nadia was telling her to stop nagging and I suddenly realised that the madame was the mother of the two girls. Jihad said something and the madame beamed at me.

But the sister was crying.

I asked Jihad what was being said but he assured me that it was nothing important. I liked the girl, didn't I? That was all that mattered. I watched the girl, through my drunken eyes, crying and suddenly felt as far away from sleeping with her as a geriatric monk. I asked Jihad again what was wrong. 'Nothing important,' he said. 'It's just that her mother is insisting she sleeps with rich old men and she doesn't want to. It's just a family quarrel. The girl's stubborn. Anyway, it's OK now. You can take her into my bedroom.'

The girl gave me a petulant, well-trained smile before turning back to her mother and grumbling once again about her disgust for old men. Being in my early 20s and looking somewhat younger, I could take some comfort in the knowledge that I was not an object of her disgust but I was, nevertheless, desperate to escape from a scene which I found utterly traumatic.

I got up. 'I'm sorry but I have to go,' I said. Jihad told me not to be ridiculous. I was just what the girl wanted. She had said so and that was half the point of her argument with her mother. The madame told Jihad crossly that she hadn't come all this way for nothing. The girl, still a pretty baby, turned to me with a clumsy come-hither smile, pouting her lips. I felt idiotically drunk and depressed and made for the door. Jihad followed, trying to coax me back. The madame talked crossly to the girl, encouraging her to do her homework; use her charms to lure me to the bedroom. The girl turned coldly to her mother and replied that it was her fault that I was going away.

I escaped down the stairs and walked gloomily back to the Golden Hotel where I tried to return Mohammed the Nubian *bawwab*'s bright smile. I went up to Salah's room. It was filled, as before, with Palestinians like communards in a tiny hall of revolution.

'How was it?' they cried in unison. 'How was she, here, here and here?' they asked, moulding their hands to breasts and hips and thighs.

'I didn't stay,' I replied. 'Her mother was trying to make her sleep with old men.' The statement must have seemed gratuitous. Salah, I knew, understood that my Western conscience had influenced me; conscience or hypocrisy or cowardice – but he understood. The friendship went from out of the eyes of the others. For them sentimentality over a tart was pathetic. It reflected human failure rather than spiritual vision. Several of them got up as one and left, barely saying good-bye to me. Soon only my two close friends, Salah and Issa, remained.

Salah said, 'I understand your feelings but the average Arab does not. We don't sleep with our fiancées. They must remain virgins until they are married. I have been engaged for eight years but my fiancée remains a virgin. Even if we lie with our fiancées we only "brush" them in bed. We must not break their hymens. We only make love with prostitutes. For us prostitution is a way of life, not a subject for moral debate. We have no time for moral dilemmas when we have lost our homeland and our friends are dying and being tortured in Palestine.'

It was evident that prostitution in Cairo during that sad, poverty-making, wartime period was often a freelance business in which married women from the slums of Bulac and Shoubra would seek a little extra money to feed their families. Despite the dictates of Islamic morality, prostitution among married women did not have the stigma attached to it in Europe.

The emphasis on pre-marriage virginity was absolute but I knew well brought-up, unmarried girls who had lost their virginity and had visited the hospital before the wedding night to have their hymens sewn up. Sometimes a loving suitor agreed to marry a girl who was not a virgin. The couple would take a phial of cow's blood to the marriage couch and scatter it on the sheets to display it ceremoniously to the eager grannies waiting outside.

Most of the Egyptian girls I knew had endured the minor circumcision, clitorectomy; the clitoris had been shorn but not completely removed. The psychological horror of this operation, and the physical horror of the major circumcision in which very much more is cut away, is described in chilling detail in Nawal el Saadawi's *The Hidden Face of Eve*. Circumcisions in Upper Egypt and in the Sudan can be truly horrible with such mutilation carried out that the girls die of bleeding. Those who survive lose all interest in sex as something pleasurable.

One evening a depressive English student from my Arabic class visited me in my gloomy one-star hotel room to test me on

Arabic vocabulary for an examination the following day. He played the clown and made people laugh but was a tragic figure and was, I guessed, at least latently homosexual. In any case, he was a lonely man and I was glad to be kind to him. He had no friends and was mentally unstable and was extremely afraid of women. But he was intelligent and a brilliant Arabist.

As he was quizzing me on Arabic economic terminology there was a knock on my door. It opened and a giant black Nubian woman appeared. I was later to discover that a sympathetic Iraqi down the corridor had observed that few woman ever visited me in my seedy room with its heavy 1930s furniture and had sent the lady to me as a gift. My colleague took one look at the colossal virago with her shining black, toothy face and turned straight back to his vocabulary list, pretending that she didn't exist.

'What is the Arabic for "Circumstantial evidence"?' he continued. I laughed and asked the woman what she wanted. She approached him and began stroking his neck with her giant hand murmuring, 'Ayyiz hagga helwa?' ('Do you want something sweet?'). He looked up at me irritably. 'Trevor, I'm asking you for "Circumstantial evidence".' For him she did not exist.

Recognising that this approach would be fruitless, the woman turned to me. By then I was bowed down with laughter and could not speak for several moments. She tried to stroke my hair but I told her politely that this was not a good day and that I had no money. 'Just two pounds for one nick-nick and three pounds for two,' she said with a good feel for discounts. I shook my head and said, 'No, not today, thanks.'

She glanced about the room with its curtain-less window and torn, flowered wallpaper and, probably recognising that money was tight and the effort to obtain it would be great, she shrugged and went to the door. 'I come back next week,' she said and disappeared.

My colleague continued in his effeminate Oxford drawl, 'Trevor, what is the Arabic for "inexorable"?' He was never to refer to the incident and I had to pinch myself to believe that it had ever happened.

2

Hobo on the run

I had lolled around Lebanon during its plump days of plenty in 1968 with my Orcadian girl-friend, Jill. We spent as little time as possible studying our newspaper Arabic at the 'spy school', the British Foreign Office Arabic school in the little mountain village of Shemlan which dominated the glittering spread of Beirut below and the Mediterranean beyond.

Jill had a bubbly charm which she spread about her without prejudice: to me, sometimes, with my *idée fixe* about her; to the witty, handsome students at Shemlan; to the tramp in a Beirut sidestreet; to the police commandant with whom we stayed in the then pretty fishing village of Tyre. With any man she met she giggled and fluttered. If she stroked a dog I envied it. No misadventure stilled her delightful flirtatiousness and my days were spent defending her from seduction.

One day we decided to visit the beautiful Roman city of Baalbek where the adored Egyptian singer, Umm Kulthum, was singing. We hitch-hiked to a village on the plain near the temple and walked along a road scattered with flowers and orange trees. A jeep filled with smirking policemen drew up and offered us a lift but we refused, I seriously, she with an adorable giggle. The policemen begged us to come but I was adamant so they drove on. Half an hour later they returned and drew up again a mile or so further along the road and we eventually agreed to drive with them.

They drove us across the plain until we reached a ragged four-storey cement building where we were taken upstairs to a drawing-room. We took our shoes off and coffee was served. One of the policemen rolled a joint of hashish and passed it round. It was strong and I felt giddy. Another invited Jill to wash her feet. 'A Lebanese custom, you understand?' he nodded at me. The hashish had made me somewhat sentimental over observing 'national customs' and I explained that yes, of course I understood. Jill was away for what seemed a very long time and I was a little anxious when she returned. More coffee was poured and the conversation, interspersed with increasing giggles, continued for a further twenty minutes until Jill decided that she wanted to go to the loo whither she was guided by the policeman of the feet washing. This time she seemed to stay away for much longer, although my accounting of time was completely impaired by now and I couldn't ascertain whether it had been five minutes or an hour. I got up, asked where 'my wife' was, gulped some more coffee, then felt so awkward on my feet that I could barely move.

At that moment Jill, somewhat dishevelled, returned with the policeman. 'There's something I must tell you,' she said.

Feeling so giddy by now that I was losing control of my senses, I replied, 'There's something I must tell you.' So saying, I drained my coffee cup and blacked out.

I came to within seconds and, seeing only a chiaroscuro of swirling, uniformed faces before me, I jumped up as best I could, grabbed Jill by the arm and stumbled with her to the door. Somewhere, miles away, I could hear the policemen saying, 'We were so glad to meet you. We do hope you enjoyed being here.' We reached the door below where the mid-day sun hit us with a scorching heat and I fell against Jill like a sack.

'We will drive you wherever you want to go,' said the suddenly desperate policemen. I slumped into the back of the car as we were driven to Baalbek. The policemen were now polite tourist guides, giving us half-baked accounts of the history of the temple and eulogising the magical wonders of Umm Kulthum. I heard them through my semi-conscious state warning me to protect 'my wife' from bad men and assuring me that, should we need help, they would ever be at our service.

When we were released on the outskirts of Baalbek I asked Jill what had happened at the feet-washing and loo-visiting cere-monies.

'Oh, he just said that I had beautiful eyes and that he wanted to marry me and were you really my husband and even if you were surely I would leave you for the likes of him, but I felt so giddy myself that I hardly knew what was happening. Why didn't you come and look for me?'

'Because I had lost all sense of time,' I answered with complete frankness.

She was a warm, smiling girl and the policemen had obviously been trying their luck. Had they managed to seduce her it wouldn't have gone down as rape, I suppose. The girl, they would have said, was willing and the husband clearly didn't care because he fell asleep. But even in those days Lebanese policemen could probably have got away with murder – or rape – in that anarchistic country.

Some days later Jill left for Damascus and I stayed in Shemlan, awaiting the arrival of Olly, a childhood friend from Oxford with whom I planned to travel to Egypt, taking a boat to Alexandria and thence down the Nile to Luxor and Aswan.

One day I noticed a rucksack in the hall of the school and, entering the coffee room, I saw my old pal, tall and healthy, all set to fulfill life-long dreams of adventure. To the envy of all of us, he had hitch-hiked through Turkey and Syria on his Australian passport. Since the war with Israel the previous year, which had been disastrous for the Arabs, Syria had been firmly closed to the British and some other West European nationalities whom the Syrians accused of collaborating with the Israelis. As Arabists we had all craved to visit Syria, the dreamland of the Classical scholar, but the borders were firmly sealed against us. Syria, then ruled by the unpopular Salah Jadid, had been through a very rough year since the war, with regular curfews and public hangings of spies in Damascus's main square.

Olly's first suggestion was that we hitch-hike back through Syria and Turkey, countries which had fascinated him. I explained the political situation to him but he insisted we try. I assured him it was out of the question. 'But let's try,' he said, recalling our childhood philosophy of life as we sat in his parents' house on Boars' Hill, drank mugs of coffee and tiny glassfuls of absinthe, smoked Senior Service and dreamed of an exotic future and swore never to say die. 'It's always worth a try.' Nothing I could say would persuade him that the ban was absolute, so I agreed to visit the border with him and prove it.

We reached the coastal border north of Tripoli at night, a beautiful night with a huge dome of glistening stars. The chic Lebanese officer gave Olly an exit stamp without demur but waved me cheerfully through assuming I would be back in twenty minutes, having failed to enter Syria. A strip of sand divided the two frontier posts. The Syrian customs officer sat at a card table on the beach beside the long customs-shed. We showed our passports and he told me pleasantly that he could not give me a visa. Olly said, 'Come on, just this once.' 'No, no,' said the man. 'You have an Australian passport. OK. But the British aren't allowed to enter Syria.'

We persisted, Olly with determination, I as a pointless philosophical exercise, and the man, wanting to seem helpful, told me I should return to Beirut and cable Damascus for a visa. 'But you won't get one,' he added even more helpfully. No Britisher had crossed the border for a year. We drank coffee with him and argued for an hour for the play of it.

Finally, we said good-bye and wandered along the seashore towards the Lebanese customs post. We sat on the beach. It was a silent, wistful night. Olly and I had never met outside England, away from the Oxford parties, the battles for girls, the gate-crashing from punts of Commem balls, the roar through St Giles on our Lambrettas.

'Think of all those dreams we shared. Think of our friends at the Turf Tavern. Think of the stories we will tell when we return. Think of our sense of failure if we turn back now. We simply can't turn back.'

My imagination, good on the inner horrors, bad on the outer hopes, filmed my public execution in Damascus's main square and I could hear the mob crying for my blood. The night was so quiet. A fishing boat with a flickering lantern bobbed on the sighing sea, sprinkling light on the little waves that trickled through our toes.

'Come on, Trev, we must do it.' For some minutes we sat in silence. I thought of my uncle who had, in the 1930s, knocked out fifteen waiters and gendarmes in a Paris restaurant because the bill was wrong and been exonerated because he was a baronet and a famous light-weight boxing champion. And then, contemplating this neurotic region of the world which I had chosen to study, I thought of my irresponsibility in even considering the adventure that Olly had set his heart on. But I heard myself say, almost under my breath, 'OK, go back to the police post and get your visa. I'll wade through the sea into Syria and see you on the other side. Go quickly before I lose my nerve.'

'Good,' said Olly, 'see you,' and was gone. I was alone with the night and with the stars. Olly would shortly be on the other side. I couldn't let him go alone. Not going was suddenly impossible just as going had seemed impossible some moments before. I drew my breath as one does before diving from a high, high board. I picked up my rucksack and stood in the sweet air and the silence. A searchlight from the Syrian customs-shed scanned the beach that ran alongside the shed and the sea through which I was about to rush. I remembered the spy films, a useful source of material now, that showed men counting the seconds to the fraction of the passage of the searchlights and rushing by during that terrifying moment of darkness. And now I, myself, was about to do it.

I crept into the sea up to my waist and waded to the outer perimeter of where the searchlight would pass. I looked minutely in all directions but could see no one. Three times the searchlight swept the water but each time I stood rock-still as if preparing to rush through the skipping rope at school at the moment that it left the ground. Then, suddenly, I accelerated myself through the water as the light withdrew, wading at a splashy run, urged on by increasing panic. I tripped again and again in the water before emerging beyond the probing of the light, soaked and barely saving my rucksack with its essential diaries. I was beyond the light. I was in Syria. I crept up the beach to a rock between the beach and the road and hid behind it. I took out a cigarette, then remembered that I couldn't light it.

I sat, cold and wet, behind the rock for half an hour. The occasional lorry revved up at the customs-shed and roared past me along the road into Syria. Eventually a figure appeared along the beach, coming towards me and completely ignoring the searchlight which swathed him every few seconds. Something straight, like a gun, stood up above his back. I huddled fretfully for some moments and then realised that it was Olly.

'They asked me where my companion was,' he said, not even bothering to whisper. 'They wouldn't give me a visa until they knew where you were.'

'That means they smell a rat and they'll be after us,' I said.

'Yes,' said Olly, 'we must get through Syria fast.'

We waved down a lorry coming from the customs-shed and it picked us up.

'Are there any checkpoints along the road?' I asked Olly.

He considered the question and after much thought said very hesitantly, 'No, I don't think so.' Almost as he spoke we saw ahead of us torches being waved up and down across the road. A striped post barred our way. The soldiers were civil, asking for the driver's papers and Olly's passport. Although I was in the front beside the window they failed, for some extraordinary reason, to ask for my passport. I felt like Rembrandt's Daniel with the gentle hand of the Angel Gabriel on his shoulder. 'Any more?' I asked Olly with a bitter cheerfulness.

The lorry dropped us off on the outskirts of the sea-port of Latakiya. The streets were dark, silent, deserted. We talked in whispers and tried to quieten our tread as if silence would make us less visible. But the clatter of our steps echoed among the houses of the sleeping town.

With engines roaring, two police motorcycles came abreast of us from behind, fat men in spherical helmets on fat, khaki machines. We chattered nothings between ourselves. The motorcycles slowed down to a walking pace. The policemen peered at us, we knew, but we did not look – never draw attention to yourself, pretend you don't exist, don't allow those vibrations to link you with them and spark off conversation. Without a word the policemen roared onwards. A baby yelled from among the houses. We hummed 'Waltzing Matilda' to keep our cool. As we came to the centre of Latakiya we heard the roar of motorcycles again. The same policemen slowed down, peered at us again and eventually drove away again. Twenty minutes later they passed again but something – Gabriel again? – seemed to prevent them from communicating with us and for the third and last time they roared away through the town. Perhaps they had by that time decided that hardened criminals would scarcely clatter through Latakiya humming a folksong.

As we passed a silent crossroads we saw a policeman sitting on a chair, a rifle between his legs. 'Merhaba,' ('Welcome'), we said. He replied with a broad grin. We had spoken to our first policeman and he had smiled! As we came through the suburbs of northern Latakiya, dawn was spilling over the palms. A bird sang. When we emerged into the beautiful, green countryside, peasant women were moving about carrying milking pails and bundles of wood. A man in a pin-stripe suit and flicking his *misbaha* (rosary) asked us politely who we were but we guessed he was a policeman. We talked to him about Australia and its beauties, I as credibly as I could manage. I had to remind myself that Olly at least had an embassy in Syria and was legally in the country all but for his entry stamp. But the man let us go and we continued along the pretty country road, leaving him fiddling sulkily with his beads as he gazed after us.

Soon a van stopped and drove us on, without incident, into the mountains and towards the Turkish border. 'You want to go to the frontier?' the driver asked innocently as the customs-sheds and Syrian flags suddenly emerged before us. 'No, please, up there,' we replied, pointing to a road to the left which climbed the steep, wooded mountainside to a little village. When we reached the top we said good-bye and bought oranges from the local shop. It was mid-day. We stepped down from the village into the forest, deciding to take a siesta under the shade of a tree until mid-afternoon when everyone else would be taking theirs.

At four in the afternoon we began making our way through the deep and lovely forests, crossing streams, our rough tread throwing up birds from the undergrowth about us. After forty minutes we reached the road. Behind us we saw the Turkish customs-sheds and behind the Turkish shed the Syrian. We were home. We were safe. Or were we? Or were we?

We reached Yeledag, the first Turkish village, and from there we hitched a truck to Iskanderun on the southern coast. In Iskanderun we met some French travellers and a German. We ate together and I became the group's general interpreter. The venal Frenchmen wanted to amuse themselves at the expense of the poor German and quizzed him about gas chambers but I would invariably mistranslate, the German would reply happily and pleasant confusion reigned. When we told the Frenchmen our story they were astonished and told us of a Syrian who had, the previous day, had a leg blown off by a mine crossing the same forest paths that we had taken.

We continued our journey to Ankara, that great, dull-grey city that represents the gloomier side of Turkey's post-Ataturk obsession with all things European. For good measure we decided to visit the British Embassy to explain what we regarded as an innocent Boy's Own adventure – we had done nothing sinister but had merely taken a short cut to get to Turkey – and to sort out the little problem of our not possessing an entry stamp. We looked on the visit as a mere formality.

The British Consul was not remotely amused or impressed by our adventure and explained that we had broken the law. He called in the Australian Consul who took the same line. They then called in a Turkish lawyer who eyed us severely and produced his files. The lawyer took an even dimmer view of our situation than the consul. Our case, he assured us, was virtually hopeless. We both began to feel confused by this turn of events, having so recently applauded the happy outcome of our little adventure. Our situation had by now become Kafkaesque, particularly in so far as we could not properly grasp what our crime was or look at it with the curious Oriental objectivity of the lawyer, who had the blimpish backing of the consuls. Up to then our only fear had been in Syria. Turkey had seemed a haven – now the Syrian alternative almost seemed cosier!

The lawyer telephoned the Ankara Chief of Police to clarify our position, which was as follows. Assuming we gave ourselves up, we would face six months' imprisonment and a £100 fine, plus a special pauper fee of £33 to the lawyer. We each had £20 left. I had to take a re-sit Arabic exam in Edinburgh four weeks later. The lawyer explained that special arrangements might be made for me to take the exam in gaol. Conditions in the prison, the three men agreed, were far from pleasant but they were not unbearable. 'One thing that the Chief of Police points out, however,' explained the lawyer, 'is that the court will want to check whether you have criminal records with Scotland Yard and Interpol. This might take five months or longer. And if,' (he stressed the 'if' ominously), 'if there is any suspicion of espionage or unfriendly political activity, then I cannot even defend you. Nothing can be done at my level.' Our adventure was definitely taking a turn for the worse. I had studied for one month at Shemlan, the so-called 'spy school'. Might that constitute espionage? The lawyer didn't think so, the first shred of optimism in the interview.

The two consuls nodded with severe approval. The three men assured us that not a word would pass beyond those four walls and advised us to decide our course of action by the following day – and warned us not to roam the streets at night without our proper papers.

Olly and I sat morbidly in the corridor. We discussed and quickly rejected the possibility of swimming the river which divides the Turkish-Greek border. That would mean sacrificing our belongings and possibly getting shot into the bargain. I was thinking of giving myself up, throwing myself on the mercy of Turkish law, when Olly again came to my rescue with childhood reminiscences. 'What creeps we'd look if we gave ourselves up. We'd never dare show our faces in the Turf Tavern again.' I found this sort of argument very persuasive. What did he suggest? Cross into Syria and Lebanon again, back to square one. 'We've done it once, we can do it again!' And the Syrian checkpoint? And the forests? And having the law of averages against us? But he brought me back to 'what creeps we'd look if we didn't' and I said yes. This way we certainly wouldn't look like creeps.

So, armed with fear fed by warnings in the embassy about not having papers, by stories of minefields on the border, and by sheer exhaustion and hunger, we went to the *servis* square and took a bus to Antioch. From there we hitched a ride in a Dormobile to Yeledag. We couldn't talk much as we were suspicious of the fat man in front of us, who kept glancing our way and murmuring '*Ingleezi*'. When he got up to buy a cold drink, we noticed the butt of a revolver poking from his back pocket.

When we reached Yeledag the local people gave us a warm, unsurprised welcome, which tied in badly with our desire for anonymity. From Yeledag we walked up through the forests along the road in search of the right-hand turning which would lead us back up to the Armenian village in Syria. We were crucially late and dusk was falling fast. We came to a well and drank. I thought it was the first path, Olly thought it was the second. With a final nervous glance to check that the road was clear, we darted into the now darkling forest. The undergrowth quickly became deeper and deeper, a jungle through which we had to hack our way in the dim moonlight.

After three exhausting hours when it seemed we had lost our way, we reached an orchard full of moonlight and saw, above and beyond the trees, the little Armenian village flickering way above us. We were tired with despair – the village, our initial goal, was to be merely the first point of our terrifying return. We had lost the glamorous bonhomie of our outward journey. As we entered the orchard, we began to pick the apples. For a moment I was scared by a bright light and ducked, but it was only the moon. We began eating the apples, which made us glow with new hope, an immediate, sensual nourishment. Laughing, we began filling our bags with apples. The moonlight in the trees was beautiful and a warm breeze dried our sweat.

Suddenly, there was a hideous shriek. We stood stock-still. Then came another loud shout from among the trees and we flung ourselves with our packs to the ground, our forms shining pale in the moonlight. A few moments of silence. 'Let's creep on our bellies into the trees,' I whispered, knowing I was frozen to the ground with fear. All of a sudden, there were shouts all around us, replying to one another. Then I could see the shape of a man holding a rifle moving towards us from the trees. As I peered round I saw that men with guns were emerging slowly from all directions. 'God, we've had it!' I murmured. Olly said nothing. Soon we were surrounded.

Nine men stood around us, pointing their rifles down at us as if we were some subterranean creatures that had arisen from their lairs and needed prodding. There is something hideously frightening about gun barrels being pointed at you, whether by one man or a group of men. From that moment, divided by about ten yards, Olly and I switched on to auto. Fear does that. Several times throughout what followed I looked at my hand and saw that it was steady as a rock. When you're frightened, you don't make mistakes – you absorb and neatly consume every ounce of the adrenalin being created. A chilling cool takes root and the coward becomes heroic, the vague man precise, the idiot erudite and the man who never learnt a language becomes a linguist.

'*Merhaba*,' we said, wiping our eyes as if awakening and grinning stupidly. But they weren't smiling. They dropped their guns a little and the questions surged. Who were we, why were we there in the border forests? We explained, cloning, that we were camping, that we had lost our way in Turkey and had decided to sleep until the dawn revealed our whereabouts. We apologised for eating their apples. I was speaking in Arabic but suddenly realised that Olly was speaking in French – in tongues, in a sense, since he had barely got through his 'O' level. 'Why do you carry rifles?' he asked. The man gazed at him with irony but without any malice and replied, as if in a poem, 'On the night of the full moon we shoot the wild pigs that eat our apples.' Fatal symbolism – I thought of *Lord of the Flies*: 'Hunt the pig! Hunt the pig that steals the apples of temptation!'

Our brilliantly feigned innocence – we had perhaps begun to believe our own story – softened the men a little. They sat down about us, their rifles between their knees. The language they spoke among themselves was not Arabic and puzzled me at first, until it suddenly occurred to me that they were Armenian, which meant that they were Christians and that they scorned the establishment. Since these issues were known to me but not to Olly, I spoke loudly so that he would pick up the trend of my conversation. The Armenians have suffered badly at the hands of the Turks and although they have not been persecuted by the Syrians, they feel themselves to be a minority and associate themselves with Syria's old Christian community, which had little time for the Baathist regime in power. Nevertheless, they are Syrians and we could certainly expect no mercy from them if they gathered we were illegal immigrants and, therefore, potential spies.

We played our Catholicism hell for leather and the Pope, holy communion, holy days of obligation, even indulgences filled the night air. The situation was becoming vaguely favourable (and very holy!) but neither of us had devised a scheme whereby they would let us go again. We kept saying how nice it was being in Turkey, while they kept politely reminding us that we were in Syria – at which we assumed looks of astonishment. However, at that moment another figure appeared from among the trees, a Syrian in police uniform with hatred in his eyes. 'Passports!' he shouted. He grabbed me by the shirt collar and told the others in Arabic that we must go up to the police station in the village. Our dreams of survival seemed shattered. I saw the firing squads quite clearly now and two sets of weeping parents in Oxford.

Olly showed his Australian passport and began chatting casually to distract the policeman's attention. By an extraordinary stroke of luck he forgot to ask for my passport – the hand of Gabriel again! At once the policeman repeated, 'Now you must come to the police station.' My reply, spun out from the minute machinery of fear, had some force and was to start an argument, the outcome of which saved us in the end.

'Yes, we'd be really happy to come,' I said, 'but we can't go to the Syrian police until we have passed through Turkish customs. That would be illegal.' This confused him momentarily. I turned to the man who had, from the beginning, played a somewhat leading role, and said, 'That's the law, that's the law.' The scales were now even and could turn either way at a gentle touch. Our fates hung upon a thread, a delicate balance between the powers and weaknesses of men. Immense patient charm on our part was a must.

I turned to the man with authority, an authority which the others had already vaguely recognised and whose recognition increased when they saw that foreigners automatically gave it to him. This in turn made him feel more responsible. 'You do see my point, don't you?' I said gently. He nodded slightly and began arguing with the beast. The beast became furious – our leader became proud and the others meekly backed him up. The beast turned to one of the others, gesticulating angrily to make his point. An angel took hold of our man, who whispered to us, 'You can go. That's the way to go.' Beaming, we shook his hand, smiled at the others, turned about and ambled off – till we hit the shadows of the trees and bolted. We ran and ran and ran and when we reached the road in Turkey twenty minutes later, we almost collapsed with exhaustion.

We found a clearing and curled up in our sleeping bags. At dawn we got up quickly, hungry and tired and unshaven. We walked down the road until we were a few yards from the Turkish customs post. Here we hid behind a boulder to survey the scene of our next tricky project. We saw the two police and customs-sheds on either side of the road and, beyond, the flags of Syria. All around us was forest. Ahead the forest splayed up on two sides into the mountains.

We made our way calmly to the customs-sheds. On the ledge along the shed to our right sat a policeman smoking a cigarette. His sub-machine gun dangled beside him. Having learnt to confront danger full frontally, we smiled at him and placed our rucksacks beside him. We then wandered across to a small café where we ordered two postcards and two Cical Colas. As we sat we began feverishly writing on the postcards. When we had finished writing, I asked to see Olly's and he asked to see mine. Mine was exotic tripe about blue skies and mountains – I had no intention of sending it. His was similar. It might have been written from a Costa Brava beach but it ended with 'lots of love to Rags!' Rags was his family's delightful but smelly spaniel. Why so much love to Rags, I asked. 'When my mother drove me to the Headington roundabout [in Oxford] to hitch-hike, she was so fretful she insisted that I have a code word for danger so I said, almost jokingly, that the code word would be "Rags".'

At that moment the policeman on the other side of the road and his armed companion began walking towards the café. We got up quickly to pay, convinced they were coming to interrogate us. We left the café and crossed in front of them, smiling greetings. By now we were completely paranoid. Any gesture from anyone was immediately interpreted as danger. We entered the customs-shed through the entrance for those coming from Syria. The card we were playing was very risky since the last stamp in our passports was an entry stamp into Lebanon. We depended on the official's pure ignorance and sloth. The official looked magnificent, resplendent in military hardware. He gazed through page after empty page of my passport. I waited for the raised eyebrows, the questioning shake of the passport, the 'Where are your stamps?' and I had no answer prepared. I could not have been in Syria and I could not have entered from anywhere else. But after much pompous perusal and flicking of the pages, he took a stamp. I held my breath and down it came with the word 'Fini'.

When we crossed to the customs desk they waved us on but then one called us back. 'Are you hitch-hiking?'

'No, no, we're travelling by bus and taxi,' I asserted. I had suddenly remembered an article I had read in Iskanderun which said that hitch-hikers were being turned back at borders and sent back to the countries they had come from.

We left the customs-shed and strode along the bright, forested road towards Yeledag – free men!

3

Bad tempers in the Hoggar

I returned to Edinburgh to complete my degree in Arabic. One day a beautiful, lazy, cynical Californian hippy called Francess appeared without invitation at our spoken Arabic classes. I barely spoke to her in Edinburgh but some weeks later she appeared at my mother's house in Oxford.

Francess was an orphan. She had recently returned from Afghanistan with an American hashish pedlar whom she, already married, had bigamously married to give his business an air of respectability. By the time that my own relationship with Francess ended one year later I had still barely cracked the surface of a very complex woman.

On that first evening she produced a block of very pure Afghan hashish, more correctly known as 'shit'. I had smoked a little marijuana and hashish some years earlier on my return journey from India but was to remain a complete outsider to the drug scene.

That evening we smoked and smoked until I was floating in another, almost perfect world in which my decisions and my actions became effortless. It was a sensual night.

Some months later, in mid-August, Francess and I hitch-hiked to Algeria, arguing almost constantly. In Paris we found a small hotel room in the Latin Quarter. We met a bombastic American negro on the stairs and when he heard that I was a 'writer' he asked me to read a chapter of his book. We went to his room where he presented each of us with carbon copies. By my perhaps naively British standards the book was repulsively hard porn and I think included coprophilia, necrophilia, any philia you cared to name. 'Unclean, unclean!' flooded my conventional mind. It was not the words themselves, however, that upset me so much as Francess's quiet absorption in the manuscript. Francess was without prejudice. She was *tabula rasa*, the perfect critic. I admired her for that objectively but I was also jealous and I suddenly got up and said that it was time to go.

Francess followed me with a superficially meek indifference, contempt, too, I think. 'Did you like that?' I asked.

'That's just normal. All modern American writing's like that,' she said complacently.

We travelled through France and Spain and crossed by boat from Algeciras to Tangier. From Tangier we travelled to the Moroccan border town of Oujda. We entered a small hotel to ask for a room. Behind the unkempt young hotelier stood two Berber girls in white lace nightdresses which were just transparent and revealed pale, young bodies.

The man asked us in polite confusion, 'Do you want the room for the hour, the afternoon or the night?' I replied, 'For the night, of course,' although it was slowly dawning on me that this was a brothel. The man, too, began to realise that we genuinely wanted a room for the night. As soon as the situation became clear to all, the atmosphere relaxed. The girls ran off happily to prepare our 'bridal' room and when we came to it they were waiting to greet us.

We sat down on the bed, surrounded by these giggling teenage prostitutes who vied with each other to question us about our relationship, our children, our clothing, about the music and dancing we liked. Then the madame came in. She wore a beautiful lace Kabyle dress. Like a strict but motherly head-mistress, she shooed the laughing girls away.

Coarse, unsmiling Moroccans waited in queues for 'quickies' in the corridor and we could see the girls, bored and lazy now, return to their rooms to work. Before entering, some would cast affectionate eyes back at our little island of stability.

'I am a good woman,' said the madame, settling cosily onto our bed. 'I look after my girls well. They are good girls. Sometimes the police come and make trouble but we never cause anybody any trouble. My girls are clean girls. We keep a clean house here.' The girls kept coming back in to sit with us but the madame would always send them back to work.

We continued through Algeria to Algiers where we stayed with Prince Ahmed, the descendant of the nineteenth-century Algerian rebel against the French whose family, exiled by the French, had reached exalted positions throughout the Middle East and Europe. Under Ben Bella's first government after independence the Prince had been invited to the Foreign Ministry. He was completely bilingual in French and English and spoke English with a considerable Oxford 'plum'. Handsome, intelligent, impeccably dressed, a womaniser, he was the perfect international emissary for the new Algeria which was desperately finding its feet after a six-year war in which almost one million Algerians had died.

But however bloody the revolution, its traces were weaker in 1970 perhaps than they are today. Where was the revolution? In the odd 'Vive le FLN' scrawled on corners of the old Casbah? Where was the bitterness of fathers who had lost sons? In the café proprietor who proudly showed me a picture of himself receiving a medal from de Gaulle? Military parades were rarely to be seen. That year's May Day parade featured an army of workers carrying saws. It was the new worker age bearing its hammers and sickles.

We met students who spent their summers in Paris, wore mod clothing and met their friends in coterie cafés. In one café a record was playing. The girl sang, 'Fear not old woman, the French have gone.' Fading revolutionary slogans were still to be seen but much more common were the new slogans 'Vive' not the 'FLN' but the initials of football teams. One of the students had lived in the street we were in. 'Our family left the Casbah to come and live in the new town in 1962 [the moment of the French panic emigration when the poor rushed to take their places in the splendid baroque buildings of central Algiers]. It was here that the real war was fought. When I was 12 I saw a schoolfriend shot by paras before my own eyes. They were usually afraid to enter the Casbah. It's easy to get lost. It was easy for a sniper to pick off a French soldier in those alleys. But we felt no feeling of revenge. Soldiers who had fought against us

and who are still recognised in the streets have even come back
to play in the national Algerian football team at Maison Carré.'
He told us of the terrible months of anarchy following
independence as the FLN marched on Algiers from the Tunisian
external *wilayats* (FLN districts). 'It was too dangerous to go out
into the streets. They were deserted.' I read some Arabic from a
notice on the wall but the students looked away. They had
forgotten the little Arabic they had learnt at primary school.

We stayed with the Prince and his sister in a magnificent
white villa in Hydra tumbling with wisteria where ministers and
top policemen lived. They took us to the yacht club where
Ahmed challenged me to swim out to sea as far as the eye could
see. For Ahmed it was a test for the women to admire but I was
tired from recent jaundice and at a quarter of a mile I could
barely move my arms. I fought my way back completely
exhausted. But the women had not watched us. Ahmed insisted
we go out again. The women were gossipping under the parasol
as wonderful sea foods were being laid out on the table. 'Did you
see us?' said the Prince, 'Did you see us swim right out there?'
His wife Safia said vaguely that she had seen us walk into the
sea but hadn't looked again. 'Right, Trevor, we'll have to go
again and show them that we're real men.' I was so drained I
could barely step into the water but I somehow could not resist
the challenge and we went out again a quarter of a mile. When
we finally got back to the waiting feast the women still hadn't
looked but the boyish test was over.

Francess and I left Algiers and the Prince for the *bled*, the
countryside. We were headed for Gardaia and Laghouat and
from there we intended to cross the Sahara to Tamanrasset in the
deep South. One of our early lifts was with an FLN *mujahid* who
had fought in the forested, mountainous region through which
we were passing.

He snarled when we mentioned the young students with
whom we had spent many happy hours arguing about Marxism
in Le Boulevard Didouche Mourad. 'The old revolutionaries
with whom I fought either have government jobs today or else
they have retired away from Algiers to forget. Today Algiers is
full of young men in gay shirts. They're all soft. They're not

Arabs. Their parents died for independence and for this their children laugh at them. The French did terrible things to us; they're too young to know. To them France means Ye-ye, shirts à la vogue, girls, girls, girls, twenty-four hours a day girls! They've forgotten what we suffered, we who today have nothing.'

He acted out for us the sort of drama that had happened in the forest we were in. 'Like now, for example. I'm smartly dressed and driving through the mountains. In front is a road block of French paras. They think, "Here's a respectable Algerian!" They wave me down, line me up with the terrified villagers and mow us all down with machine guns. The paras used to go into a village and if they saw a pregnant woman they would take bets of ten francs whether it was a boy or a girl and then JAAAWWW! They would cut her open to see.

'Another time they would ask a mother of three children, "Which one do you want to die?" The woman would scream, clutching her children and crying, "None, none," and the laughing soldier would fling them away one by one and shoot them.' But the man was careful to add before leaving us, 'After independence we had no feeling of revenge or hatred. We forgave completely. The French never forgave the Germans, did they?'

We drove on to Laghouat and from Laghouat to Gardaia, the holy city of the Mozabites and capital of the Mzab region from which this puritan yet cosmopolitan sect come. Twenty miles beyond Laghouat was written on an enormous notice in French 'Notice to all travellers to the Great Sahara'. Below, the warning advised that the tarmac ended at El-Golea and the tracks began. All travellers must report to the El-Golea police post in the interest of their own safety to give their passenger quota, have the vehicles tested for durability, have water and petrol supplies carefully checked, and travel in convoy.

It was mid-August when temperatures reached 140 degrees Fahrenheit. Few trucks crossed the Sahara because of the heat. It was a deathly month. The police in Laghouat told us, 'Between Laghouat and Ain Salah there is nothing, only sand, often no track. Sometimes the track is swept away by sand storms and drivers panic. They drive off in search of tracks but the tracks they are making are erased by the breeze. When they try to retrace their tracks there are no tracks to retrace. The secret in the desert is never panic. If you lose your way the first thing to do is to retrace your own tracks if possible.'

A drunken Berber drove us from Laghouat to Gardaia. Voices in the *souq* whispered 'Be careful of this man!' but he did nothing to justify our caution. Soon the brimming fertility and the little French villages with their uniform churches and squares were behind us and we were in the Africa of the Sahara. The wind smelt of Africa. Djerbas like tiny kangaroos leapt in the headlights and from time to time shuffled away from the sidings into the night's heart of darkness. Suddenly, beneath us, the lights of the oasis of Gardaia sprang into life and our old Chevrolet wound its way down the mountain towards this glimmering city. When we reached the palms of the oasis the three of us spent the hot, windy night under a shelter beside some petrol pumps.

Gardaia lies in the Mzab, 'the desert within a desert', on the edge of the Great Western Erg, one of the two great dune seas of the Sahara. Gardaia is built of glistening white or luminous pale blue houses and tiny streets twisting and weaving in a web around the market places. The people are ultra-orthodox Ibadi Muslims. Smoking, drinking and usury are forbidden. Music is anathema to them. Their women are strictly hidden from all strangers, but in spite of their reactionary puritanism they have for long been wealthy cloth and spice merchants throughout Africa and in France.

Several Mozabites told me intriguingly that every young man must go to Paris before settling down and that girls refuse to marry their fiancés until they have done so. The men all wear black beards and long white muslin scarves wound round their turbans. Because of their orthodoxy Mozabites working in France cannot take their wives. When children are born shortly after their return, the women maintain that the 'foetus slept during the father's term of absence', a story which husbands have accepted gullibly for many years.

We visited Beni Isguen, the Holy City of the Mozabites. Smoking is forbidden in the streets and the city gates are closed at nightfall. As we entered the horseshoe arch a shaikh approached us and explained that it was forbidden to enter this maze of a town without a guide. We were thirsty and scooped water from one of the round goat-hide buckets hanging nearby which kept water cool in the fiercest heat. 'We are looking for a café,' we replied.

'There are no cafés here,' he said. 'We are Mozabites, we do not drink, we do not smoke. We have no cafés, no hotels. People eat at home. It is forbidden for foreigners to enter the town without a guide. There are many, many streets. You will get lost.'

Some girls in Algiers had giggled when I told them we were visiting Beni Isguen. I asked them why and they put their hands over their mouths.

'Shall I tell him?' said one to the other.

'No, you tell him,' the first girl said. 'If you go into Beni Isguen, don't go alone, that's all.'

The second girl said, 'OK, I'll tell him,' and turning to me, she said, 'You see they don't welcome strangers as it's a Holy City and if the women catch a man alone in those winding streets they kidnap him and they rape him one by one. All of them do, the old ones, the young ones. And they go on and on, egged on by each other, until he dies of exhaustion.'

I laughed, but a little nervously, and decided to keep Francess firmly by my side throughout our visit.

When we entered the town unobserved we realised that our shaikh had told us the truth, for among these winding alleys there was nothing but a primitive grocer. There was a ghostly air of puritanism in the sleepy market-place. The men wore brilliant white *gandouras* (long, flowing cloaks). There were no Westernised teenagers, no urchins pestering for *bakshish* in seven languages. We were left utterly, strangely, in peace. Our eyes were dazzled by the whitewash of the buildings and there was nothing to indicate where we were. The sight of a pretty girl at a window now filled me with dread after the story I had heard in Algiers.

A merchant was laying out his supply of *gandouras* and *cheches* (head-cloths) on the cobbled stones. Way above us and the medina stood Beni Isguen's Mozabite mosque, brilliant white like almost everything else, its slim minaret tapering at the top to a battlement of four fingers pointing to heaven. A shy youth came up to us, inviting us to spend the heat of the afternoon by his private swimming pool. He lived on the edge of the town. Beyond stretched the open desert. He insisted we remain outside the high mud walls of his house for some minutes while from within we heard him frantically calling, 'Layla, Samya!' clapping his hands and urging his sisters into the house lest I catch a glimpse. We spent a lazy afternoon under the palms around the pool as our host brought us dates and mint tea.

The next day a lorry took us to El-Golea, 'the end of the asphalt'. El-Golea is an oasis city bursting with plantations of fruit enclosed in high, ochre-coloured walls, a city of murmuring doves and the smells of flowers, and thousands of tiny streams that are its life source. Dominating the city is the ancient Kasr (castle). Beside the central square was a tiny government tourist office. Inside sat a large, jocular man and behind him in a little alcove festooned with tourist wares sprawled his assistant dressed in *gandoura* and turban. Without so much as hinting we should buy anything they invited us to stay in the office until the expected convoy of lorries heading for Tamanrasset arrived.

On the first day we visited the tomb of Le Père Foucault which stands by the white, Spanish-style church among the dunes on the outskirts of El-Golea. The church was run by the White Fathers who run educational and medical projects in the Sahara and make no attempt to convert Muslims. Le Père Foucault was a former soldier of the late nineteenth century and one of the earliest Frenchmen to penetrate this deeply into the Sahara. He went to live the life of an ascetic at Tamanrasset where he lived in his hermitage as Assekrem and worked on his Tifiniq dictionary, the written language of the Tuareg. He devoted his life to the Hoggar-Tuareg tribes and tried to win their confidence, despite the fate of other Frenchmen who had tried the same. 'I became', he said, 'an outlaw to the outlaws to win over the outlaws,' echoing the words of Christ. He became almost a saint to the proud Tuareg and the ordinary Saharans, the Haratin. But in 1916 the Sanusi, allied with the Central Powers, invaded this part of the Sahara and persuaded some of the Tuareg to revolt against the French. Foucault built a *bordj*, a little tower, to defend the wretched Haratin but he was finally enticed out and slaughtered by a group of Tuareg invaders.

The few tourists who came to the Tourist Office were regaled with food and tea but our hosts seemed to have not the slightest interest in selling anything. Every day Kadr, the assistant, would artistically arrange his shoddy imitations of *Takoubas* (Tuareg long swords), rugs and trinkets. Then he would recline back on his ottoman as we ate and drank tea. One day I bought a *djerba*, a goatskin tied up at four corners which looks like a dead dog and is treated with a kind of sticky tar inside. It is the conventional water carrier in the Sahara and keeps water cool on the hottest day. I was told to wash it daily for ten days by the end of which it would be clean of excess tar. Unfortunately I tried to accelerate the process by washing it in Tide. After three days it had disintegrated.

In the evenings we would go to bathe in a tiny natural lake among the palms and dunes. A crowd of village children always came with us. They would scramble up the palms and bring us armfuls of dates and plunge about in the water with us. We would often see camel trains on the horizon. Sometimes a stork would come and stand beside the pool as if watching us.

On some days Muhammad, head of the tourist office, would take us to his plantations filled with pomegranates, clementines, apricots and lemons, but most of our time was spent with the languid Kadr who would often quote a favourite verse from the Qur'an: 'Did he not find thee an orphan and protect thee?' or would beg a kiss from Francess in exchange for a tourist trinket while my back was turned. When we went to the local café for a *cous-cous* the bill had always been paid in advance.

One day we noticed a Mercedes mini-bus standing in the main square. It belonged to three Germans, two young men and a girl, who were travelling overland to the Cape. They agreed to take us and another German student who had appeared that day to Tamanrasset. We obtained the necessary police permit, told the police how many days we intended to take to reach Tamanrasset, and drove out of El-Golea.

We had fifty litres of water and sand tracks. It was a terrible squash for six people in the little bus and the German girl was seriously ill with dysentery. For fifty kilometres we travelled on asphalt. There was loose scrub on the desert and scattered groups of yellow dune. Suddenly with a crash we were on the track. The asphalt had ended.

From now on it was almost impossible to make oneself heard through the explosive bumps and rattles. The track was indicated by small piles of stones or red stone markers above huge rocks showing the ancient caravan route. A jeep, making a local journey into the desert, passed us the other way and asked us if we needed water. 'Do you need water?' is a virtual greeting in the Sahara. Driving needs great skill. Either the track is hard and corrugated by heavy wear and knocks a machine to pieces, or it is *fesh-fesh*, soft wind-blown sand which is like quick-sand to the wheels. The mid-summer heat was intolerable and the hot winds as we drove were scarcely more comfortable than the oven the bus became if we stopped. Stop we often did! The German girl had to use the portable lavatory at regular intervals while we all sheltered in a delicate line of shade beside the bus.

Our first well was at Fort Miribel, a small, crumbling fort reminiscent of Beau Geste and built in the Bandera, or Spanish colonial style. The fort was couched in the lee of a big isolated rock. Two hundred yards away in the wadi among four palms was the well. Beside it stood a lorry unloading goats while a few shepherds counted them beyond. The camels stood undisturbed as the tin rattled in the well on the end of a rope which the drivers were pulling up. When our turn came we drank feverishly and delightedly, and drenched each other with bucketfuls.

We drove on into the huge Tademait plain. Flat in all directions, it was covered with a thin shroud of black pebbles which made it look bleak. That night we cleared a space of stones and laid out our sleeping bags. Having eaten a dinner of hard bread dipped in milk and drunk tea from a saucepan, we slept peacefully in the cool of night. The desert heat is a time for quick tempers and strange imaginings and the cool evenings are a time for laughter and joy.

We drove on in the early light, skirting the Great Erg. Tiny dunes had been blown across the way. On the hard desert we often drove several hundred yards parallel with the track, but always within sight of the markers, following the wheel patterns of lorries which had created intricate artistic designs for a quarter of a mile on both sides of the track, looping and intertwining. But now all was sand and the explosive track was the only hope. We slid around horribly even on the thinnest patch of *fesh-fesh*, a cumbersome bus on tiny wheels.

Soon we saw a slim pillar of smoke on the distant horizon behind us. We stopped. The wisp became a billowing cloud of sand and through it, in a blaze of dust, sped a convoy of lorries. They roared past us like an accelerated tank column and in a few minutes were once again a puff on the horizon. Now we were driving in nauseous mid-day heat. Mirages of lakes appeared and faded away.

We saw a Deux Chevaux stuck in the sand a little way off the track. It was heavily weighed down. A young man was at the wheel, and his girl-friend, screaming at him abusively in her hysteria, was trying, in vain, to push. They clearly thought they were doomed. We all ran over laughing and virtually lifted the little machine out of the sand. The boy sat, deeply humiliated, at the wheel, while his girl-friend cursed him incessantly. It was a repulsive scene. We told them never again to leave the track. They had 50 litres of water, quite sufficient, but one must always offer water in the desert. It might be your turn next.

We had only driven on for five minutes when we, too, were stuck in a mound of *fesh-fesh* that Hans, our driver, had tried to 'rush'. Out came the spades and the sand tracks and for two hours we dug, and pushed, and steered at different angles, but the bus slipped deeper and deeper into the sand. The girl was still dreadfully ill and there was no way of knowing when another vehicle would pass, whether after hours, or days, or a week.

The three Germans didn't speak English. Stefan, the new-comer, did and was our friend, but the girl saw us as a threat to their water supplies. She shunned us and was frightened. After an hour of dribbling sweat and of drinking great quantities of water, we tried savagely to dislodge the bus. But after some hours we gave up the task as hopeless. We decided to sit it out and wait. The day had cooled and we became more cheerful. Throughout the day we had to vacate the bus at twenty-minute intervals for the sick girl. During the worst of the heat and the crisis I'd had a row with Francess who'd finally screamed in misery, 'I never wanted to come to the wretched Sahara. I wanted to go to Paris!'

Despite this mid-day neurosis, we had all joked to hide our worry. But it was evening now and someone pointed to a puff of sand in the distance. A mirage? No, it was real. It was an old Peugeot whose driver we had met in Gardaia. Our fears were groundless. Out stepped two men in *gandouras*, *cheches*, and baggy Berber trousers. Hans said 'Ahmad' with a cynical smile. But the driver and his companion were not Arabs. They were German-speaking Swiss. Their battered car was enormously overloaded and they drove like madmen, ostentatiously confident in their skill at desert driving. Behind them was a convoy heading for Tamanrasset. They quickly produced some efficient sand tracks and the bus, after a few speculative squirms, at last freed itself, and we were heading for Ain Salah, 40 miles beyond.

In Arabic Ain Salah means the Spring of Picty. The Fire of Hell would be more appropriate. It is one of the hottest points of the Sahara and was being slowly swallowed by the sand; the streets were sand and dunes pressed high against its mud walls in the very centre of the city. We were actually bogged down in a dune in the main street. It was like a dying city, its negroid inhabitants shuffling through the sand like ghosts.

It was a truly Saharan city, not the last point in North Africa but the first indication of black Central Africa, a sister city to Timbuctoo and Fort Lamy. Until the turn of the century it was one of the most important slave markets and caravan cities of Central Africa and among its exports were ostrich feathers, ivory and gold dust. Its great mud walls, its unbearable heat, its sand-filled air, and its handsome negroid people gave it an air of splendour.

The Germans hated Ain Salah but had to have some papers stamped by the police whose office, like everything else at this time of day, was closed. So we couldn't leave till the next day at least. We went to the market-place in search of food. Most of the people were negroid Haratin (the name for the original inhabitants of the Sahara) and wore brightly coloured *gandouras*. Few of the women were veiled. Food in the café was Western, and expensive, imported from the north. In the little market-place, with its square, covered, market-platform in the centre, groups of old men and women were selling incense and spices. Hardly any young people were to be seen. Most had emigrated north. I photographed a woman in the market-place and she screamed and threw herself down onto the ground and into her veil as if she was having a fit. The men laughed. 'She thinks it's magic,' they grinned. As we passed through one of the streets some ragged girls who were lounging in the sand smiled at us wistfully. The men told us they were prostitutes.

Two days later we left Ain Salah. Soon the great plateau of Tademait was behind us. Flat-topped mountains which appeared to be the same height however far apart appeared singly or in groups. Then came a notice telling vehicles to change down into first gear and we found ourselves plunging at an alarming angle through hairpin bends towards the desert far below. At the bottom lay two lorries smashed to pieces, a permanent warning. Half way down beside the track lay a fine white camel, decapitated. It must have been killed earlier that day by a lorry taking the corner too fast. When we reached the desert, the Reg (vast expanse of stones) had turned to fine sand.

Soon the track and its markers disappeared and for a few miles we had to rely on instinct. It is surprising how easy it is in the desert to lose all sense of direction where there are no land marks. The markers returned but the *fesh-fesh* was becoming worse. There had been a recent sandstorm. Hans was trying to race through the mounds of sand as fast as possible. Once the sand hurled the machine off the track and we were flung headlong, but by chance and driving skill the bus managed to slide back onto the track. Eventually we were really stuck. Before us lay a large, impenetrable mound, but we were now secure in knowing that the convoy would follow shortly.

Soon the happy convoy arrived and at once this minute spot of the Sahara became a scene of festivity. Some minutes later the Swiss Peugeot arrived and behind it a Deux Chevaux with a French teacher wearing a *cheche* and a French hitch-hiker. As the day cooled, the fiesta began. We all crowded the sides of the *fesh-fesh* and placed spades on either side as finishing posts. The Peugeot rushed the sand, a few squirms, success! We all cheered in five languages. Then with fifteen of us behind and Manfred at the wheel, we were pulled out of the sand. The bus wriggled grotesquely in the *fesh-fesh*, but with a final bound cleared the mound. The French Deux Chevaux rushed the sand but was stuck. At once thirty arms dived for it as for a rugger ball and lifted it to freedom. The three Land Rovers took it fast and made it in style to wild cheers. As the sun set figures were seen running out into the desert to take photographs. One of the Scots said, 'If only the world politicians could see this there'd never be another war!'

The convoy's clever Algerian guide, the desert fox, knew every grain of the desert. It was night and we were soon a weaving snake of red lights following him in spirals through the sand. Whenever a vehicle was stuck we became festive as we struggled to free it. This happened four times that night. Finally the Deux Chevaux broke down, its accelerator cable broken. But, ironically, there was among us both a doctor, a medical student from Cambridge, and a Land Rover mechanic, the co-driver of our guide. The car was soon repaired and again we were on our way.

We came to some low mountains, portenders of the Hoggar. The track was now harder and sandless. But here the Peugeot of the Swiss broke down. The convoy, unaware, rippled away into the night. The car had a puncture but when we took the wheel off one of the screw threads broke and there was no hope of repairing it. The Land Rover with the two Scotsmen appeared back but soon we all went into the gully to sleep.

The sky was full of stars, many shooting. Having finished off our tin of orange jam, the last of our provisions, we slept. It was wonderful to wake up among the rocks. The sky was a soft blue and for once there were no flies. The Peugeot had to wait for a lorry and we promised to pass on the message when we saw one. We set off again. The road was badly corrugated. We entered among impressive naked mountains, contorted into extraordinary sphinx-like shapes. Desert shrubs and *latin*, little Sahara trees, appeared. The latter, lacking moisture, flopped sluggishly over the sand, a mess around themselves. Soon we came into a wadi between two great table mountains. To our right was a big spinny of *latins*, more erect than before, and a sea of tall reeds bending in the breeze, and beyond, couched in the side of the mountain, stood the mud walls of Arak, a tiny courtyard barracks, the size of a large house. Here was our vital water. We had almost passed by unnoticing.

As we stopped two Algerians leapt from the reeds as if by magic. They led us through the reeds to a well where we hauled up water in a bucket with a hole in it. We drenched each other in the heat of the day. Four young men ran Arak as a substitute for military service. They had been there for twenty days. It might be for three months.

'What do you do all day?' I asked.

'Oh, we just sleep!' one of them replied without a smile.

They were in their early 20s and from Ain Salah. Their commandant was with them. They took us to a cool pre-fab shed without doors standing by the fort. The walls had been scrawled all over with schoolboy graffiti and naked women.

'I'd hate to be left here alone!' sighed Francess.

I tried to explore the fort but the commandant said proudly, 'Mamnoo' (forbidden) and having proved his authority in this one word, began asking me to bring him provisions when I returned from Tamanrasset, above all tea.

In the shed making tea sat our first Targui, his face veiled except for his eyes. Sacred amulets hung around his neck. There was bleating outside. A goat meandered in and, noticing the old tea leaves, began devouring them avidly. We began feeding it on bread and jam. Among the graffiti on the wall was scribbled the lonesome phrase 'Solitaire on domine'.

As we drove on patches of rough vegetation began to appear and the latins were bigger. We saw houses of reeds. In front stood stern, blue-robed Tuareg. A little girl, standing in a field of dry earth, shyly watched us go by.

We came to Tesnou, the well some miles before the grave of the marabout who discovered it. But we found no well. According to local tradition those who failed to stop here brought the evil eye upon themselves. We searched amid the twisted rocks but found only beautifully made stone fireplaces and walls built by shepherds to protect the sheep from jackals. Three miles further on stood the convoy, a little way off the road. By the track Algerian flags fluttered from a little white shrine. To our right was a nomadic tent. Outside stood a Targui in bright blue. The British were roasting a goat they had bought in one of the villages. The guide told us the tale of the marabout, Moulay Hassan, whose grave this was. In 1836 he had helped to open the Tuareg south to the French. When he came to Tesnou he died of thirst. No sooner did he die than water burst from the rocks and the spring appeared. The Tuareg had another story. Once there was a terrible drought. The Tuareg prayed for water. God cleaved the rocks in two and water gushed forth. In the tent, said the guide, lived an old white-haired man who guarded the shrine and claimed direct descent from Moulay Hassan.

That night the British brought out whisky and we ate the goat. But first we had to drive three times round the shrine. Local superstition believed that the traveller who failed to do this brought down terrible misfortune upon himself. Everyone had done it with great amusement but when later that night a lorry calmly wound round the shrine three times before continuing its journey, we realised that for most people it was no joke.

The guide told us of the tragedies of people who had lost the track as they drove and panicked. Instead of calmly retracing their tyre tracks, they would hysterically search for the stone markers until they were lost in the desert. 'I had a German friend who died like this. Just a few weeks ago a tourist car was lost. The police found the bodies a few days later.' He told us of the few solitary Frenchmen who had for many years been settled at Tam or Djanet. There was one old Frenchman in Djanet who had become a Muslim, lived for years in great luxury under French rule and had stayed on. Once the guide was with him. The Frenchman stopped at a house and said, 'Just a minute. I must go in and see my wife.' He did this at four houses in the same street. It transpired that he had eleven wives.

We stopped for water at the village of Ain Eker shortly before Tamanrasset, and drove on. We began passing through the table-topped mountains of the Hoggar. It was high and cool. Suddenly we came onto perfect asphalt. It was like driving in the silence of a Rolls Royce after the machine-gun rattle of days. A tiny airport appeared. This minute stretch of asphalt to Tamanrasset seemed like a cunning government manoeuvre to persuade the visitor landing at the airport that the crossing had been asphalt all the way although our ragged, dusty state must have belied this to those who saw us arrive.

The neat clay city of Tamanrasset, dominated by the strange, chunky Hoggar mountains, lay before us. Around us was the great plain. A caravan of Tuareg in their blue veils wandered through the shrubs in the distance towards a mud village. On the outskirts we found a primitive camping site of African reed huts. We settled into them, six in each.

The next day we wandered across the plain. In one place all was dust and emptiness. A few hundred yards further on we came to villages, groves of trees scattered with fruit and goats, a child in a ragged cloth trailing on the ground, the huge scattered carcass of a camel, its fur the colour of the dust still clinging to its long skull, and the unveiled Haratin women carrying invaluable firewood through the scrub. All over the plain there were dots of life. Hour after hour shadows and colours changed, the mountains turning to a strong blue and the ruined Targui forts to orange at sunset. At night the silhouettes of camels were seen winding through the rocks and quite near by we could hear the child-cries of jackals.

The once noble Tuareg tribes who, until their ultimate subjection by the French, ruled supreme in the Sahara and who exploited huge numbers of negro slaves, were already a declining race. The *litham*, the veil which covers all the Targui's face except the eyes and which he will not remove even to eat or sleep, a veil whose blue dye leaves its imprint on the face and gave rise to the mystique of the 'Blue Men of the Sahara', is worn today by many people in Tamanrasset and the Hoggar. Slaves have copied their masters. The *Takouba* long swords which were once the terror of the Sahara are now seen only in the arms of the tourists who come down from Algiers in little plane loads on Saturdays 'to look at the Tuareg'. The modern world has crippled the power and the economy of this cruel but noble race and it won't be long before the still untainted Tuareg of the mountains find it more profitable to mass produce their sacred amulets for tourists than to raid the few passing camel trains.

In Tamanrasset a young Frenchman in a skimpy black *gandoura* and I were discussing the comparative evils of anti-Algerian racism in France and anti-Pakistani racism in England. Some minutes later a policeman approached us and asked us to come to the police station. There we were taken into the office of the commandant, a handsome, arrogant young man whom we discovered was half Italian. Sitting in a chair beside the desk was a man we recognised from the café. The commandant did not ask us to sit down. He put on an air of severe authority and accused us of being 'sales racistes'. We asked why.

'Our colleague heard you saying how excellent it was that Algerians were beaten up in France.'

'No, monsieur, we said the opposite.'

'Our colleague speaks perfect English,' said the young stud, wagging his finger at me, 'and he heard precisely what you said.'

I turned to the Judas and said, 'Then, will you kindly recapitulate our conversation in full.'

'Candly?' replied the confused man.

'Yes, please recapitulate.'

'Repulee catee?' replied the man.

'Do you speak any English?' I asked.

'Yes, me veery, veery gud spik Eenglis.'

Then he went completely silent and said no more. The commandant looked annoyed but was clearly unwilling to backtrack.

'Well, you can go, but don't do it again.'

'Don't do what again?'

'It is forbidden by law to question a policeman,' he said. We went to the door and out into the desert heat.

On the following day Francess and I arranged with two kindly lorry drivers to take us all the way into Morocco, a journey of three days by lorry which would have taken us at least ten hitch-hiking. But as we entered the lorry the commandant approached and asked the man for a lift to Ain Salah. His position, he explained, entitled him to a front seat. As the man, I was relegated to the back where I lay among bags of wheat. The two drivers were petrified of the policeman and would not even discuss the matter when I suggested they refuse the dreadful man a lift. We reached Ain Salah after a long day's drive with only one stop. I was tired and aching from twelve hours flung about like a stone in a tin can.

Francess looked anxious and when the policeman was out of earshot she said, 'He told me that unless I agreed to elope with him, he would have us arrested for pretending that we are married.' My pent-up exhaustion led me to rage. I stormed towards the policeman and asked him in the presence of others whether the story was true. He looked worried and assured me that he had never said such a thing. I had caught him completely off his guard. He had somehow decided that Francess, who was not in love with me, would be easily prised away and I easily intimidated. Although I didn't care very much any longer, I almost doubted her myself. However, I immediately threw away my advantage by saying, 'I have important friends in Algiers' (the Prince who I knew could never help me over this sort of thing) 'and shall report you as soon as I reach Algiers' (to which we were not returning).

He replied quickly and with authority, 'Are you trying to threaten a police officer?'

I let the matter drop since he was no longer a threat and I had so quickly cast away my own advantage. But it was interesting to find this intelligent, rather venal man playing out the role of one's unjust public school prefect here in the central Sahara.

We drove on without the commandant from Ain Salah, and the drivers, two good, warm men, became completely alive once we had left him. For three days we travelled with them across barren desert which they seemed to know by instinct, inch by inch. The huge wheels of their lorries could negotiate virtually any terrain. When they stopped it was either to pray or to eat. They prayed with fastidious regularity. When they ate they insisted on sharing all their food with us, big steaks and every kind of fruit. They were true Muslims and never tried to take advantage of us. Francess was a natural attraction to lust and this had made our journey very tiring. But these men treated us both with dignity. They seemed to be living completely outside of themselves, and spiritually.

We crossed Morocco and when we reached Rabat we sat at dusk on the beach, unsure of where to stay. A very sexy Moroccan woman approached us and squatted down beside us to talk. We could stay in her house, with her friends, she said. We thanked her and agreed to come. She said that she would go away and check and come back and tell us. When she had gone a polite young man approached us and said that we should not be speaking to that 'bad woman' but would we kindly agree to stay with his family. We agreed and went with him.

The family devoted themselves to us slavishly for a week. Day after day we tried to leave but they wouldn't let us. We soon felt imprisoned by their hospitality. Day after day we tried to pay or buy food but were warned that it would be extreme impoliteness to do so. I could barely get through the meat they lavished on us, we had become so accustomed to living on dry bread and the one big tin of jam we had bought. And theirs was a poor family for whom meat must have been a lavish expense.

Finally, we had virtually to beg them to let us go and escape from what was becoming an unending cycle of hospitality. We took a boat to Spain and when we reached Paris we brought our now chilled relationship to a formal end.

4

The feminine battle of Algiers

When I left Edinburgh University in 1972 I visited the Algerian Embassy in London in response to an advertisement for English lecturers at Algiers University. As I had never taught English, I was convinced that I would not get the job. I was sent to a room in the embassy where a small, fat man with harassed brow and bitten nails sat behind a desk.

I told him why I had come.

'Do you have an MA?' he asked.

All the Scottish Honours degrees were MAs, I explained, so that technically, yes, I was an MA.

'Fine,' he replied, handing me a document and a pen. 'Sign here, please.'

'What's that?' I asked.

'That's a contract.'

Having prepared myself for heavy interrogation I felt cheated by the ease of my selection, particularly when I remembered the agonising BBC news traineeship selection board into which I had just put so much effort and still failed. 'Is that all?' I asked lamely.

'Yes,' he replied, peering distractedly out of the window. 'Just sign,' he yawned.

I glanced at the simple document and, wondering how much of my life I was signing away, I signed. A week later I was on the plane to Algiers.

Having spent the morning before my flight punting on the Cherwell in Oxford with friends, I sat sad and nostalgic on the plane. The embassy assured me of red carpet treatment when I landed – 'Worry about nothing, we are responsible for your well-being, everything will be taken care of.' I spruced up as we touched down. I wore a suit and tie. I wanted to make a good first impression on the education ministry people waiting for me at the official reception lounge. When I entered the terminal building late at night I was shocked by the chaos and the rudeness of customs officials. They took apart my suitcase aggressively and confiscated my tape recorder.

I glanced about for the reception committee but could not see my name on any of the hastily written placards for visiting businessmen. I was sent to a small office to reclaim my tape recorder and at once came up, bang! against the horrors of Algerian bureaucracy. 'Come back with a letter from the ministry and you can have it back,' said the fat, gloating officer. I explained that I was a teacher and needed the machine for my work and that ministry officials would be there – somewhere – to greet me. The official scoffed at my recourse to status and I left in search of the committee. But reception committee was there none.

I took a taxi into Algiers and asked for the centre. 'Which centre?' asked the driver. That was a question that had often bedevilled me on first arrival in Middle Eastern cities. 'The centre of the modern town' ('you ninny!' I whispered under my breath). We drove through the white, stuccoed buildings of Algiers, the hills of the city glimmering palely above us to the left and the ships and fishing boats bobbing and sparkling in the lovely wide bay on our right. We reached the edge of the Casbah where we visited six pensions that were all full, and when I realised that no hotel was to be found, I asked the driver to deposit me at a café in the Place des Martyrs.

I entered the smoky, noisy café, dragging my five suitcases behind me like a tortoise drawing behind it its own, disunited, shell. I ordered a coffee wondering where, at three o'clock in the morning, I would sleep. Ten minutes later the café began closing. The waiter told me to pay and leave with that cold abruptness which combines French hauteur with Algerian roughness.

I pointed piteously at my suitcases but the waiter shrugged and walked off. Hateful with anger, I paid and hurled case after case out into the street to the laughter of waiters and late-leavers.

I was almost weeping with exasperation. From the pavement I could see a small hotel on the edge of an alley which led up into the winding streets of the old Casbah. I managed to leapfrog my cases to the hotel to be told by the owner with arms crossed and a frigidity surpassing that of the French themselves, that it was 'complet'. I sat outside on my cases in despair. An old drunkard in a tattered jacket slouched by and disappeared into a dark alley. A big, black rat leapt up like a wineskin from the gutter. I sat with the patience of a believing Muslim for the decision of fate.

In a few minutes two smiling students from the café came over and invited me to spend the night in their hall of residence and I slept soundly on a sofa.

My arrival in Algiers had been inauspicious but one year later I was to leave the city with a love and a great regret that I have never known in any other city on earth. I was to discover that beneath that rough Algerian crust lay a fascinating charisma which eventually takes hold of one, and that friendships made were to become deep.

On my first day, the university authorities, without any explanation for their broken promises, arranged for myself and the other teachers to stay in rooms in a teachers' hostel. The hostel lay in a tiny, dirty side street where rats scampered by night. One night I found the alley barred to me by battalions of rats running to and fro among scattered garbage across the road and I had to take a series of alternative streets to approach the hostel from the other end.

Our haunts throughout the year were the pavement cafés of the Boulevard Didouche Mourad, Rue Michelet to the old 'pied noir' colons whose seedy frenchness was still reflected in the crumbling Rococo of the buildings and the untidy chatter of the Algerian crowds who had replaced them. The girls in our faculty would not enter the cafés. So open and cheerful on the campus, they would barely nod at us in the streets which they saw as threatening obstacles through which to hurry home. Frightened, they looked neither right nor left.

The cafés were for men in a world where men had atavistically reasserted their authority since the bloody war against the French. The French had tried to lure Algerian womanhood through emancipation, so that Islam and suppression

soon became symbols of reaction to French colonialism. The
streets were full of young people in this, one of the youngest
cities in the world. Fathers, uncles, brothers, cousins were dead.
'Didouchka', as the street was known to the teachers, teemed.
You sat drinking your *moitié-moitié* coffee and marking homework
beneath the lime trees and the proud, noisy crowds moved
among the tables like a guerrilla army.

You chose your café according to your whim, your pocket or
the status of your meeting. If you were with students you went
to the Cercle des Etudiants beside the campus gates. The
scruffiest and cheapest of the cafés, it buzzed with revolutionary
rhetoric and eternal analyses of the progress of the Agrarian
Revolution which was to dominate politics throughout the year.
A faded photograph of Ali le Pointe hung behind the bar. Ali le
Pointe was the adventurer student hero during the Algerian war
who had been blown to bits with his friends in his Casbah hiding
place by Colonel Massu.

Across the road was the Cafeteria where meals were served
behind a long window and where the quieter teachers sought
refuge from the turmoil outside. A little way down, on the same
side, was the Milk Bar where you might drink a Pernod and eat
mille feuilles as you prepared your notes for the next lecture. The
Milk Bar was the café in which the beautiful revolutionary
Djamila Bouhired and her tragic, obedient accomplice, Djamila
Boupacha, had placed a bomb, killing many young *pieds noirs*.
Djamila Bouhired, whom I came to know, is still beautiful and
runs a pharmacy. Djamila Boupacha, scarcely out of childhood,
was deflowered by French paratroopers with the neck of a bottle.
After the war she roamed the streets in despair, obsessed, it was
said, by the fear that she would no longer find a husband. Soon
after the war she committed suicide.

Algiers represented the soul of Algeria's 'French', fertile
northern strip, a perfect copy of southern France, which comes to
a stop at mountain ranges no more than thirty miles south of
Algiers. A foreigner deposited in a little village in this northern
tier would think himself in France. From the neat little red-
roofed villages, fields of ripe wheat, olive groves and vineyards
spread out in all directions and Algerian peasants in French peasant
jackets and berets, with Gauloises hanging from their lips, roam

the country lanes. Tall young men with elegant *bernouses* hanging loosely from their shoulders stand chattering and flicking their prayer beads at street corners. Women in Muslim head-wraps hurry from shop to shop with bulging bags of groceries.

This ripe northern tier gives way abruptly to series of mountains, among them the high arc of mountains which hides the gorgeous world of Kabylia, so close to Algiers yet as far away in spirit as Tibet. The Kabyles are Berber, related to the Tuareg (Tuariq) of the deep south. Thanks to France's divide and rule policy the Kabyles rose to eminence under colonialism and had much closer contact with France than with their Arab brothers. Today the best educated at the university tend to be Berbers, either Kabyle or Auresien. The peoples of Kabylia have, ironically, retained their native customs, including colourful national dress.

At the beginning of one of the first lectures I gave on Orwell's *Animal Farm* I publicly asked the class taboo question number one, who was Arab and who was Berber. 'Oh, but we're Algerians, sir,' the sixty, mostly girl students, said in one voice. I knew at once that I had blundered and moved quickly to another subject.

A day later, however, a girl came up to me and explained that she was a Berber and that her family lived in a small village in the Kabyle mountains near Tizi Ouzou. Like most Kabyles, many of her relations lived in France. If I was interested in learning Kabyle and knowing more about the Berbers, would I like to meet her and her friends at the ice-cream shop on the following day? she asked. When I went there I found some of my most conscientious students eating ice-creams and crowding around a secretly printed news-sheet on Berber cultural activities like innocent communards. There were poems and stories but nothing remotely political. 'The education system is entirely Arab,' they told me. 'Although Algeria was Berber before the Arabs came, there is virtually no allowance for our culture and we are forbidden to print books in our own language.'

Nearest to Algiers you come to the Mitidja mountain with its cool pine forests and, beyond, you rise interminably to the mountain ridges which dominate Kabylia and from where you gaze down into myriad green valleys with scattered red-tiled hilltop villages and profusions of trees and flowers. During the war of independence the Kabyles were among the fiercest fighters and French troops were loathe to enter the perfect guerrilla terrain of hills and valleys.

Unveiled women in bright red dresses move like flowers through the valleys, bearing sheaves of yellow wheat. At night you can hear the child-cries of jackals and the hideous baying of wolves. Kabylia is like a huge, natural fortress of rock. No invader, whether Roman, Arab or French, ever really managed to impose themselves here. The French army could only enter the hills in massive numbers after heavy saturation bombing which has left hillsides blackened and dead to this day. Beyond, the mountains fall into the huge deserts, Algeria's 'third' tier, the biggest, the emptiest and, in summer, the most terrible. Here you are among the immense, knife-ridged dune seas of El Oued and Laghouat, a world of mud houses, palm groves, and great Arabian camel caravans with their ladies swaying within creaking, tasselled *houdajes*.

This was the country to which a dozen clever idealistic teachers had chosen to come, seven years after the end of the war of independence, to set up a department of English. None had come for the money, there was little to be had. None had come to escape. Each one of us had come to Algeria because the country drew us, either for political or cultural reasons. Partly because I came to love an Algerian girl, I also came to love the country. Almost all the other teachers left with a sense of deep disillusion, if not disgust. This was because almost every promise made to us by the authorities, both the ministry and the university, had been broken. We worked the year with complete dedication but the Algerian authorities never, for one moment, stood up for us. The other teachers quickly became so cynical that they became insensitive to the real beauty that lay beneath the surface of the country and its people.

The teachers that first year were an interesting and eccentric group of people. It was long before the days of high-tech EFL, English as a Foreign Language, or TEFL or what you will. It was still the era of freebooting dreamers and idealists. There was Alfred, the middle-aged, urbane intellectual with an air of David Niven. Alfred had never married or managed to compete in the practical world. He was loved, knowledgeable and witty. In one way he was a loner. In another he leant upon those of us who were able to resolve the impossible practical problems that were the very tapestry of our lives in Algiers. He had a child-like humour. On one of the endless days in which we were seeking out an official on the campus to get one of our everlasting documents ratified Alfred lifted a dust-bin lid in vaudeville despair. 'He couldn't be in here, could he?'

There was Henry, the middle-aged Australian intellectual whom the students were constantly complaining was drunk in class. We all stood up for him for, although he drank of nights as we all did, he was never drunk in class. He had a lazy drawl and a lazy movement that gave the impression of perpetual inebriation. He had taught throughout the Middle East for many, many years and wherever he went he took his MG coupé sports car which was our transport night after night to visit the exquisite sea-food restaurants along the coast, which looked down upon the sea and the little fishing boats that bobbed upon its waves.

There was the brilliant Marxist couple, Henry and Jane, who had come to Algiers through genuine idealism. Despite a year's experience that would have disillusioned the most ardent erstwhile supporter of the FLN, they never altogether lost their belief in the Algerian revolution. Henry was a mathematician, the son of an Oxford scholar and expert in West African affairs.

There was the little English girl with the rasping London accent who was living with her Algerian boyfriend. She completely ignored the myriad interests that were the hub of our lives and saw Algeria through a relationship that appeared to be constantly falling to bits.

There were the Menaces, correctly the Menzies, the social core of our group. Edgar was the quiet, clever witty intellectual married to the frivolous Marie whose aim in life was to stand as far away as possible from her South African, coloured past. She, perhaps, hated Algeria more than anyone. She was abused in the street for consorting with foreigners, by young Algerians who thought she was one of them. Waiters sometimes refused to serve her in cafés. In Ramadan, when Muslims were forbidden to eat in public during the fasting hours, she would be virtually spat upon for eating with us.

Marie flirted innocently with all of us and Edgar ignored her flirtations as only an English intellectual could. The Menaces had names for everything. The main boulevard Didouche Mourad was Didouchka. The bureaucratic horrors we faced were LRT, 'Life's rich tapestry'. They managed to find a flat in central Algiers and it was here that the group came to drink, discuss literature and opera, and groan about the horrors. As time went by I became embedded in my own Algerian life and moved away from this witty, cynical group who were themselves moving away, in isolation, from Algeria itself.

The glory of Algiers is the reflection of the glory that it had been, that it had been because, like Cairo, the flamboyant once-white Rococo façades are crumbling and the great rooms with their *fin-de-siècle* furniture and chandeliers are lived in by peasants from the Rif. Muslims, fanatically puritan as a result of Algeria's stormy history of revolt in which Islam and tradition became the rallying cries of identity, ignore the naked, plaster maidens that trail the beautiful stucco beneath elaborate, floral balconies. The soul of the inhabitants of Algiers, the *pieds noirs* who reflected all the nostalgia of a France they had never known, has flown away. The new dwellers are often squatters.

In place of exotic families reclining on deck chairs sipping good French wines on the balconies, mounds of washing hang from dirty pieces of rope. When the Queen visited Algiers the buildings along her route were given a quick, superficial whitewash, but Algiers is a city evacuated and reoccupied by peoples for whom it is an enigma.

On one of my first evenings I sat in the Baroque dining-room of a restaurant with the tall ceilings and chandeliers of an English club to down a bottle of Cave du President in my solitude and eat a steak. The restaurant was virtually empty but at the next table sat a young European with horn-rimmed spectacles reading Trollope. He looked up and invited me to join him. He was English. 'I love Trollope when I'm alone. He reads so easily.' He was Peter Sluglett, another teacher at the university, who was to become, in face of the multiplying bureaucracy that lay ahead, our leader.

During one of my first lectures to my sixty girl students there was a scuffle with shouting in the courtyard. Always deferential, the students at first looked at me to see whether I would approve of their running to the window. When I shrugged the whole class rushed to the window and soon began shrieking with delight. 'They're killing a rat,' one shouted. I could hear the university concierge yelling to the accompaniment of the clacking of a broom against concrete.

I returned to my desk and stood there quietly. I heard the rat squealing as it was crushed to the applause of all the classrooms around the quad. A student who had peered round to see where Monsieur was nudged her neighbour and the warning that Monsieur was 'not amused' rippled through the craning bodies. Carefully, they peeled away from the windows and returned, heads bowed, to their desks. I made no comment.

I never really understood whether their dignified silence reflected natural deference and hospitality or whether they were morally ashamed. Much later, when I fell in love with one of the girls and we planned to marry, I asked her whether she, too, had run to the window but she maintained that she could not remember the incident. For me it was to become symbolic of the schizophrenia that has existed in every Algerian since their bloody war.

In my class were twins, two beautiful, smiling girls. Walking back after a lecture one day I said that I felt that they were happy and could never have really suffered. 'Oh, yes, we have, sir,' said one. 'During the war the French took our father and our brother in front of a wall and made us watch and shot them before our eyes.'

For most of my year I shared a magnificent white, crenellated villa with rollicking gardens full of wisteria and jasmine with the friend I had stayed with when I crossed the Sahara. He gave me a suite of rooms for a nominal rent. In exchange for that I was to be his companion, a sort of Greek chorus to his extensive philanderings. 'I have mistresses for six days of the week,' he joked. 'On Sunday I see my children.' I soon found that I was ferrying mistresses back and forth across Algiers and trouble-shooting situations that belonged to a Shakespearian comedy.

On one occasion the mistress of the moment, a beautiful blonde-haired actress, appeared at the gate and I brought her in where Ahmed embraced her rapturously. Ten minutes later the bell at the front gate rang. Ahmed glanced through the window and saw to his horror that it was his long-standing mistress, Farida, a famous freedom fighter in the war. 'For God's sake, keep her at bay for as long as you can,' said Ahmed. I went to the gate and fumbled for ages for the key to the infuriation of Farida who threw stinging glances at the house. When I finally let her in she was livid with me but Ahmed had managed to smuggle the actress out by the garden gate.

Farida was so venerated in Algeria that President Boumedienne, hearing that she had a lover (he didn't know who) would occasionally telephone her to implore her to remain respectable. I was fascinated by her war record, indeed obsessively interested in the revolution in those days. Farida had carried arms through the dreaded Maurice line from Tunisia for the *moujahideen* in the internal *wilayats* (FLN districts). One day Ahmed had to meet an official at the airport and Farida and I went with him. We had had a lot to drink that evening and Farida was bubbling with heroic memories. When Ahmed went in to the airport, I turned to Farida and said, 'You must be very proud of what you did for your country.'

'No, Trevor,' she said quickly, 'I am horrified, I am ashamed.' She lifted up her rather powerful hands and holding them as if to strangle, said, 'You don't know what it is like to kill a man with your own hands.' I trembled.

The freedom fighter I had been fascinated by since going to university was Djamila Bouhired. Djamila had been accused of placing a bomb in the Milk Bar in which three people were killed on 30 September 1956 and in the Cafeteria and the Coq Hardi on 26 January 1956. A beautiful 22-year-old woman, she was shot down by the French paratroopers while fleeing through the Casbah and discovered with important documents belonging to the FLN liaison officer Yacef Saadi, the protagonist of urban terrorism, although she was in time to warn the rebel Ali le Pointe.

For seventeen days Djamila was tortured by the paras by electric shocks to the forehead, the feet, the vagina and the breasts. Her brother, the 11-year-old Hadi, and her 14-year-old nephew were also interrogated and tortured. The trial was manifestly unjust, the judge declaiming, 'One arrests the doctors who cure the rebels. One would do better to arrest the advocates who defend them.' Her advocate was Jacques Verges. Her fiancé, Taleb, was tortured and confessed everything, apparently adding a statement which led to her condemnation to death.

Her defence was Greek in its drama. 'For what you are about to cut off my head', she announced, 'it is true that I said it but for what is without consequence and concerns someone else with whom I am only attached by sympathy of ideas, I did not say it.' She was referring to her fiancé.

When the judge condemned her to the guillotine Djamila laughed. 'Don't laugh,' said the judge, 'it's a serious matter.'

'Sirs,' she said, 'I know that you are going to condemn me to death, for those whom you serve are thirsty for blood.' The sentence was commuted to life imprisonment at the eleventh hour.

I met Djamila at a New Year's party in Ahmed's house and was astonished at how young and vivacious she had remained. I danced with her for much of the evening and far from being diffident about the war, she poured out her reminiscences. 'I am proud of what I have done for my country, I have no shame at all.' Friends nearby laughed. 'Is Djamila telling her war stories again?' said one. She was now a pharmacist and resentful of the way women had been treated since the revolution. 'We fought alongside the men but Algerian women have lost everything they won in the war. Look at me, I'm just a pharmacist while the men have top government jobs.'

The grievances of women were justified in those days. My students told me of a very sophisticated Kabyle girl the previous year who had had a liaison with a man. Her parents, simple people from the Kabyle mountains, came down to Algiers to see her. They treated her with every affection and took her to their village for the weekend. When they got there they tied her, under the gaze of the entire village, so I was told, to two horses, which tore her apart. Honour had been seen to be done.

In class the girls were very free and positively flirtatious. Their favourite set-book was D.H. Lawrence's *Women in Love* and in their essays were told their pitiful stories about their search for love and lovers and their yearning to escape from Algiers to England where they would be treated well. In the streets, however, they would scarcely dare acknowledge my existence. For many months I received love notes from a girl with pictures and pathetically sentimental poems attached. Naturally, I never replied and soon the anonymous notes became a kind of independent correspondence with the girl complaining about how I had deceived her, how I had shown her my love and suddenly withdrawn it. I became disturbed by the correspondence but, not knowing who the correspondent was, could do nothing about it.

It represented the torment of many Algerian girls who had been educated to expect freedom and who had glimpsed freedom on holidays in France but were completely oppressed in their own society. After six months the girl revealed herself. She was one of the plainest and most sulky girls in the class. I explained very correctly but completely hypocritically that teachers were forbidden to have any liaison with their students. I then began receiving notes of furious despair and betrayal and ignored them as best I could.

One day I took my students to see Beckett's *Fin de partie* at the Hogar Rooms near the Aletti Hotel. After the performance three of them, including my love-sick correspondent, came with us to a café at the beginning of the Bab el-Oued area nearby. We went upstairs to the café and ordered Coca Colas. Almost as we sat down three scruffy men surrounded the table. One of them, a plump, ugly, dirty man in his early 30s, shrieked cruelly at the girls: 'You are minors! You know that you are forbidden to consort with foreigners, bitches!'

'Who the bloody hell are you?' I said.

'*Sûreté nationale.*'

'Show us your cards.'

The policeman plunged his hand into his breast pocket and flung a grubby plastic identity card on the table. One of the girls looked at it. 'Yes, it is,' she said pathetically as she began to get up.

'No, they're not going with you,' I said. 'I'm their teacher and they are here quite correctly.' It was four in the afternoon.

The man looked at me with loathing, a decadent cruelty, and said with calculated menace and confidence, 'If you're not happy we can take you somewhere and show what the f . . . we think of you.' I stood for a moment looking at him in astonishment.

A tall, long-haired student, Mahmoud, who was with us, got up and said, 'Don't worry, I know these people. I'll go with them. You stay here.' The two other teachers, a young American academic and Henry, the Australian, continued talking as if nothing whatever was happening as frightened people sometimes do. I asked Mahmond where the police would take the girls and he said 'home'. The group left, leaving me to worry about whether I should have insisted on going or not.

The other teachers continued discussing Beckett, completely ignoring me, so I got up to go and went into the street, feeling like Peter by the brazier. After a few minutes I saw Mahmoud and the girls across the road. I rushed across. It transpired that the police, if police they were, had immediately insisted that Mahmoud leave the car. Otherwise they would take him to the police station and cut his hair off. 'They've done that three times to me; I don't care any more.' The girls were chattering with the excitement of the event. I felt mortified. It now seemed that the 'police' had had no intention of taking the girls home. Mahmoud had refused to leave them and the men had finally kicked them all out. The problem, Mahmoud explained, was that the Bab el-Oued area was a red light district. I had no more love letters from the girl.

One of my students, whose husband held an important position in the Department of Forests and Water, became a personal friend. I often dined at their flat. But she was a lazy student and inevitably missed her lectures. As the exams approached I warned her that she was in danger of failing. 'But, sir,' she smiled, aggrieved, as if to say, 'You can't fail your friends.' I explained that in England friendship didn't count and that although we had set the courses and were to set and mark the exams, I would not look at the names on the exam papers. We were tipped off by the authorities to pass as many students as possible for what I assumed were political reasons and had agreed to mark the papers as generously as possible. However, we were all sincere and there was to be no question of favouritism. Indeed I, who now had so many friends among my students, found myself in the most vulnerable position when the exams came.

As I expected Fadela failed, although I had been so generous in my marking that she only failed by about 5 per cent.

However, failure meant taking the entire year again and she came to me pleading. I explained regretfully that the die was cast and that I could do nothing. 'In that case,' she said, 'my husband is a friend of the Principal.' The Principal happened to be the nail-bitten little director who had interviewed me and with whom I was barely on speaking terms. I told her that if she wanted to pull strings with him then that was her affair. A day later the man called me to his room and tried to charm me. 'What's 5 per cent?' he said with a hang-dog look. 'Say you'd erred by 2 per cent, then you can just add another three. Otherwise she'll have to take the year again.' I told him that this would be unfair on the others but if he wished to take the initiative then it was up to him. 'No, only you can do that,' he said. He begged me and I began to gather that his head was on the line. But I refused and eventually left the office. My relationship with him was to become quite frigid. Strangely enough the girl and her husband bore no grudge and I dined with them on each return trip to Algiers.

Fatiha had been in my class from the start. She was one of the prettiest and quietest girls in the class. She was certainly the cleverest and I could barely put red ink to her essays. She never flirted with me as the others did but worked dexterously and left the class when it ended. I sometimes found myself thinking about her as I lectured and if I asked her a question about a modern English novelist I would find some weeks later that she had read virtually every book the novelist had written.

I decided to put on a play at the end of the year, Shaw's *Arms and the Man*, and canvassed for actors. The role of Bluntschli, the chocolate-cream soldier, went to a blind boy called Taleb who turned out to be lazy and completely ineffective. Fatiha wanted a role and she became Raina. It was leading her through her part that made me completely alive to her and when she declaimed her love for Bluntschli I realized that it was to me that she declaimed. The play was aborted by the university authorities and we were soon told that it could not be put on. Perhaps the memories of a previous year's demonstrations in which armed police flooded the campus and numbers of students were arrested had frightened them.

I soon began to woo Fatiha. This consisted initially of

meeting her and her girl-friend at the ice-cream parlour. These meetings took place at four o'clock and became routine. I would usually arrive first. The trim, dark-haired figures would approach tidily through the crowds. They always carried their ruled exercise books and wore simple child's frocks. We never drank coffee but ate ice-cream which I hated. I hadn't yet dared lead Fatiha across the line that divides childhood from Western sophistication. The girls would choose ice-creams with coloured ripples. The café with the red seats was our usual haunt. It was expensive but you were paying for protection from the vigilant moral police.

'Shall we meet here tomorrow?'

'As you like it,' they would sweetly smile. I never tried to correct the grammar.

'But you must learn to decide for yourselves.'

'As you wish,' they would reply obediently.

Sometimes teachers would join us and settle to unreeling endless lamentations about bureaucracy, eternal visits to ministries and banks and offices to gain documents which would justify more documents which would win more documents which would in theory get you paid or lodged. Documentation was a game for those who could stand the course. A document whose meaning was 'residence permit' would turn out to be merely the first of ten documents which would end, if no errors were made en route, in your actually being permitted to reside. Luckily the process was so slow ·that some of us realised in time that residence actually carried with it all kinds of new legal and fiscal problems.

The teachers who joined us would inevitably ignore Fatiha and her friend in fear of such association leading to the sort of dramatic confrontation with the authorities which we had experienced at Bab el-Oued.

A day came when I decided to risk all and invite Fatiha to come for a drive in the country alone. Perhaps less aware than I of the dangers but more likely with the quiet daring of a woman in love, she agreed without a murmur.

We decided to drive to Chrea, a small village in the pine-clad Mitidja mountains above Blida. My battered VW Beetle surged through the hectic rush-hour traffic that cacophonically honked

its way through the twisting streets of the city's many hills. Soon
we were out into the green, fertile valley which was France if
you blinked but became pathetically Third World if you gazed
too long. It was springtime and the trees were full of sweet-
smelling blossom. Peasants sold fruit from the side of the road.
Little boys were forever running out with arms laden with
oranges.

But as we rounded a corner, we heard sirens. Plump
motorcycles ridden by policemen hidebound with paramilitary
trappings screeched to a halt 20 metres ahead. I stopped quickly,
as short of them as possible, and told Fatiha to sit quietly. She
smiled and said nothing. Was she afraid?

The police had that sting of authority which is universal in a
world where dull men absorb such power.

'Your papers!'

'Certainly,' I smiled, commenting on the beauty of the
countryside as I fumbled for papers that proved that I existed,
that I was allowed to exist, that I was present, that I was who I
said I was, that the car was mine. I had, of course, no papers to
give me dispensation from immorally consorting with a minor, a
Muslim girl and a pupil. I mused on counting the criminal
charges as I fumbled, then shattered the framework of analysis
by commenting again on the prettiness of the countryside.

'Where are you going?'

'To Chrea.'

'Who's your friend?'

'Oh, just a friend,' I said casually. The police glanced at the
car. Then I played my only card, a master card throughout my
many years of travel in the Arab world. 'How many kilometres
to Chrea?' I casually asked, this time in Classical Arabic.

Puzzled, the policeman took off his helmet, unwittingly
humanising himself, and scratched his head. 'By God you speak
better Arabic than we do,' he said in his barely comprehensible
dialect. I told him where I had studied Arabic and why. 'Look,
he SPEAKS Arabic,' the policeman laughed at his companion.

Suddenly they became jovial peasant men, pouring out their
aborted hopes. 'I'd love to visit England,' said Policeman
Number One.

'The girls are pretty there, eh?' said Policeman Number Two.

'Yes, why don't you come and visit me,' I said, scribbling down my Oxford address. They took the address with moving gratitude and said they would love to come in the way that people say they would love to become millionaires. When we said goodbye we were slapping each other on the back like childhood blood brothers.

Fatiha and I spoke little as we drove on across the green valley that is northern Algeria, with its French villages with their little squares, overgrown *places de boule* and boarded-up churches; so French until you peer into people's faces and realise that the spirit of France never penetrated the surface of Algeria. The landscape is French, the architecture is French, the language, the clothing, the Gauloises, even the berets are French. But nothing else is and that nothing masks what is truly Algerian. One million Algerians had died to a man to preserve what even many nationalists claimed did not exist. Yet today Algeria has perhaps more of its own, proud, somewhat severe identity than any other country in the Arab world.

We drove across Blida's pretty little square with its *fin-de-siècle* gas-lamps and its elegant wrought-iron concert pavilion in the middle. Wealthy Algerian commuters live in Blida which transcends the squalor that hangs like a pall over many Algerian towns. Middle-class Algerians were wandering across the square with carefully-studied, Parisian hauteur, the women neatly scarved and carrying bulging shopping bags.

Blida is dominated by the great Mitidja mountain which was our destination, our romantic exile. On the other side of Blida, the valley burst into a puzzle of bends up the hillside. Villages of five thatched houses appeared. Little girls in tattered, muddy skirts smiled at us from the roadside.

Girls, tumbled into puberty, realising that their days of spontaneity were cast off, peered giggling behind their mud hovels, making a show of masking their faces with their hands; girls a year deeper into puberty wandered proudly by without a glance. Peasants tramped forever up the luxuriant hillside carrying scythes, women as old as the hills trudging up with immense packs of hay on their backs and with a vigour which contrasted with the sloth of their menfolk.

We drove eternally upward until the bends multiplied at acute angles. At every second bend we confronted the valley, rolling brightly, green, away in all directions, slipping away into the coast and the sea's silver arc. Blida had drawn in on itself, pretty with its desolate church and slim minarets. We came among elegant chalets and the rich smell of pine. Soon we reached the precious little hill town of Chrea with the crisp winter air of a Tyrolean village.

We left the car and wandered along a little path which wreathed through the pines along the lip of the hillside. All was cool and green, clear fertility. We heard a saw rasping timber in the valley deep below. We embraced by a rock and wandered through this forest, for the first time ever alone and unafraid. Spears of light burst into pools or exploded in the valley. As we came to the forest's edge we gazed upon a sea of breathing mist which protected us from the cold unreason of the world below, a world of bureaucrats, police, memories; above all, a world of fear.

Fatiha and I were drawn together by risk. One day in Algiers we decided to walk through the Casbah. I had been many times before through these winding streets which had been the labyrinthine heart of the war. As we entered I heard a man mutter to his friend, 'This Roumi [Roman, i.e. foreigner] is eating the bread of our house.' When we were deeper inside a young man shouted across to his friend, 'Ahmed, look! Our sister is betraying us.' We decided to abandon our journey and return to the comparative anonymity of the modern town.

One day I took Fatiha to the café with the red seats and told her casually that I didn't know whether our relationship could ever work since there would be so much conflict at family and social levels unless she wanted to sacrifice her Algerian identity entirely. She began crying quietly and I was in the impotent position of being unable to put my arm around her to comfort her or even to touch her. The mildest fanatic would surely have reported us.

A similar incident occurred in the beautiful Bois de Boulogne about which Gide wrote so ecstatically. I took her behind a palm tree and kissed her, then suddenly noticed that even there a gardener was eyeing us bitterly.

We walked among the trees until we reached a wall over

which we could gaze onto the corniche road and the sea.

'I've never been here before. It's so beautiful,' she said.

'Yes, it's a pity we can't be more natural.'

'Yes,' she replied quietly, 'it's terrible to be in this country. We fought for freedom but we can do nothing without being watched. It's quite different in England, isn't it?'

I told her that yes, it was freer but in that freedom there was often little idealism. I loved Algeria despite the viciousness it bred. I loved it because of the idealism that existed everywhere in those days, among my students with whom I sang as we traipsed off to the fields to dig as part of the agrarian revolution, among my pupils who after a lecture ran to read every book the writer had ever written, even among the obscurantist Muslims who eyed us with hatred. Even there there was some belief. It was not mere jealousy. It was genuine resentment that a frivolous 'Roumi' could wander into this vibrant country and draw its women away to decadent lands.

I said, 'There is so much to separate us but we are stretching our hands over the universe to touch. Yet I am your teacher. Your affection is in the context of your own despair during an ambiguous period. I don't want to create scandals for you. You must think carefully about the possibility of living forever away from your own country, from your family. You must think carefully about the possibility of never coming home again.' When I turned to her she was crying.

For some moments she was silent and then she yelled: 'I don't mind who you are. I don't mind if you're my teacher. I don't mind if you're English. I just love you.' I could not touch her as the warden was peering at us lecherously through the shrubs wherever we went.

We spent the summer together in Oxford. Unfortunately for our relationship so did numerous other girls from my class whom I had arranged to stay with families in Oxford. For two months my house became a little corner of Algeria. Most of the girls were longing to marry an Englishman, partly because Englishmen were kinder to them than Algerians for whom machismo played an important role, and partly because Algerian puritanism and the problems involved in Algeria's 'revolutionary experiments' held little attraction for pretty women who craved for lives filled with love and freedom.

Thus was I wooed by these Algerian belles and my vanity succumbed to the wooing. A girl from my class arrived without warning one day and immediately began tidying my drawing-room. When Fatiha arrived there was an air of conflict which I had to use all my diplomacy to subdue. Another evening a girl arrived with an enormous bouquet of flowers for me. On another a recently divorced Algerian woman turned up at two in the morning, pleading for a bed for the night. The summer became a dreamlike 'Thousand and One Nights' and tested to the utmost that loyalty towards Fatiha that the responsible persona within me wanted to retain. But, alas! the spirit and flesh are weak.

At the end of the summer Fatiha and I drove back through France to Marseilles from where she was to fly to Algiers and I was to take the boat. We judged it risky to take the boat together for fear of being betrayed to the police once we had arrived. There were two boats, one was Algerian with elegant first-class facilities, the other was French and a virtual cattle-truck for the wretched Algerian workers who came to and from France, broken, blank-eyed men. The boat that lay in the harbour appeared to be the Algerian boat so we decided to risk it and go together. We were to be sadly disillusioned. Once aboard, we realised that it was the terrible French boat.

We were stuck in third class, deck class, surrounded by a thousand stupid, lusting eyes. As the boat left harbour the lower floor had turned into a general lavatory of screaming women and children. There were no deck chairs on deck. In other circumstances we would have been flung together for comfort and warmth but given our situation, in which any suspicion would lead to trouble on arrival, we had virtually to pretend we did not know each other.

I felt with horror that we might never be together again. It was a beautiful, quiet, moonlit night and we had many months of memories to share. If I looked away an Algerian would creep up to stare or touch Fatiha and I had to push him away quietly to avoid a riot. Once a man crawled across the stenching deck and asked Fatiha in Arabic where she came from. She was pretending to be Spanish and she replied in fake astonishment in English.

'You're from the Aures [Mountains], aren't you?' said the dreadful man with grotesque precision.

All night we sat deep in gloom on the boat and we arrived in Algiers exhausted with depression and mental chaos. It was strange spending the next few days in Algiers with Fatiha. After months of lyrical freedom in Europe we were back into the fulcrum of risk, only able to meet by day and never able to show any signs of open affection. We had agreed that Fatiha would complete her studies in Algiers that next year and it was implicitly agreed that we would marry the following summer. After some days I returned to London and our love-affair of correspondence began and was to continue until we met in Spain for a mid-year holiday the following February.

For those few months we wrote to each other daily, passionate letters, but my own life, as a teacher of English in Oxford, had become increasingly hedonistic and philanderous with my little house filled every evening with Latin American girls. Fatiha, pathetically faithful to her first romantic love, suspected this, and I realised later, in my despair at losing her, that the ambiguity of my own letters was traumatic for her. She wrote comparing my own 'experience' of the world with the fact that I was the first man that she had known and lived with.

In February we met for two deeply romantic weeks in Spain, spending the days drinking sparkling wines on the warm hillsides and watching flocks of goats tinkling down the slopes, dressing up in the evenings and dining out in different restaurants. One night in Cordoba we roamed the old Muslim alleys and came to a shop full of wedding dresses. Fatiha tried to draw me to the shop but I smiled and led her away, responding to my own inner doubts.

When our holiday had ended and I had returned to London and Fatiha to Algiers our correspondence continued to reflect our passion. To words of unbridled endearment in English and French Fatiha would add 'Yeki dabi', 'My darling' in the Aures dialect of the Berber language. But my own letters became fewer as my doubts increased.

Suddenly her daily letters stopped and the next letter three weeks later was addressed 'Dearest'. The letter included a description of her friendship with her now constant companion,

Mohammed Omar, a Syrian friend of mine. I was glad of this friendship with a man I had liked. I did not recognise the sting. But then it arrived, the coolest farewell letter I have ever received, and so ended in sorrow my remaining link with Algeria and so died a little bit of my life. Six years later I was in the hall of the Marriott Hotel in Amman. A young man tapped me on the shoulder and said, 'Do you remember me? I'm one of your old students, Mohammed Omar.' He was in Amman, he said, with his wife. When I left him he quoted a line of verse in Arabic which I failed to understand. 'It means that I'm pleased to see you even if you are not pleased to see me.' So I did not need to ask who his wife was.

5

Sharing salt in Saudi Arabia

I first went to Saudi Arabia in 1974 as a 'technical consultant' consulting who on what I did not really know. During my few weeks' training in my plush new Park Lane office I had pushed pieces of paper about my desk and absorbed the important knowledge that we were not recruitment agents but were offering 'technical services'. It seemed a broad enough mandate and I carried to Riyadh a little brief-case with neat, headed paper, a few notes on our philosophy and general outlines of the services we could offer. As our office was new, had four members of staff including me, and I had been given the go-ahead to offer almost anything to anyone, I sat on the plane with considerable peace of mind. No need to worry about detail. Whatever the problem, we would sort it out sharp for a nice, fat fee.

On my first night in Riyadh my taxi rattled through the billowing dust of Batha Street whose central drainage ditch stank like a sewer, nerving myself against the howling cacophany of car horns, and searching for a hotel. I finally left the taxi and fought my way through the 'Kuwaiti' *souq*, avoiding crowds of poor Yemenis bargaining for army shoes and surplus jackets and leaping the broken pavements. I finally found the Riyadh Hotel, a monolithic building all of five years old, antique by Riyadh standards in that first destructive era of the great boom. A newer building across the road was already being bulldozed. It would later be replaced by a jerry-built concrete block which would make its owner a millionaire and collapse a few years later.

The dingy Riyadh Hotel, whose air conditioning smelt of damp rats, was filled with pathetic Western businessmen almost crushed by gloom, sipping after-dinner 'American' coffee, a cup of lukewarm water with a Nescafé bag in the saucer. Such are the whims of Saudi clients, that many foreigners had had to postpone their returns to wives in Guildford, Dorking or Pennsylvania ten times over in order to complete their business.

On the first day I went out consulting, practising my patter over and over again under my breath as I wound my way among savage cars and taxis. Despite the professional excellence of my company I could not resist musing as follows: 'I represent Technical Services Worldwide (i.e. my boss, his dreamy partner, our secretary and me) and we have had ten years' experience of recruiting top-level middle management through-out Asia (the odd fitter in a small Asian country) and the Middle East (a secretary in Dubai), and we wish to offer you our complete range of services. You may like to know our philosophy. Well, our philosophy is based upon the premise that we tailor our man for the culture that suits him best – in your case somebody with a proper feel for the Arabs (i.e. watched *Lawrence of Arabia* and eats shish kebab from his local takeaway). We have an almost limitless list on our computer (i.e. two unemployed stockbrokers scribbled in a file somewhere) and we believe that we are the RIGHT company for YOU.' Although this was how I mused, my company was to win many important contracts after my first 'scouting' year.

Having mastered my spiel, dusted my Samsonite, tightened my tie, polished my shoes on the back of my trousers and put on the smile that I had been practising for hours in the mirror, I entered the General Motors car showroom. Two languid Saudis leaned on a Buick, fiddling with their prayer beads and giggling girlishly.

'I would like to see the Director,' I asserted politely but just a little severely.

One waved his hands at a staircase. I climbed up, went along a corridor and entered a room from where I had heard considerable noise. It was filled with bedu.

Behind a big desk sat a grand old man with a wise, lined face and a pleasant smile. Everyone was shouting. A tea-boy lounged against the desk arguing with the shaikh without a hint of respect. The telephone rang constantly and the shaikh patiently

answered everyone in turn, in a complex sort of way. It was the
falconing season and two tall bedu carried immense, hooded
tiercels on gloved wrists. Two obsequious British businessmen
sat with cups of constantly circulating tea on a sofa, waiting for
their turn which I could have told them would never come unless
they imposed their presence.

'*Salaam alaykum*,' I said to impose mine.

'*Wa alaykum as-Salaam*,' said the shaikh, turning to a friend to
point out that the *afrangi* spoke Arabic.

'By God,' said the clerk, 'here are the invoices for the new
consignment.'

The shaikh signed the document, the telephone rang. 'Yes
we'll buy three,' he muttered into the telephone, 'but only
against pro-formas.'

'How are your sons?' shouted a bedouin with something
more personal on his mind.

'*Al-hamdulillah*,' replied the shaikh warmly, meaning,
'Well!'

'I have an Englishman here,' said a smarmy little Lebanese
with an expensive French attaché case and gold cuff-links, 'who
represents Samazuki motorcycles.' The Englishman's eyes lit up.

'By God,' said the shaikh, 'Do they go fast?'

'As fast as the wind,' said the Lebanese.

'Yes,' said the Englishman daringly, 'they have three
cylinders, automatic declutch and they will do 200 kilometres to
the gallon,' said the Englishman. 'Look here's the brochure. You
see the diagram here, now here on page 64 is the breakdown of
the. . . . '

The phone rang. 'By God,' said the shaikh. 'May your years
be long!' to the caller.

Meetings in those days in Saudi Arabia were easy, even at the top
level. When I went to the Ministry of Agriculture and asked for
an appointment with the Deputy Minister to discuss recruiting
management for agro-businesses, I was ushered into his presence
immediately by a tea-boy. I was astonished by the one-to-one
meeting and began explaining my mission as tea was served.
Hardly had three minutes elapsed, however, when the doors
burst open and twenty chattering bedu ran in and surrounded the

man's desk. The Deputy Minister rose as if greeting dignitaries. He asked each in turn how were their parents, their children, their camels, their goats, their fields. They all replied at once.

The atmosphere was suddenly bedlam and I was quickly forgotten. They each replied, '*Be-kher, al-hamdulillah.*' ('Well, praise be to God.') Then the whole cycle was repeated and repeated until the ignorant observer doubted the purpose of their visit. The bedu might as easily have been visiting a bedouin camp in a wild desert place as a big room in one of Riyadh's Airport Street ministries.

The leader of the group eventually took the floor and embarked on a highly theatrical soliloquy in which he praised God, he praised the minister, he praised the earth which gave of its fruits and finally, pointing to a photograph of King Faisal, he burst into hysterical weeping, crying. 'Praise be to his Majesty whom God has taken from us, alas! Praise be to His Majesty whom God has taken from us!' He then began wiping tears from his eyes with the ends of his red chequered *gutrah*. Then he fell into a chair beside the Deputy Minister, weeping, and as he wept he quietly whispered his petition: 'Ahmad so-and-so has put a fence across our land and we have no room to graze our sheep,' or the like.

The twenty bedu began making their farewells, a virtual carry-over from their welcome, but each one, as he embraced the Deputy Minister, whispered his petition and you could see from the Deputy Minister's face that he was carefully absorbing the laments, for these were cousins on whom his position within the extended family and power structure depended.

When I first arrived at the Riyadh Hotel, I decided to spend my siesta away from the gloom of the cliques of unhappy businessmen in the foyer and sunbathe on the roof. There I found an American hippy doing the same. Somewhat astonished – who has ever heard of a hippy in Saudi Arabia? – I struck up a conversation. He was teaching English to Lockheed employees on the outskirts of Riyadh. It was enjoyable to meet someone who was not in a hurry, someone so much closer in that respect to the Arabians than the harried, hurried businessmen who flew in and out of Riyadh like darts. Soon another American joined us, a pleasant young man with short back and sides. A sensitive, academic person, I thought. 'He writes beautiful love poetry,' my hippy friend told me when he left, 'but he's very unhappy. He was in Vietnam. He told me that when he was there he used to burn out the eyes of children to obtain information about the movement of the Viet Cong.' The story was so little bearable that we quickly changed the conversation. The young man belonged to that quite large population of Vietnam-niks who had been so brutalised by the war that they had been unable to re-adjust to life in the West and had gone to Saudi Arabia and Iran to train their respective armies.

Wandering one day down Riyadh's al-Wazir Street I stopped to watch one of the *mutawwa'een*, those ragged old religious policemen with henna in their beards, waving his stick and calling out, 'Close the shops, close the shops, pray, pray!' Two Saudi girls, veiled and shrouded in *abayas*, stood nearby. When the old man tried to wave them off the pavement one of them suddenly lifted her veil and stuck her tongue out. It was a magnificent act of rebellion. The *mutawwa'a* was so astonished that he merely stood for a moment, speechless, and the young girls were able to slip away giggling.

The women of Saudi Arabia and the Gulf become completely indeterminate under their shapeless, black *abayas* unless they wear the very expensive version which is like a one-piece dress tight at the waist with the *abaya* over the top – there at least you can see their figures. Until that girl's act of defiance she might have been an old hag, rather than an imp of 17, so impenetrable was her camouflage. On rare occasions as I wandered through the modern women's *souq* off Deera Square a girl would wink at me. That was as far as flirtation ever went and, in the early days, was my only contact with Saudi women. Muslim women are veiled, say the cynics, because their own libido is strong and must be restrained. But the erotic mystery of the veil has the most disturbing effect on foreign men.

When you fly to Jeddah or Riyadh from London you sometimes see Saudi girls on the plane wearing the latest fashions from the King's Road, heavy make-up and copious silken hair, their 'crown of glory' which must be hidden by Islamic custom as it is considered sexual. When you approach Jeddah airport and the girls hear the landing announcement they go one by one to the lavatory and reappear in their ghastly black cover-alls, suddenly indistinguishable from the Abyssinian servant-women who gabble and cackle throughout the journey.

Staying one day with a grand Yemeni publisher, now a Saudi national, in Jeddah I came to know his charming Czech wife who was on a visit from Beirut. When, later, I stepped into his Cadillac and sat in the front seat I saw that the back was filled with a row of veiled Saudi women. I sat in silence in the front. Then one of the cowls leaned foward and the lady raised her veil. 'Don't you recognise me, Trevor?' We were both quite suddenly laughing. It was strange leaning back and chattering amiably to a liberated Czech among a uniform line of factory-made black sacks.

Taxi drivers in Saudi Arabia in those days were notoriously crooked. Many were in the chrysalid state betwen bedouin and urban dweller. The guide-books advise you to bargain before getting in. My policy has always been to bargain as soon as I am out and free. If I am being driven to a private home I always get the driver to stop some houses away lest we squabble and he calls the police. The problem with the police is that most homes have alcohol and a casual visit on other grounds can easily lead to exposure.

I was once particularly disillusioned with a taxi driver. I sat in front as usual and began talking in Arabic. He begged me to become a Muslim without more ado. Had I read the Qur'an? If I had read the Qur'an, then I knew the truth; I knew God was One and that Mohammed was his Prophet. I responded with my pet replies, that Jesus is the Son of God (he responded with the usual gasps of horror!) but assured him that I had great admiration for Muslims, etc. He passionately extolled the virtues of Muslims, their piety, their honesty, their hospitality. I agreed, with some reservations which I did not utter, and we were friends. When we reached my destination the driver asked me for 20 riyals, three times the regular price. I have never in my life been so angry and leapt out of the taxi, thrust 7 riyals into the driver's hand, and shouted for all to hear, 'Munafiq', 'Hypocrite'. He was astonished, totally unaware of his inconsistency.

6

Oh Arabia –
my new-found-land

Skirting soft, desert sands near Riyadh in a Land Rover one weekend, we came upon a shepherd and his flock. On the horizon was a cluster of black, goat-hair tents and, extraneously among them, a lorry with a tall aerial. 'Peace be upon you, oh my brother!' we greeted the smiling old man whose shining eyes and wispy white beard were framed in a tattered red-check *kafia*. 'And upon you be Peace and the Mercy and Blessings of God,' he replied, using the most complete welcome to show that we were, indeed, welcome and should tarry with him awhile. We followed custom and exchanged greetings for several minutes, asking how were his sons, how many sheep he had and responding with *'wallahi'* (by God) to his *'wajid'* (many), constantly returning to the original greeting until we felt that the cycle was complete.

We asked the shepherd whose were the tents yonder. 'They are Sudeiri, oh my brothers,' and, after a pause, 'Go, you are welcome there.' Hassa bint Ahmad al-Sudeiri was the favourite wife of King Abdul-Aziz, known to Westerners as Ibn Saud, the founder of theocratic Saudi Arabia. Among the seven children she bore him were Fahd, now King Fahd, the Defence Minister Prince Sultan and the Governor of Riyadh, Prince Salman. 'Which Sudeiri, oh my brother?' we asked. He replied, simply, 'Fahd,' for among the bedu there is no kingship. The shaikh is an arbiter not a leader and until the assassination of King Faisal in 1975 any man could approach the king, clutch his *thobe* as he shouted his request, and call him 'brother'.

We drove on to the camp. There were no guards hugging sub-machine guns, no barbed wire, indeed nothing except the lorry and the aerial to distinguish it from any other bedouin camp in the Kingdom. A giant kettle, big enough to serve twenty people, sat cock-eyed on a fire of gleaming twigs. A young bedouin came out and took us in among his friends who served us tea. They apologised that Fahd (then Crown Prince) was not there to greet us. 'But he is away for the weekend,' they sighed. Away? Jeddah, Rabat, Washington? They didn't know. They had made barely any tryst with a modern world that had lurched into their once clay cities.

Some months earlier, in my squalid Riyadh hotel, I telephoned Juffali Brothers. Juffali are one of the great merchant families whose multifarious divisions import anything from a bolt to a Mercedes. A cheerful, well-spoken English voice came on the line. No, this was not Juffali's headquarters. It was Juffali's Computer Centre. But who was I? 'Oh, a Mostyn. I knew your cousin at Ampleforth. I'm Peter Morrogh.' I was picking up on the expatriate old boys' network. Thanks to one wrong number I was talking to one of the best travelled people in the Kingdom. Peter invited me for a strong (hush!) coffee.

I took a taxi to his flat in Number 4 Street, just off Number 6 Street (don't look for numbers, just turn right at the *shawarma* stall) in Malaaz. It could easily have been 4, 14 or 140 Street, so uniform are Riyadh's housing complexes. We talked travel over a *sadiqi*, that repulsive liquor made from fermented yeast and sugar that was in vogue until, some weeks later, the flogging of a few back-street distillers forced contraband whisky back onto the market at £30 a bottle. I told Peter I had travelled across the Sahara to Tamanrasset by track, neglecting to mention that I had been a passenger and had not a clue about the complicated skills of desert travel.

Shortly after this visit the Kingdom closed down for the Hajj, the annual Pilgrimage to Mecca incumbent on every Muslim who has the means and ability to make it. Although the Hajj only takes three days, business and government come to a stop for the best part of two weeks. As I sat bowed with boredom, scribbling notes in the dull light of my musty hotel room, the telephone rang. It was Peter. 'I want to go down to the Yemeni border via the edge of the Empty Quarter tomorrow. They're stick-in-the-muds here and nobody wants to come with me. Will you?' I agreed at once.

As instructed by Peter, I went to the 'Kuwaiti' *souq* off Batha Street to buy two of the flowery quilts that the Yemenis sell in piles, a number of giant jerry-cans, green for water, blue for petrol, skewers, tarpaulin for protection from the icy dew of the Asir mountain ranges, and sand tracks. I then went to a tiny hillock surrounded by the high-rise glass and concrete glories of modern Riyadh. On its peak stood the cockeyed, ramshackled hovel of the charcoal-maker. His cottage was a spiritual island, a stranded relic of the pre-boom years to which he had obstinately clung. I had to clamber up the rock and peat sides of the hillock to meet him. He was black like a Victorian chimney sweep but had a huge smile through which big, white teeth shone like pearls against the soot. I could imagine him, like Rodin's Penseur, leaning forward to watch a frenzied boom world growing up like a jungle around him, drawing in around him, almost submerging him. I paid about £2, took my big sack of charcoal, and trod back down into the technological age. When I returned one year later the hillock had disappeared.

For our trip we had three guides, the stars by night, a heavy-duty compass, and an out-of-date version of the United States Geological Survey map of Arabia which covers everything except routes, whether roads or tracks. We left Riyadh in the late afternoon, forging our way through the chaotic rush-hour and cacophony of horns of the holiday traffic. We drove south on the tarmac between the Jebel Tuwaiq range of escarpments and the sands of Al-Biyadh. It was night when we reached the little concrete town of Layla, a far cry from the tale of Qais in Persian literature, Qais who, refused in marriage to the lovely Layla, wandered the valleys insanely singing to her and earned the sobriquet Majnoun (mad for . . .) Layla.

We camped beyond Layla between the Qasr Himar (the Donkey's Castle) and As-Sullayil, made a charcoal fire on which we cooked a chicken, drank some *sadiqi* and fell asleep to the trumpets of Mahler's Fifth Symphony beneath a huge sky of tangled, glistening stars through which one, moment by moment, would shoot and burst like a firework. We awoke amid scrub desert scattered with pebbles and, here and there, flat-topped acacias which reminded me of my early childhood in Africa. Returning to the road, we found a desert café of such clumsy, concrete architecture that it seemed about to tilt and cave in. Outside stood a row of lorries painted all over with bright coloured Qur'anic phrases in the tradition of lorries from Morocco to as far as India where cautionary phrases become the crude paintings of semi-naked Sivas, the elephant-god Ganesh or snow-capped Himalayan peaks. The lorries were filled with poor Yemenis huddled together from the cold like crows with battered wings. They were heading home after perhaps fifteen months working in pathetic conditions in Saudi Arabia from where they would remit most of their savings to their families at home. Entering through an arbour we came among wide, raffia-seated, tall-backed benches on which Yemenis squatted in their *futahs* (kilts) and untidy tartan headcloths before glasses of sugary tea and sheets of grey bread.

We took our tea and bread and returned to the Land Rover, waving good-bye to the poor, shivering Yemenis. As we drove towards As-Sullayil, the crags of the Jebel Tuwaiq on our left went pink in the dawn light. As we approached this small town crenellated mud cottages appeared amid green fields and trees that became increasingly bigger and more assertive. The more one travels in the desert, the less one thinks of it as empty. Where a few seconds of rain have moistened the sand, a rich film of grass and flowers will appear after several days from seeds that may have lain dormant in the ground for years. Walt Disney once made a film called *The Living Desert* about California in which the apparent death of the desert was shown to be a deception. And this is right. Day and night there is always something happening. There is always the noise of some bird, some animal or just the hiss of the sand blowing from the dunes. But it is a land where the noises never irritate; they are the cries of freedom from the repulsive and agonising sounds of the world's great cities. The mind and soul are free – 'far from the outer roar' of Virginia Woolf, and in some ways free from the inner devils, the 'nimbus of furies' that a lovely girl called Amani once suggested to me in Cairo.

When we reached As-Sullayil we were in rich countryside. As-Sullayil is the first oasis in the great Wadi Dawasir and the

last before you enter the sterile wastes of the Empty Quarter
(Rub' al-Khali) itself. Coming up onto a knoll in the centre of
this town with its gleaming white, clay houses, we gazed down
upon an oasis of palm groves that spread out in every direction
and upon green fields with cottages. But the line between the
desert and the sown was as sharp as a knife. Looking south, to
our left, the fertile land stopped abruptly as it does in Egypt, as if
the land of the living and the land of the dead were joined by a
tight seam. Beyond the yellow sands the dunes and the flats fell
away into the horizon of the Empty Quarter. As we sat and
mystically mused, eight teenage girls in the flowing, flowery
'evening' dresses of the bedouin emerged on a parallel knoll some
hundred yards away, tidied their skirts and sat down to watch
us. They were like beautiful jungle birds in the crisp sunshine.
They gazed at us with intense concentration and when we gazed,
smiling, back, they smiled too. By their colourful dress and air
of social freedom, we knew that we were leaving the puritanical
heartlands of the imperial Najd and entering the south and the
freer influences of Arabia Felix. We wanted to photograph the
girls but as we raised our cameras they disappeared as if by magic
down the other side of the knoll.

We drove several kilometres until the tarmac came to a
sudden end at a point called Khashm Fardah on the map. As we
came off the tarmac we were entering a void; it was like sailing
out of port into the open sea. The skills of desert driving are,
indeed, similar to those of sailing. The tracks were clear at first,
probably those of the two-weekly lorry convoy into Yemen.
When we were confused by two, equally neat tracks, we
discarded the right-hand track leading into the Bani Khurb and
took the left-hand one leading towards the centre of the Empty
Quarter. Soon, however, this track disappeared as if its maker
had flown away or been swallowed by the sands. Suddenly, we
were driving around in crazy patterns trying to pick up a 'lead'
which we eventually found in the form of a delicate line
scratched through the soft, blowing sand. On our right the
desert was scattered with the camels' favourite fodder, the
brambly *unayfah* bushes.

According to Saudi law desert travellers must get permission
from the police to undertake off-the-road trips and such

permissions can take months to obtain. It is also obligatory to travel in a convoy of at least two vehicles. The rules are sensible and we had broken both, and many others, too. However, it made us better drivers in the knowledge that there was no one to dig us out if we were stuck. In summer such a venture would have been foolhardy but it was now mid-winter and we knew that we could survive for several days in an emergency.

Sometimes we entered areas of very soft sand and at the first hint of stability would halt and take our bearings and move off to better ground. In open desert the imagination becomes rich on every level and many things become deceptive. We thought we saw a series of gigantic domed buildings but as we drove closer they became sand dunes. By now we were constantly using four-wheel drive to negotiate squirming sand, driving neither too fast nor too slow, Peter fighting with the steering wheel as if it were the tiller of a yacht in a storm-tossed sea. The dunes stood up in front of us, barring our way like leviathans, another deception since according to the map they should have faced us end-on. Although it is difficult to reflect on the ground map readings in the desert, we also guessed that there had been considerable dune movement since our map was published in the mid-1960s. The track turned right so we headed across open desert to the left towards the Tuwaiq al-Arid escarpment. A huge bird which we thought, narcotically, was an ostrich, appeared on the sand in front of us and we had to drive round it although when we discussed it later we were unsure whether we had merely imagined seeing it.

Soon the tracks improved and we returned to two-wheel drive. The sand dunes were on our left and the Bani Khurb on our right. The position of the escarpment became more and more confusing, seeming to change angles. When we reached the end, we saw that it had either altered its position or we had mis-read the map. We stopped at a solid point of ground and refuelled with one of our eight giant petrol cans, then we entered a wide, thinly green prairie to which a little moisture had given immediate life.

We saw a bedouin encampment of black-tarred goat-hair tents and some hundred camels munching the soft grasses or roaring with pleasure. The bedu showed little surprise at seeing us and confirmed our directions. 'Drive on to the Black Mountain and keep to the right,' they said. We came through a hard rock bed scattered with big yellow gourds and saw ahead the 'Black Mountain', a dune of muddy-coloured sand. When we came around it we saw with astonishment a Pepsi Cola sign above a corrugated iron shack. Beyond lay a huge wide plain that ended in a distant escarpment.

A 10-year-old boy came running out with delight to greet us. He must have been dreadfully bored. 'Come in, come in, have tea with me.' We sat outside the shack drinking tea. The desert was very still. A cool breeze blew across the plain. Winter days in the desert are a delight like an English spring-time. He asked us for the '*Akhbar*', the news. The bedouin delight in news. They will spend hour after hour exchanging news and gossip, going over the same story again and again, each time elaborating it or looking at it from different angles. The rock was called Jebel Sinh, he told us. We explained our travel plans and he nodded seriously. 'Do you have enough water?' he asked as a reflex question. This is the first question of every bedouin, as if he is asking, 'Have you enough air to breathe?' It is the question of life – and of death.

The plain was hard and a joy to race across after days of negotiating subtle changes of rock and sand. The mountain at the corner of the escarpment we reached was called Jebel Kawkab, 'Star Mountain'. In the scree of Star Mountain was another corrugated iron hovel. This was a tiny shop run by Yemenis whose clientele were the Yemeni workers passing every two or three weeks south for home, the Promised Land, after working in Riyadh as construction workers or road sweepers to save and remit their savings to their families. The results of their labours are the beautiful houses of stone with stained-glass lunette windows that are built in Sanaa today. The Yemenis gave us tinned Japanese fruit juice, a disgusting chemical-tasting cocktail which was then in vogue in the Kingdom thanks to the clever sales talk of a Japanese sales rep. Then they gave us coffee flavoured with cardamom, ginger and cloves in tiny cups, that bedouin delicacy called 'Arabic' as opposed to Turkish coffee.

They talked passionately about girls and begged us to discuss the sizes of girls' breasts, the smoothness of girls' thighs, the bright, almond shapes of their eyes and the silkiness of their long hair. They cupped their hands to remember breasts and stroked their thighs to remember waist-lines. They spoke of girls as if they were by now mythical creatures. They wanted us to remind them about every detail of mother earth beings whom they craved for in their agonising frustration. 'In Yemen you can have girls like this [cupping the breasts], like this [stroking their hips], like this [making moonshapes with their hands to show faces].' They lived in dreams of jungles of girls and had almost forgotten that the girls in Sanaa are covered from head to toe in flowery table-cloths made in Pakistan beneath which you could barely distinguish hag from pretty virgin.

One of the boys went into the shack and brought out a goat. 'Please buy it. Only 200 riyals.' We laughed: 'We have nowhere to cook it.' He looked perplexed. A goat is food. Everyone needs a goat. Anyone can prepare and cook a goat. How can one travel through the desert without goats? Despite his hurt entreaties, we declined the offer, exchanged elaborate farewells, promised to drop in again one day, and continued our journey.

We passed through a small, mud village where pretty unveiled girls in their flowery dresses smiled at us. Between a narrow defile that split a big rock from the escarpment a camel emerged through a curtain of dust filled with glimmering sunlight and behind it wound a slow, long herd of exquisite white camels, flaming in the sunlight. It would have made an extraordinarily subtle Orientalist painting but the light needed great skill and quick reaction to photograph. The procession of now several thousand camels spilt out of the gleaming dust into the plain, almost like molten silver through the neck of a bottle. The camels seemed to emerge from some hidden crack in the mountain, stirring up the golden dust through the dazzling aperture of the sky.

As we drove on tracks began to appear from all directions. We drove wildly, baffled by the labyrinthine patterns. If we followed a track, it would promptly die out where soft sand had erased it. After endless indecision over what were and what were not tracks, we reached the low, black tents of a bedouin encampment. The men wore *futahs*, Yemeni-style kilts, silver-hilted daggers attached against their stomachs to their rifle-belts. They spoke to us in impeccable Arabic but were abrupt in directing us and did not invite us to drink tea with them. When we drove a hundred yards on past the neighbouring tent, we saw why. In the tent, its curtains pulled aside to reveal its marvels, sat a long line of women in full ornamental attire, beautiful black silk dresses, silver jewellery glimmering from every part of their bodies and face veils studded with filigree silver, silver coins and gold. I thought for a moment of the extravagance of the Royal Enclosure at the Ascot races in England. We had intruded on a marriage in the midst of the open privacy of the desert.

We came past beautiful, table-topped Jebel as-Saba (the Mountain of Sheba), solitary in a great plain of scattered, slanting acacias. Then, without warning, we hit the asphalt and soon saw to our right the tiny airport of Najran. After days of rattling track, the silence of the road was like flying through air. Plots of neat cultivation appeared. But, as we came over a small knoll, something happened. We stopped abruptly and turned off the engine. We were suddenly peering into the most beautiful panorama I have ever seen. We were gazing on Paradise. After moments of silence Peter whispered, 'Oh America, my new-found-land', John Donne's ecstatic cry to his mistress in which he compared her beauty with newly-discovered, virgin America. An immense valley plain filled with the tall, tapering pale clay buildings of southern Arabia lay spread out before us amid fields, thick palm spinneys and varieties of trees. The castles of a mythical Arabia, they were so perfect as to seem deceptive, a perfect cardboard cut-out of a Hollywood film set through which Sheba in all her glory might have appeared before a huge army of shimmering armour and fast, chafing horses. Herds of camels loped from grove to grove among these lovely palaces. After rough desert it was a land of sensual epiphany. A line from the Song of Solomon ran through my mind: 'Arise my love, arise my dove, arise my beautiful one and come. For winter is gone, the rains have come and been, the turtle-dove is heard in our land . . . '. The landscape was filled with every kind of cultivation, bright, ripe wheat, trailing vines, red blossoming pomegranate orchards, banana trees and ripe alfalfa, cattle and sheep and children running, laughing among the palms. The palaces were pale and clean in the sunlight, their sides black with shadow, their crenellations neatly carved above the rows of tiny windows through which their inhabitants would once espy hostile tribes. But no more. The buildings are empty. The America to which the people of Najran turn today is now the bright, new America of concrete and corrugated iron, Toyotas and Pepsi Cola of a twentieth century to which the whole sad, lost Third World aspires.

We stopped at a village of adobe and wattle houses couched into a rockside. Teasing children surrounded us as we got out. A black camel knelt, still, among the trees. I clambered up the rock, followed by children who tried to outpace me. When we reached the top I gazed about me upon the valley. The children's eyes followed mine with wonder, then looking from me to it, from it to me, trying to fathom what I was looking at. They could not know that their home was my epiphany. On one side of the holy view was a gleaming white plain as if of salt which led out into more palm groves and the towers of distant castles. I came down again to be told that the camel was to die at dawn, a victim of the Id al-Adha (Festival of Sacrifice) when a camel, sheep or horned animal is sacrificed in every household as it is at Mina near Mecca on the Tenth of Dhu-l Hijjah according to the Muslim calendar, the following day.

We drove on into the pretty town of Najran, whose clay houses have brightly painted, carved wooden doors with huge brass locks which are opened with equally huge keys. For us Najran was Yemen, as it was in reality until it was captured by Ibn Saud's Ikhwan in 1934, a far cry from the austere Wahhabi 'wee frees' of the pitiless Najd. The Romans visited Najran, which they called Negrana, on a military expedition led by Aelius Gallus in 24 BC to explore the mysterious incense country and control trade. But they failed, defeated by exhaustion and thirst. It was an important city long before the Romans came, belonging culturally to Yemen, or Arabia Felix. Indications of the splendour of this civilisation can be deduced from the dam and temple at Marib in North Yemen and the ruins of Shibam in South Yemen. Najran was probably the most northerly outpost of the city states of Arabia Felix. Since we were there the town has quadrupled in size and one traveller, Rosalind Ingrams, had difficulty in 1982 in finding the real town, the area around the old governor's palace, Qasr Aba al–Saud, in which Philby once lived but which is now crumbling away.

We asked a young man the way to Ukhdud, the ancient Christian city which was out of bounds when we were there. Ukhdud, which means 'trenches', is mentioned in Sura 85 of the Qur'an and refers to a massacre of Christians in about AD 522 by the Jewish King Dhu Nuwas in which the Christians are believed to have been burnt alive. The pompous young man put his nose in the air and said '*mamnoo*' (forbidden) so we took our directions from someone else and drove off. Since visits to the site were, indeed, then forbidden and no excavations had taken place, Ukhdud was well preserved and, as we quickly discovered, unplundered. We gazed at undamaged walls with sharp Sabean hieroglyphics and roamed from crumbled room to room, looking at pieces of pottery. Peter picked up an exquisitely carved stone horse and put it down again. Barely broken shards lay scattered everywhere. We took dozens of photographs and moved about in a frenzy of creative inspiration. We were gazing not at a cold reflection but at the brightness of living history.

Peter and I then parted company, exploring different parts of the site, clambering from pit to pit and wall to wall. We were about to encounter some unpleasant bureaucracy and I wrote in my diary, with tongue in cheek, that the ensuing incident drew Peter to treachery. My own adaptation of his diary entry is as follows: 'Trevor and I parted company but I was soon interrupted by screams. A 16-year-old Saudi [known hereafter as 'the creep'] leapt out of a crowded Toyota pickup and rushed towards me, shouting that it was utterly "*mamnoo*" to take photographs or to be here at all, that I must give him my film, that I must leave and that, above all else "Where was my brother?" Choosing to respond to the last question first I pointed to some ruins where "my brother" pleasantly roamed. So obsessed was the creep with catching my brother, that he ignored me and began running over the knolls yelling for him. I, meanwhile, raced for the Land Rover to change my film for a virgin film. Little boys from the Toyota wanted their photographs taken so I said "Wait a minute" while I implanted my virgin film. I had just completed my film change and was lining up the children for the sports day pic when Trevor, hotly pursued by the panting creep, appeared over a hillock. The creep shouted that "it", presumably everything up to life itself, was thoroughly "*mamnoo*" and ordered me to take out my film which I did with a theatrical reluctance. Trevor protested with more passion since, having not had time to change his film, he was clearly the loser. The creep said that he would take us to the police station if we didn't comply so Trevor finally gave in his non-virgin film, too.'

My version of this tragic story is as follows. As I roamed, mesmerised by these living ruins, a nasty, plump 17-year-old in dirty *thobe* and *gutrah* and all the authority of an adult Saudi appeared on a mound and began yelling and whistling at me as if I were a pi-dog. Despite the odious whistles I assumed at first that he came with a message from Peter but quickly realised that he was foe, not friend. Deciding to play it cool, whenever he shouted '*mamnoo at-taswir*' ('photography forbidden') I raised my camera, asking whether he wanted to be photographed. This sent him apoplectic and I dreamt for a second that he had burst with rage and disappeared so that I could roam joyously onward. But the screaming and whistling continued and I ambled down the other side of the knoll, out of his vision. My attempt to lose him angered him further and the wolf whistles became vicious. When he glimpsed me among the ruins I picked up a piece of pottery, studying it with a keen eye, and wandered on, disappearing again like a magician from his sight. I was aiming for the car, my only escape route, hoping to exhaust him and reach it in time to change my film. But as I reached it he emerged, hard on my heels, puffing and panting and red with anger and exhaustion. Peter was calmly aiming the camera at him as I waved to warn him, little realizing the immensity of his treachery. We both had to sacrifice our films, mine full of exquisite shots, his, as I was to discover despite his feigned reluctance, an unused film.

Irritable, we drove down from Ukhdud into a lily-white plain, fringed on one side by drooping palms, which curled like a dew-drop away from the white pool of the plain to our left. The plain and the palms were like the beach of a deserted Pacific island. Coming through a group of pretty buildings with elaborate whitewash patterns and four white streaks running upward from the windows, we photographed them – no sooner done than two youths approached us, asking 'why we photographed the houses?' We told them in impeccable Arabic that we photographed them because they were beautiful, an explanation which considerably increased their suspicion. The buildings reflected, perhaps, a past from which they recoiled, yearning to replace them with the Kingdom's now ubiquitous breeze-block and corrugated iron.

We returned to Najran in search of a chicken for dinner. A policeman led us to the chicken room, a long low room full of chickens running about a bloody, sandy floor. The chicken seller demanded 12 riyals for a chicken which would only have cost 7 riyals in Riyadh. He held up two struggling birds for me to choose from. Sentimentally, I told him to choose himself. Chatting idly with his friend he held the chicken to the ground, slit its throat and, true to the Islamic rules of slaughter, allowed the blood to drain away into the sand. He neither looked away from his friend nor slowed down in conversation. The chicken glugged, vexed to a moment of nightmare until the eyes glazed over and the head fell sideways. He flung it into a huge machine which roared for some seconds, then retrieved it, now completely naked, then flung the entrails to the ground, put the chicken into a plastic bag and handed it to me. He barely looked away from his friend for a moment during the entire operation.

We took a road up into the mountains but quickly realised from our map that we had crossed into Yemen, so we turned back. When we asked our way in one village, the man explained by way of introduction, 'Our land was once ruled by the Jews and the Christians.' We gave him a lift as far as the turning to Khamees Mushayt, then we turned off the road and up into the rock where a wadi looped through the mountains like a serpent. Whenever we were tempted to stop and camp, we came upon bedouin encampments which we did not wish to disturb. Finally we found a loop in the rock surrounded by small acacias and stopped for the night. We made a charcoal fire for the chicken, which we called Ethel, but, despite the technical marvels of the chicken room, she was too stringy to eat so we buried her solemnly in her plastic shroud. The night was cold so we drank sadiqi to give us warmth to sleep.

We awoke at early dawn in icy cold, and hungry, but the damp and high altitude made it impossible to light our fire. We waited eagerly for the sun to rise high and warm us. We climbed up the escarpment which faced us and separated. I came up onto a ridge which, on both sides, overlooked ranges rippling away into hazy blue horizons. Looking down into the valley I could see Peter walking towards a smooth water-course in the corner of the wadi. I heard a clear trickle of water as if coming from close below me but I then realised that it was an aural illusion and came from that brook which he was approaching far below. I stared up into the cliffside at massive, twisting roots which would reappear as healthy trees higher up the cliff. I returned to the wadi below and Peter and I climbed rock as smooth as soapstone until we reached the feeder pool of the brook.

We returned to the Land Rover and continued through the mountains, down through Wadi dhi Kuhl and thence to Mayzah and Wadi al-Muslahah and from there to Ghayl and Basrah where the tall plains buildings are built of mud not stone. We passed through neat, irrigated fields to Ya'oud with its flintstone houses and their whitewash line patterns and high parapets. A tiny girl with big black eyes and tangled hair trailed her flowery dress through the dust and a lamb followed her affectionately but she ignored it to gaze at us with her baby astonishment. Two young men appeared in a village on a motorcycle of flamboyant, psychedelic colours. Pretty, unveiled women strode through the dusty streets. We drove on through the villages of Al-Sharayi and Al-Bassam and by mid-afternoon we reached the asphalt road leading to the mainly expatriate town of Khamees Mushayt in the centre of the plain.

We found our way to the British Aircraft Corporation base whose superficially surly but inwardly delightful manager, Gus Hughes, was a friend of Peter's. His Scots assistant Kilo Wate greeted us with some astonishment; we had not seen a mirror since Riyadh and would barely have recognised ourselves had we seen one now. We were bearded, our faces and clothing were caked with sand, and our noses had peeled, red layer after red layer. The tough BAC men seemed impressed by our journey but were extremely discouraging about our proposed return to Riyadh through the central deserts. Since our dynamo had

broken we spent several days at the camp, eating, drinking and
sleeping well and our friends spent the time trying to persuade us
to return by the asphalt route that passed along the coast and
through Taif. 'The route you want to take is nothing but dull,
empty desert,' said Gus, 'nothing to see at all. The coastal road,
however, is really spectacular.'

Of course the warnings encouraged us the more. Although
none of them had taken the desert route, their argument was that
since there was no regular traffic through it there would be no
one to dig us out if we were stuck. But we were adamant. We
had promised ourselves a desert adventure, not a spin along
asphalt. It was finally agreed that if we did not reach Riyadh by
Christmas, ten days later, Gus would be obliged to send out a
police search party. 'And that'd get us all into a hell of a lot of
trouble,' he added. On this we agreed and said farewell to all the
warm, tough men of the camp who so envied our freedom of
movement.

We drove back up into the mountains to the immense, garish
palace of King Saud perched on a clifftop. It is an ugly pink
plaster building of the 1950s with simple balconies. It looked to
me more like an East European ministry than a regal palace. But
Peter was fascinated by its location. 'It absolutely dominates the
valley. Just think of the sense of power.' The view below was,
indeed, splendid, the valley scattered with smaller mountains on
whose peaks stood the Turkish forts that follow the line of the
coast through the Tihama. The mountain-tops were shrouded in
trees. Range fell behind range in a ripple of grey and blue. Flocks
of birds flew back and forth like scattered silver in the sunlight.

We drove on through dry-stone wall cultivation, then dipped
into a valley in which the corrugated lateral lines of the houses
merged with the dizzying terraces which spiralled down the
mountainside. Until very recently, until oil wealth drew the
peasants into the towns, this complex terraced cultivation had
continued unchanged and unimpaired since the original terraces
were constructed in Sabean times. On the mountain-tops were
white markers for the bedouin caravans that passed through the
valley below.

Near Wadi Sirhan we came around a little farm and along a
very rugged track of black, volcanic stones. Up and up we went

until we reached a huge plain where we parked the Land Rover. Walking across the plain, the light volcanic rock tinkled to our tread like glass. We were walking through the heart of the Asir. Looking down at the mountains and deep valleys beneath us, we felt that we were almost in the sky.

We walked across the plain towards a hamlet couched against the side of the mountain-top in the distance. When we came close to the silent, thatched houses we heard laughter and then saw two pretty teenage girls giggling at us from behind a haystack. The village was almost Italianate in its neat arrangement of stone houses, trees and cultivated fields clustered on the edge of a hard, black, barren plain.

A smiling woman emerged from the village, beside her a little boy of 10 in a clean white *thobe*. The woman pointed to us and the little boy ran towards us. He was an intelligent boy with an open, smiling face. He shook my hand and then kissed it as a sign of respect and welcome. He possessed the self-contained charm of a child prince up on that black plain from which you might believe that you ruled the world. He spoke clearly and at ease in impeccable Classical Arabic. He showed no impatience if I failed to understand but would simply repeat the sentence quietly. He told us that the village was called Sufhan.

I asked him what happened in the mountain-top above his village. He replied with dignity, 'Nobody lives up in yonder mountain. Nobody goes there. But one day people lived there. They were our ancestors. Then bad men came down from Asir yonder with guns. The people of the village asked the jinn that live in the rock to save them. But the jinn told them that in order to be saved they must sacrifice a sheep on the highest rock and that the people must come down from the mountain to the place where we live today. So they sacrificed the sheep on top of the mountain and they came down from the mountain to the plain where the men from the Asir were. And the men from the Asir fired at them with their guns, but the bullets fell off their bodies without harming them and the men from the Asir were afraid and they ran away and left the people in peace. None of us ever go up into the mountains.' He spoke of the jinn as if they were living creatures. 'Are the jinn still there?' I asked. The little boy laughed and replied with kindness, 'Yes, they are still there. But don't be afraid [*matkhaf*]. They are *salihun* [good].'

The Wahhabis do not approve of the worship of jinn which they regard as *shirk* (association of others with God) but the northerners have still made little impact on the bright individualism of the south where women go unveiled in bright dresses and singing and dancing is still popular in the villages. The men from the Asir must have been Turks from the Tihama coast, attempting to establish some foothold on the rugged interior.

We said good-bye to the little boy and scrambled up the rock. Almost vertically above us scattered goats were munching, perched on little ledges or hoof-holds. The shepherd boy shouted down instructions on how to climb but when we reached him he asked for money. 'One who is already poisoned,' murmered Peter. When we asked him to indicate where were the inscriptions we had heard about he pointed to another mountain which had not revealed itself to us below. Indeed, we were to find that each time we reached a peak, higher and higher peaks appeared beyond it as if by magic. We wandered across a small, volcanic plain, then up another crag which led us along a tight ledge which dropped massively into the valley far, far below. Above the little ledge from which we peered was a sandstone canopy like an awning. Suddenly I heard a mooing and peering into a cave at the back of a ledge I discovered two red-brown Jersey cows. They must have been the nimblest cows on earth and we felt quite ashamed of the gingerly steps we had taken across the ledge.

We clambered up another crag and came to the deserted but undamaged village of stone houses. We could imagine the village being evacuated exactly as the boy described. We climbed up the peak of this last part of the mountain and huge eagles, whose black shadows were massive against the sun, swooped down on us. They were probably aiming for small animals or for their eyries but they came down fast as if attacking us and we crouched in cracks of the rock. It would have been easy for local lore to have confused these huge birds with magic beings of great power in this awesome fastness.

We made our way back down to the plain and set out for the Hanging Village of Habala. Habala was the home of the Bani Malayk, a family belonging to the Qahtan clan. We had been told that the series of footholds that reached down to the village was marked by a whitewashed oil drum on the cliffside. When we reached the drum a strong wind was blowing at the cliff so we lay on our bellies and peered down the cliffside into the great sterile rock trough of a valley below. There, like the planet of the Little Prince, stood the village of Habala, its little houses and its midget fields and its peasants toiling in them, all over a knoll jutting out of the rockside, nearly 800 feet down. The valley below is sterile so that the villagers' entire contact with the outside world is upwards onto the plain with villages such as Sufhan. Very precarious footholds lead down the cliff face but for the last fifth of the descent you must take a rope (*habal*). The villagers can make the journey in fifteen minutes but strangers take very much longer at some personal risk. However, after two accidents in 1979 many of the villagers moved to a new village about 13 kilometres away and built at the private expense of the governor of the Asir Province, Prince Khaled ibn Faisal. The people of Habala were an exotic and joy-loving people, perhaps a little mad, with wild flowers in their long hair. Today, however, in their new purpose-built village they are likely to have become Saudi-ised and bland.

We continued our journey towards Bishah and camped on the white plain of Wadi Houran. We slept in frigid cold on stony sand by a dead tree which glimmered a wicked blue in the light of the full moon. On both sides gleamed escarpment screes. Foxes, disturbed by the awesome light, coughed in the rock. We had made a roaring fire to cook Gladys, chicken number 5. It was a pagan night, a blue, trembling night, but when dawn came we were awoken by beautiful birdsong. We made Earl Grey tea before our start.

We came through a wadi of palms and slow, wide streams that spread about the sand like ice, disappearing and reappearing. In the wadi a man in trousers and *kafia*, half bedouin and half urban, waved us down so we gave him a lift. We should have guessed that he would become our Judas. The bedouin is by nature free and steeped in deep social values but after one year in the city these often disappear and he becomes the greediest and most primitive man on earth.

We were about ten miles before Bishah. The man had local

knowledge and told us the names of various trees such as small camel thorn (*nufoud*), the big camel thorn (*samr*), the tamarisk (*nidha*), the big evergreen tree (*nidhar*), the rough bush (*raqa*) and the flat-topped acacia (*sarh*). We passed through the village of Haris in which a tiny river glistened in the sun. We came to a wide, palm-laced plain and a shallow but very wide river with little white birds on the water. In the distance a stone Turkish fort looked down from the mountain. Stone huts stood along the crags to protect sheep from wolves.

We made a detour among palms through the village of Hazimi which was full of smiling black women in bright dresses, descendants of Abyssinian slaves. I tried to photograph them but our passenger stopped me. '*Mamnoo at-taswir!*' We grimaced. We had given a lift to a delegate of the Kingdom of Killjoy. We came out onto a plain and a series of barely visible wadis, wadis Houran, Tirj, Baqara, Harf and finally Bishah. The wadis were merely tracks across the sand, representing the waterway during the rains. Big, dry gourds were scattered about. At Wadi Bishah, however, a soft, green veldt appeared. The veldt turned to small trees and bushes, the bushes to a plain of *sirh* trees and the *sirh* trees to forests of trees and rich cultivation similar to the landscape we had found at Najran. We soon reached the mud buildings of Bishah.

We parked near a big fruit and vegetable market in the heart of the town. Our passenger left us in a hurry. We entered the *souq* which was run by guffawing, unveiled black women. They seemed far from puritan but were physically indescribable. Indeed, they were veritable terrors! Peter negotiated for and bought a *bizri*, a baby's leather cradle with multi-coloured tassles. In another stall he bought a reed mat. I also asked for one but seeing another one asked for that instead. As soon as I did this the woman raised the price by 50 per cent. 'But why?' I asked. 'Because you changed your mind,' replied the Amazon with as much logic as the March Hare. I tried to insist but the relentless woman was obdurate.

A fascinated crowd began to form around us. Men and women noisily took my side but their consensus made not a whit of difference to the woman who seemed to revel in her decision. It was strange in a land where contact with women is so limited to be so openly cheated by these viragos. As I wandered off an immense woman grabbed my arm and virtually dragged me to her stall to try to persuade me to buy a bag which was identical to the one I had already bought. I showed her this but she wasn't convinced and I had virtually to fight my way away from her.

As we returned to the car we saw a leather bag with a tight neck from which dates were spilling. It made a good abstract picture and we photographed it. No sooner had we taken the photograph than a slim Saudi in *thobe* and *gutrah* approached us with a chilling courtesy which I suspected at once. He had a narrow rat-face. He asked us why we were taking photographs. We replied, somewhat cynically, that the folks back home would be impressed by the elegant Saudi leather-work (local handicraft is almost non-existent in Saudi Arabia today). He was too much of a coward to prevent us from returning to our car or reject our gushing farewells, but as we stepped in he came over and said, 'I'll lead you to the petrol station. Please follow me.' I suggested to Peter that he might be an informer so we put virgin films in our cameras. We followed him and, as we suspected, he led us straight to the police station.

We parked our car beside his outside the police station and, in order both to pre-empt the authorities and frighten the traitor with our bravado, we marched into the police station of our own accord. It would have been easy to drive out of Bishah but it would also have been risky entering open desert and leaving a hostile town at our rear where we might need support. The main room inside the police station was full of people and the policemen were surprised to see us and treated us with respect. The rat was sitting, talking earnestly with a policeman in the corner, probably embellishing our crime as far as he could. When he saw us, however, he leapt to his feet and disappeared through a back door. We never saw him again. The policemen didn't know what to do with us. It appeared that they had expected us to wait meekly in the Land Rover until the police chief came. They sat us down, brought us tea and marvelled at our Arabic.

For half an hour the atmosphere was pleasant, then suddenly a big angry man entered. People stood to attention or looked busy. We sat and watched, at first bemused, but were suddenly the victims of a bitter interrogation at the hands of this man who had a severe inferiority complex with Westerners. His first question was a chilling; 'Why do you photograph women in the wadis?' I couldn't understand the question at first. Did the policeman have extra-sensory perception? How did he know what had happened in the wadis? The only picture we had taken was of a date bag in Bishah. Then to our horror we suddenly realized that our passenger had made straight for the police station on our arrival. We were so accustomed to admiring the honour and dignity of Arabians, particularly the bedu, that we had almost forgotten that such treachery and ingratitude could exist. I said that we had not photographed women in the wadis and asked what made him say that we had. Luckily, the police chief was unwilling to reveal his source or develop this line, reflecting, perhaps, our disgust. Nobody likes an informer, even a policeman.

He changed tack, asking where we had come from and whether we had permission to come from there, where were we going and had we permission to go there. Saudi officials are obsessed with permissions but are often confused in their knowledge of the law itself, as in this case in which we should have had permission to enter any trackless desert, whatever desert, a rule that the police chief seemed unaware of. If you take photographs of buildings in Riyadh, people will approach and ask whether you have a *tasrih*, a letter of authority from the police. People who have visited the police station, however, have been assured that photography is not illegal and that no such document exists.

The policeman wanted to know what we were doing in southern Saudi Arabia. 'Adventure? What means adventure? Inscriptions? Who wants to look inscriptions? Camping in desert? Can't afford to stay in hotel? Did we have other camera films?' This question worried us as there were ten bottles of *sadiqi* in the Land Rover and their discovery would lead to our imprisonment and, perhaps, a public flogging. Luckily he didn't push the point hard and eventually became bored with the dialogue and let us go. As we left we felt a general air of sympathy for us among the policemen and gathered from this that the police chief was a hated man at the station.

The policeman who led us to the petrol station was a kind man who wanted to make up for the bad hospitality we had received. When we told him that we intended to go to Riyadh by the trackless central deserts he became very concerned and tried earnestly to dissuade us. 'There is nothing in the middle,' he said. 'No people, no water, no petrol. It's impossible by vehicle. You must take the asphalt road via Taif. That is very nice. Good road. Good straight road, very good.' At the little garage children peered into the dusty chaos of our Land Rover, filled with Yemeni quilts and leather Moses cradles, as if they were looking through the window of a Victorian junk shop. When one man saw the cradles, he began laughing hysterically and tried to drag one out to show all the others who were fighting in a shrieking scrum to have a better view of the possessions of these dusty madmen. Perhaps a European would show the same amusement towards an Arab who, with artistic possessiveness, carried a pile of soiled nappies about in his car.

We drove out of Bishah as the sun was falling towards the horizon. We wanted to rid ourselves of the town and shook the dust off our feet to symbolise our disgust. The menace of the void that lay ahead was welcome after the town's unkindness. In our untidy haste to leave we had forgotten water so were relieved to see a water truck standing in the desert some miles beyond Bishah. Simultaneously with us a Toyota jeep arrived at the tanker that stood amid scattered tools and bits of machinery. A bearded European in a *shammagh* stepped out and with authority called a Yemeni who filled our water galoons. He was a Greek working on a local irrigation project. He pointed us in the direction of the desert route for Riyadh and drove off.

We crossed small hills and sandy plains where herds were loping, then across a plain with immense, isolated, round or contorted stones. We then reached another sandy plain where townspeople were trying to free a Datsun pickup from slipping sand. We helped pull them out. As we were doing this one of them crept into the Land Rover, hoping for a more comfortable ride, but we politely ejected him. As he was ushered out his friend, hoping for better luck, crept in from the other side. He, too, we politely sent packing. Their truck was crammed with men, women, children and goats and they evidently thought they would have a better ride to their village with the *afrangis*.

Following our trackless map we turned right at the track for Tathlith where they turned left. After leaving the escarpment on our left we came through low rock to a bedouin encampment. The bedu came out and lined up in front of their tent. A dozen women peered out from their tent on the right. Despite our flamboyant greetings, the men remained cool and made no attempt to invite us in or develop any kind of intimacy. When we asked the route to the 'Black Mountain' marked on our map, they waved their hands brusquely in a certain direction, eager to be rid of us. A marriage or circumcision ceremony was taking place and the bedouin abhor exposing their women to strange men – round, dust-covered *nasranis* (Christian men).

We descended into a wide, white plain where, on the far horizon, stood a Datsun pickup. As we approached we saw that two bearded bedu were drawing water from a well. The well was marked as Ishmas on our map. When we reached them, the bedu greeted us kindly, smiling. We asked them for land-marks and they asked us where we were going.

'To Riyadh,' we replied simply.

'Have you enough water?' asked one of them.

'Yes,' we replied, pointing to our six giant galoons.

'Then God be with you,' replied the old man.

Standing in the midst of this great white plain with two wise men, we knew that they considered the journey feasible and we were relieved.

The plain was covered with a gentle film of young grass. We came along a good track which led us into a deep gully where camels lay in the shade. Then, some kilometres later, we saw a thick black line spread across the horizon of the steppeland. The black line trembled into the form of a herd of several thousand camels being urged forward by tiny boys running about like sheepdogs in the dust with sticks in their hands.

On our right we saw a bedouin camp of several big, black goat-hair tents. Some forty bedu came running out to greet us. We exchanged the fullest palette of greetings for about ten minutes. 'How are your sons? How is your mother? Is she well? What is the news? Praise be to God! Everything well? Praise be to God! Peace be upon you! By God! How are your she-camels? They are well? Praise be to God! By God! All well? And your mother, and your sons, and your goats, and your she-camels, all well? Praise be to God!'

We took our shoes off and entered their tent. Inside it was like a meeting of the French communards. Hundreds of bedu surrounded us and immediately deluged us, battered us with a symphony of questions. 'How were our wives? Were we not married? No? By God! Why not?' (i.e. were we queer, impotent, mad, etc.) And how did we like our women, like this (cupping the hands like breasts), like this (brushing the hands downwards to represent waist-line)? Their questions tumbled out in that slightly hysterical manner which always makes the bedu seem a little mad to foreigners. Their movements and responses were rapid, brooking of no hesitation in our own responses.

They handed me an immense bowl of smelly, uddery milk. For a moment I hesitated over the slimy slosh. They all leant forward to witness my satisfaction. I raised the wooden bowl of sludge to my lips. It was rich, thick and sour and, behind the screen of the bowl, I grimaced and choked. As the lip of the bowl came down over my eyes my bilious grimace gave way to a broad smile. '*Laziz katheer, mumtaz, Wallahi!*' I quoth ('Very delicious, marvellous, by God!'). 'It is camel milk,' they said. 'It makes you strong,' one said, raising his forearm in an erotic symbol. Like all bedu they had the tendency to break into girlish giggling but this, I think, stems more from a sort of refined nervousness than contempt. I have always found the movements of the bedu very sudden, as sudden as their decisions, their likes, their dislikes. They have a hysterical frenzy which is, perhaps, only controlled by the tight oral laws of hospitality, the practical rules regarding blood money and the like.

They passed us heavily spiced Arabic coffee in tiny cups. You toss it down the throat more as a taste than a drink. They liked my Classical Arabic better than Peter's Najdi dialect. I, too, felt more at home with these men whom the angry puritanism of Wahhabi Arabia had not touched. After an exhausting hour of rapid repartee in which, as in a good legal debate, you must always hold your ground and exchange a quick and clever piece of witticism for the like, the shaikh suddenly asked us if we wished to spend some days with them or leave. When we replied with courteous reluctance that we must, alas, leave we expected one of those long drawing-room leave-takings usual in the town. We were, therefore, shocked when the whole clan leapt up as one and led us out at a fast trot to our Land

Rover. We realised that this was their 'way' and that it did not reflect their wish to get rid of us. There is something fine about this life in which all bluff, all protocol is dispensed with and decisions are swift and final. The stranger only has to kiss the hem of a bedouin tent or drink from a cup to qualify for hospitality lasting 'three days and one third' at the end of which the tribe may ask him his identity. Even if he is a deadly foe they must see him off with provisions and gifts. If he has committed a crime against them, they may wish to kill him at the next encounter but he is a sacred guest during his sojourn and can depart in peace.

They gathered around our Land Rover with the excitement of children. As we stepped in, one of them spotted our cradles piled onto our quilts in the back of the machine. This discovery made them quite hysterical. They jumped, tugged, pulled, ran around the Land Rover, then began rocking it violently to and fro. For a second we thought they were trying to turn it over but they were merely giving uninhibited vent to their feelings of pleasure. What would have been severe provocation in the town was fun and games in the desert. We moved the machine slowly forward, smiling and waving, and they fell back into a laughing crowd as we drove on past the *hareem* tent from which a dozen women peered at us with shy interest.

We came down among grey hills brightened with patches of yellowing grasses. On our right was an escarpment and on our left a low mountain, Jebel Dalfa. We drove on to Jebel Hadad where we noted camel spoor leading north and then through a sandy plain scattered with camel thorn. We saw a white camel giving suck to its shining wet new-born on our right and passed a bedouin camp by a wadi of dried mud. We crossed soft sand wadis which tested our skill. The car slid as if through water. Big yellow gourds like giant apples lay plentifully in these wadis. We drove in violent and complex zig-zags through mounds of *sabkha* and when we reached the fifth wadi a big white bird with blue wings flopped lazily past.

We camped among the rocks of Umm Matirah. It was a night of whining, sand-filled winds and the blue moonlight filled the escarpment and the valley bowl about us. We camped before a dead, black tree near a rock where our fire burnt ferociously in this hot tempest. We heard the rook-like cries of birds and the whimpering of jackals in the mountain. The moon threw figures and patterns in immense relief against the mountain, trembling against the lashing flames. If the rains had come – the terrible freak storms that wash through desert valleys from time to time – we would have become an island. We both felt a strange joy in this void, like being on the moon.

The following day we passed through a plain with yellow bushes, acacias and meandering black camels and distant escarpments, a perfect balance of mountain and desert. At Jebel Shukayr we passed an escarpment ridge where we saw a herd of long-haired black sheep with white faces, then a sole bedouin bathing in a pool of catchment water. Then we saw an immense herd of camels moving across the plain, herds of sheep, bedu, a jeep and a water tanker. We were approaching civilisation once again. The bedu pointed the way to Riyadh and we knew that we were on the final lap of our odyssey.

We stopped for sardines at Adhqan an-Najran, then continued through the dunes of Ghawdah from where, in the distance, we could see Jebel Ghawdah. We were now on a track crossing Wadi Sabha and we passed through a narrow defile in the mountain which led us to the mud village of Sabha and then up again through mountains of up to 500 feet. We camped among small mountains some 10 kilometres from Sabha. We had driven 520 kilometres from Bishah.

We awoke the following morning to damp and cloud and drove across the plains that were pools of *sabkha* sand amid screes of rock. We saw large herds of camels munching camel thorn and herds of Indian humped-backed cows, and reached the village of al-Abd which was surrounded by palm groves and fields of sweet-corn. Soon we came through wet sand, the aftermath of rains, puddles and pools which we had to rush. The deadly sludge of wet sand is far more difficult than soft dry sand to negotiate. In trying to avoid the marsh we lost the track and became disorientated. Having crossed a plain of 40 kilometres we reached a bedouin camp with a Mercedes truck beside it.

Having spent the required few minutes on greetings we asked the bedu where we were and they directed us to the village of al-Raya. There an old man surrounded by children insisted on writing down our directions to impress them. They all peered over his shoulder, crying '*Wallahi*' as his trembling hand slowly put pen to paper. On the paper he drew with immense concentration a straight line and then wrote above it *Bismillahi ar-Rahman ar-Rahim*' ('In the Name of God, the Compassionate, the Merciful', the Qur'anic prelude to any statement). The instruction was merely to drive straight ahead in the direction in which he turned the line. We drove through more escarpments, more sandy plains and then came through pretty red sands.

When we hit the asphalt of the Jeddah–Riyadh road, the sudden silence was awesome. We had become so used to shouting above the rattle of the Land Rover on corrugated track or on *sabkha* that we now had to struggle to keep our voices down. When we reached Riyadh we drove straight, without washing or shaving, to the house of friends, the General Manager of the British Aircraft Corporation and his two daughters. When they opened the door they stared at us for a moment in astonishment. They did not recognise the two sand-caked, unshaven, sunburnt, smiling travellers with red chequered *shammaghs* wrapped around our heads, arriving from somewhere in the Empty Quarter. We sat down with them and drank delicious French wine as we told our tale.

7

Saudi Arabia – the gloamings

In May 1979 a morbid event took place in Jeddah which sparked off a campaign of repression aimed at the lifestyle of foreigners, whose decadent influence was seen by Saudi Arabia's puritan 'wee frees' to be eroding the pious fabric of the God-fearing Kingdom.

A small party had been given in the flat of a British doctor and his wife near the hospital in which he was Chief Surgeon, Jeddah's Dr Bakhsh Hospital off Siteen Street, and it had ended in two violent deaths. Dr Arnot and his wife Penny and others at the party had been promptly imprisoned and the fate they might expect in a Kingdom where beheading is the penalty for both murder and adultery was the talk of every party when I was there, researching for a book on Saudi Arabia. Single foreign girls working in the hospitals or for the national airline, Saudia, scarcely dared leave their hostels for fear of savage reprimanding by the religious police, the *mutawwa'een* ('Those who must be obeyed'). The police raided companies whom they suspected were illegally employing women, for women in Saudi Arabia are restricted to the professions of teaching at women's institutes, nursing and broadcasting.

The charismatic King Faisal had made some courageous progress in emancipating women, responding to puritan anger at women's voices being heard on the radio by saying sharply, 'You'll soon be seeing their faces on television.' But progress and reaction oscillate under the pressure of Western influence in Saudi Arabia and an 'incident' can release fanatical reactions. After the Arnot affair foreign liquor stills were raided without warning and their owners imprisoned and threatened with public lashings, and the angry *mutawwa'een* with henna in their beards whipped the legs of women whose dresses were too short or whose bodices were too low. Foreigners became frightened again, remembering periods when friends had, indeed, been flogged for distilling *sadiqi*, that dreadful yeast and sugar brew which made do for the whisky which was sold for £30 a bottle by the very traders, it was said, who talked so piously about the evils of alcohol which is forbidden by Islam.

When I returned to Jeddah in February 1980 I stayed with a British Embassy friend and went to a series of dinner parties which represented the lifeblood of the Western diplomatic and journalistic set. On my last evening he and I went to a dinner party given by a young American journalist called John Close. At the end of the dinner a tall, handsome and very pleasant man approached me and introduced himself as Dr Richard Arnot. He had heard that I was a publisher and wanted to know whether I would be interested in arranging the publication of his 'story' when he managed to return to Britain. We sat together and he told me his terrible tale, although throughout my entire month in Saudi Arabia the ever-gossipping expatriate society had never whispered a word about the murder theory that was to make British newspaper headlines for several years.

Richard Arnot had come to Saudi Arabia to work as a surgeon at the new hospital in Jizan where he had made many Saudi friends and gained what appeared to be a genuine affection for the Kingdom. He had then been appointed Chief Surgeon at the Dr Bakhsh Hospital and he and his beautiful wife had quickly become key figures of glamour in a bored, glamour-thirsty expatriate society.

'The irony was that I wasn't even giving the party,' he said. 'I had offered my flat to a friend to say good-bye to people. I was tired and went to bed early. At dawn I was woken up by a friend who had slept on the sofa. Waking up with a hangover he had wandered to the balcony, looked down and gazed upon a horrible sight. Two bodies, those of a man and a woman, lay dead in a state of some undress. The girl was on the pavement and the man was impaled on a railing. I ran down and felt the bodies. Both were cold and in a state of rigor mortis. They must have been dead for some hours.' The doctor had contacted the head of the hospital, Dr Bakhsh, the police and the ambulance and then – 'We just waited for the explosion.'

When the police arrived they asked for the names of everyone at the party and the poor doctor was obliged to give them. Then they began asking one of the questions that was to be repeatedly asked at the 'investigation': 'Did you have alcohol?' Everyone had been drinking heavily. Everyone was jailed, the men in the men's jail and the women in the women's. 'It was bad enough for me,' said Dr Arnot, 'for Penny it was terrible. We men were crowded into our cell, a small room with one working loo. We had a ladle of water a day to wash with. Food was brought to us by our friends – no other food was supplied – and the other inmates fought for it as it was handed through the bars. Because I am tall and a doctor I had some advantages. I didn't get buggered or anything like that. Eventually my cellmates asked me to be their cell leader as Arabs have much respect for height. I was able to help the other foreigners to some extent. We weren't barred into our cells and they all led out into a corridor so we could move about a bit and I kept in touch with the other expatriates in for manslaughter, drugs and alcohol-related crimes.' Dr Arnot spent five months in jail and Penny three.

When I met him he and Penny were attending investigatory sessions with a judge each Monday. 'It's just one little man in a dirty *kafia* picking his nose as he asks me continually whether I gave my wife permission to dance with other men. He seems obsessed and fascinated by the question.' In an article on the whole story the *Daily Mail* of 10 September 1985 wrote: 'The judge asked Penny: "Did you allow Mr Hayter or any other man to kiss or touch you?" Penny replied: "No." He turned to Hayter: "Did you kiss or touch this woman?" Hayter replied: "No." He then began asking each individual present, "Did you dance with . . . drink with. . . . " Suddenly the judge got bored with the whole thing, remembers Arnot. He finally said, "Hands up all those who danced . . . hands up all those who didn't . . . hands up those who drank . . . hands up those who didn't. . . . " Various hands shot up and down and "it was a total farce. I could hardly believe this was a court of law," remembers Arnot.'

A week after that dinner party Penny, who had admitted adultery, was sentenced to a public lashing, a sentence she appeared to be willing to accept if only as a means of being allowed to leave Saudi Arabia. As the *Daily Mail* put it: 'In despair she had just confessed to her interrogator that at the time she and New Zealander Tim Hayter were supposed to be murdering British nurse Helen Smith and Dutch seaman Johannes Otten, they were in fact making love.' But the *Daily Mail* also drew attention to the ghastly catch. For according to the diktat of Islam and the practice in Saudi Arabia the penalty is death for adultery as well as murder. 'You see,' she told the *Mail*, 'the police had been going on and on about me being a murderess – and then, as soon as I made my false confession of adultery, they said, "Fine! Now we know you're telling the truth. Obviously you can't be guilty of murder."' Nobody apart from the police was ever remotely to suggest that she was guilty of murder, only that some person or persons at the party may have been.

On 24 March 1980 Penny and Tim Hayter were sentenced to 30 lashes each for the alcohol offence and 50 lashes for having lied to an earlier court about the adultery. Richard Arnot's sentence was 30 lashes plus a year's imprisonment for illegal drinking, holding an illegal drinking party in his flat, and for allowing his wife to talk and dance with other men.

Both Richard and Penny Arnot were eventually reprieved and released but at a time when Penny would have welcomed her flogging she told the *Daily Mail*: 'The only thing I really hated about those prison beatings – flogging is too violent a word really – was the fact that they made them kneel when it was being done. I thought: I won't kneel for them, I won't be humiliated like that. They'd have to force me to the ground. . . . '

I remember coming out of the smart Queen's Building in Jeddah one day. In the street outside was a crowd. Standing on a high point I gazed down at a man being flogged. He lay front down on the ground as if doing press-ups and a policeman with a thin cane and his elbow held tightly against his side was merely brushing him with the stick. Every time the stick touched the man's clothed back he howled but I had the clear impression that there was only humiliation and no pain involved and that the howls were simply a part of the concordat. A man in the crowd told me that the victim was being beaten for refusing to close his

shop during one of the four daylight prayers. Penny described
the beating of a woman to the *Mail*: 'If the guard flogged her too
violently,' she said, 'the women would all shout and jeer at him
and tell him to lay off. And when it was over they'd all crowd
round her and congratulate her and generally make a great fuss of
her.'

Minor crimes in Saudi Arabia are punished either by
floggings or by imprisonment while third-time theft is punished
by the amputation of the right hand. Wilfred Thesiger in his
Arabian Sands tells the tale of a young boy nursing his amputated
hand. It had been cut off, through no fault of his own, because
the circumcision rite had been carried out incorrectly. Today,
such penalties appear to be much rarer. Three crimes carry the
death penalty: murder, adultery where there are four reliable
witnesses who have seen the actual penetration of the penis, and
renunciation of the Islamic faith.

In 1982 a film called *Death of a Princess* was screened by
British television. A young and beautiful member of the Royal
Family, Princess Misha, had eloped to a hotel near Jeddah's
Creek with her lover. Her uncle ordered her execution,
presumably on the grounds that she had confessed. King Khaled
apparently protested against the execution but could not overrule
the wishes of the Princess's own family. The scandal of the film
led to the expulsion of the British Ambassador, James Craig, and
a down-turn in relations between Saudi Arabia and the UK.
Saudis were as horrified by the execution as the British. One
Saudi quoted to me the story of the adulterous woman who
approached the Prophet Muhammad and confessed her crime.
He told her to go away and repent but the woman came back
three times insisting that she must suffer according to the Law,
and the Prophet finally consented, on her own insistence, to her
execution.

8

A noisy night in Beirut

I had first known Beirut in its plump days before the civil war, and as a poor student was repelled by its brash wealth. I next visited it nine years later in 1977 when the forces of darkness had become a self-perpetuating cycle of horror. Only then, and I say it with shame, did I look at the city with fascination and empathy. Damnation seemed to have broken its fragile surface of slick satisfaction.

Had the Lebanese come into their own amid the blasted buildings, the bodies dragged behind '*voitures verolées*' ('bullet-poxed cars'), the traffic jam on the airport road while the car ahead was having its passengers kidnapped and dragged off to a repulsive death? Yeats could have written for Lebanon: 'The best lack all conviction, while the worst Are full of passionate intensity.'

In April 1977, shortly after the short-lived ceasefire which was mistaken for peace after a year of internecine savagery, I put Beirut down on my itinerary for a visit as Macmillan Publishers' Middle East Manager and no director questioned it.

At the airport I was astonished by the efficiency and friendliness of officials who barely glanced at my baggage. The taxi driver immediately tried to cheat me, a cosy reminder of Lebanon before the war. I had misunderstood that his £20 charge was danger money. So absorbed was he in haggling for his bloated fee that my attempts to discuss the 'events', or get him to comment on the massive security force checkpoints, or identify the shattered buildings, were to no avail. But the devastation was partial and when I reached the elegant, efficient Bristol Hotel in Al-Hamra I relaxed into the assumption that, as usual, the whole affair had been exaggerated by the press.

I paid the taxi £10 and entered the hotel where a phalanx of porters greeted me with genuine pleasure. 'No need to book a room, sir,' gushed the reservations clerk. The porter refused a tip. The only stipulation was that everything had to be paid in cash. No cards or travellers' cheques: hard cash and everyone was happy. The credit card companies had long ago crossed Lebanon off the map. My first visitor was the German Ambassador, a friend of a friend in London, who had been running a one-man show for one and a half years. 'I have no staff so have to don a hundred hats,' he told me jovially. 'I am everyone from Ambassador to tea-boy.' The French Embassy was, by comparison, top-heavy. Everybody seemed to have stayed put throughout the war. They had not cut back on a single staff member although two gendarmes had been killed. Two years later the French Ambassador was murdered.

When the German Ambassador had left I telephoned one of my closest childhood friends, Charles-Henri d'Aragon, who was now Second Secretary in the French Embassy. He had recently arrived in advance of his wife and was delighted to hear from me. 'I'll come round immediately. Just wait there.'

Within fifteen minutes he had arrived. I told him that I felt that reports of the civil war had been exaggerated. 'Have you been through Beirut yet?' he asked. In the Bristol Hotel I had lost all sense of violence. There was no shooting in the streets. I was to spend five days in Beirut and Charles-Henri suggested we dine each night in a different quarter. That night, in order to traverse the whole city, we decided to eat in Ashrafiyah.

As we drove through central Beirut I was at first surprised by its brightness and efficiency. There was no hooting, unlike Cairo which is a cacophony of car horns. But as we reached La Rue Fouad Chehab which leads into La Place des Martyrs, the heart of old Beirut, the lights disappeared. We were driving through the darkness of utter devastation and emptiness, buildings either blown to bits or half tumbled with huge chunks of masonry hanging down above us at horrific angles. Sometimes we would skirt around them lest they fall and crush us.

Rats cowered on the smashed pavements. I saw what I thought was a corpse slouched in an armchair before a fragmented building. On looking more closely I saw that it was a soldier asleep in his greatcoat with his machine-gun slung between his legs. For ten minutes we drove through this silent, apocalyptic darkness – the pure tranquillity of death. Utter silence. It was Berlin, April 1945. Then we saw bright red lights ahead. Flamboyant, smiling women were lounging outside the doorway of a house, brightly dressed women with voluptuous breasts. I have never looked upon prostitutes with such affection. Their imploring smiles as we drove past were almost virginal.

We drove on over the flyover, later to be called Death Ring because it was the target of snipers from the empty buildings on either side of the notorious and empty Damascus Road, the dividing line between West and East Beirut. That night we dined in a small restaurant and we were glad to leave.

The following day I began visiting bookshops to sell my 'academic list'. I expected the usual haggling, complaints about lost invoices, all the dreadful machinery of the book trade where the rep takes the brunt at both ends. When I reached the first bookshop, Levant Distributors, the manager took one look at me and cried, 'You're the first publisher we've received for two years.' I was lionised. All my sales-talk, my catalogues, the homework wrought over into the early hours, had suddenly become completely irrelevant. 'Come and have lunch.'

'I'd love to,' I replied but, totting up the revenue I was expected to earn to prove that Beirut really was worth visiting, I said, 'Can we go through the catalogue first?'

'The catalogues, my friend, the catalogues! Forget the catalogues. You're here! That's what matters. Give us £3,000 worth of books. Choose them yourself. Now let's go and eat.'

One night Charles-Henri and I decided to eat in Sabra, the Palestinian refugee camp that was to suffer the terrible massacre in 1982. Everywhere young Al-Fateh officers stood around eyeing us sardonically. The following day I heard that the Syrian peace-keeping force had stormed Sabra and killed several Palestinians two hours after our departure.

One evening, some great friends, apolitical Christians who ran a smart shop in a big, modern building in West Beirut, took me to dinner in a restaurant in Phoenicia Street near the Damascus road dividing line. The splendid building,

in the heart of Al-Hamra, stands all marble and glass, completely
untouched by gunfire or artillery in an area where no building is
without its token bullet. Before visiting the restaurant they took
me to their warehouse. We wandered through the shop into a
tiny courtyard. 'Look up,' said Bachir. Obeying, I suddenly
saw the blackened windows of the gutted Holiday Inn looming
immediately down above us. 'The Palestinian guerrillas would
knock politely and enter with bazookas and cannons, place them
in the courtyard and fire away night after night at the Phalangists
who occupied the Holiday Inn,' said Bachir.

We went out to the restaurant. As we entered we were given
a warm welcome by the doorman. 'Some Christians have just
phoned to ask us whether it's safe to cross the line,' he said. 'I
told them it was a good night and it was OK to come.' At that
moment a Mercedes drew up and some of the Debs' Delights
whose photographs filled the pages of Beirut's society weekly
Monday Morning bundled out in evening dress, giggling and
clutching champagne bottles. Earlier in the day I had seen pretty
women in mini skirts leading poodles down the streets of Al-
Hamra or sipping Pernod in the cafés. Beirut is like that: glamorous
business as normal until the shooting starts, then everyone
wanders off to the cellars. You go to the beach which is full of
girls in bikinis to the background tara-tara of machine-guns.

In the restaurant Bachir's beautiful wife told me, 'Every
morning I would come out and see a tramp on the other side of
the ceasefire line. I prepared soup and took bread. Then I would
squat down on the road and run across every morning to feed
him. They would start firing at me. I don't know whether they
aimed to kill me or were just playing. Once I had fed him I
collected the plates, squatted down again and sprinted back again
with machine-gun bullets flying past me.'

Another trader I knew in Al-Hamra had had his seven-floor
building destroyed in the war and was trying to persuade the
Liverpool insurance brokers that it had burnt down by accident
and had not been bombed. He was having difficulty proving his
case. Bachir had not blamed the Palestinians but the Christians.
He showed me a photograph of the burnt-out and mutilated
corpse of his Sudanese *bawwab*.

When I left Beirut I took a taxi from the devastated Place des Martyrs, otherwise known as The Bourj (The Tower). The taxi driver was friendly and talked about the war, identifying which group had destroyed which building. He was a Druze and claimed to have taken no part in any of the 'events'. It was a relief to climb the hillside above Beirut, away from the horrors and up among the olives and elegant stone houses of the rich. We drove on to the mountain village of Aley, a favoured town of the Druze leader Kemal Jumblatt, the eccentric intellectual who enjoyed complete devotion among the Druze guerrilla groups, was one of the dandiest dressed men of Beirut and visited his Hindu guru each year in Benares.

Aley was silent when we reached it. It was siesta-time. We had passed through several road blocks of the Syrian peace-keeping forces but in Aley there was not a Syrian to be seen. The driver suggested a drink in a bar. I was keen to continue to Damascus, but I finally agreed. Three girls leaned against the bar and smiled when we entered.

'How long do you want to stay?' the barman asked the driver in Arabic.

'About an hour,' he replied.

'No, no, we're just staying five minutes,' I said and, glancing at the girls, added, 'Just for a drink.'

The driver went to the other end of the bar with a girl and I took my beer to a table. A girl followed me and began murmuring dreamily, peering romantic magazine-wise into my eyes and telling me they were beautiful as she stroked my thigh. Soon the barman brought two more beers to the table and I remembered the brothel routine from many years ago in Piraeus where I had visited a bar and before you could say 'kalimera' you had spent £20 on two gins and a cuddle and couldn't afford the bus back to town.

I told the barman that I was paying for one beer and no more as I glanced at a bill for about £20. The driver sat away from me with one of the girls and completely ignored me. Everyone stood around in an ominous silence for a moment, then the girls scampered away, frightened. Perhaps they assumed that some-body would draw a gun in a trigger-happy world, a possibility that had certainly occurred to me. 'OK, I shall call the Syrian security forces,' I shouted naively. No one said a word. It was like a sleepy cowboy film. I went out into the hot, silent street of this small town but the street was completely empty.

When I returned I was given silent, threatening looks. It occurred to me that I could simply dock the money from the taxi fare when I arrived in Damascus and, fearing for my life, I very quietly paid the barman and we left. I was livid when I entered the car and threatened to report the driver to the next Syrian control post. He became very frightened, insisting that he knew nothing about what was happening and didn't know the people. However, the passionate embraces of the whores when we first arrived made it clear to me that many a passenger had been menaced by the driver in this way and many a pleasant afternoon of love-making enjoyed by him, at his passengers' expense.

When we reached Damascus the driver meekly accepted the reduced fare I paid him.

9

Chewing over affairs of state

I visited North Yemen in October 1977 some days after the gruesome assassination of its popular President Ibrahim al-Hamdi, his brother Colonel Abdullah al-Hamdi and his brother-in-law Colonel Ali Kannas on 11 October. Two French courtesans had been murdered on the same night and their bodies were found alongside al-Hamdi's corpse as if to question the ruler's reputation. Behind the peaceful and exotic surface of Yemeni life lies an underworld of Byzantine intrigue which remains secret to even the most perceptive foreigner.

As soon as I arrived in Sanaa I made my way through the fantastic gingerbread houses of the old city to the university to discuss the adoption by its library of Macmillan Publishers' university text-books.

As I sat discussing book sales with the jolly, fussy Egyptian librarian Mr Fathi, an elegant young Yemeni called Ahmed Sharaf ad-Din came in carrying three antique Islamic manuscripts. One, he explained, was a thousand years old. I wanted to interview him for a magazine so he drove me to his home on his scooter through Sanaa's lovely, labyrinthine alleys. Little girls peering through the alabaster lunettes of the *mafarij* (drawing-rooms) of the stone buildings shouted 'Sura, sura' ('Photograph, photograph').

Ahmed's father was Shia and claimed descent from the Prophet Muhammad's cousin and son-in-law, Ali. His father's father had had 15 wives and 28 sons and daughters but all but 12 of these children had died in a series of epidemics. He showed me pictures of his family's mountain-top castle near Kawkaban. When I mentioned the October coup in which al-Hamdi had been assassinated he whispered, 'It was a revolution, not a coup. Seven thousand people died.' Sanaa's little, medieval, tapering buildings are alive with gossip but very few people ever know the truth, even long after the event.

Next door to Ahmed Sharaf ad-Din lived North Yemen's most eminent painter, Abdul Jabbour Nu'man, whom we visited. His house was filled with his gaudy, realist paintings and he allowed his children to crawl all over them as if they were cardboard toys. 'This is true art,' he said as he watched his son smearing butter all over the body of a girl drawing water from a mountain pool. His paintings were of Yemeni village scenes but in the neo-Classical French style, stylised girls carrying Italianate jars to the side of a stream amid a Tuscan pastoral landscape. His epic paintings of Queen Bilqis, the Queen of Sheba, were bright and bloody enough to make comic-strip material. Nu'man had painted portraits of Hamdi, also the Saudi Crown Prince Sultan.

He showed me an erotic painting of his Egyptian wife. Her breasts burst from her silk cleavage and at her head sat a young boy playing a *na'y*, a flute. The boy was Nu'man himself, the husband playing son to his wife.

In the afternoon I was invited to attend the daily afternoon *qat*-chewing session in the *mafraj* of my old friends the al-Wazirs. Their two-storey palazzo stands just off Nasr Square. Al-Wazir means 'Minister' and the family had been ministers to the Imams (North Yemen's religious and secular rulers) for centuries. In 1948 the Imam Yahya was assassinated and the father of the present al-Wazir brothers, Abdullah, was proclaimed Imam. Although Abdullah promised to rule as a constitutional monarch, his rule lasted barely one month. Yahya's son, Ahmed, secured tribal support, defeated him and had him and other leaders of the revolt against Yahya executed. An additional penalty was to have most of the storeys of the al-Wazir palace destroyed, leaving today's truncated building.

The long *mafraj*, scattered with cushions, was filled with tribesmen among the brothers and a few dignified Yemenis wearing Western suits. Each man lounged on cushions against the wall, his cheek plump as an apple with *qat*, the mild narcotic which looks like privet and takes exhausting hours to

chew enough to get high on. In front of each man lay green
bundles of the bush. Beside each bushel stood a tall, bubbling
narguileh pipe with a glass stem and beside it a press-button
vacuum flask filled with water.

I took my shoes off, bowed my '*Salaam alaykums*' in every
direction, found myself a cushion and got down to the
complicated business of stuffing my mouth with privet and
making polite conversation from the side of my mouth which
was unfilled. The tribesman beside me in his copious turban, his
futah (kilt) and his *gambia* (dagger) was virtually asleep as he
puffed at his murmuring *narguileh*. But questions shot at me
from all around the room and my assessment that to talk
endlessly and chew at the same time was biologically impossible
was clearly not shared by anyone else.

Zayed al-Wazir began to comment, between puffs, on the
world economy at large, on a bombing in Beirut, on Thatcher's
monetary policies – would they or would they not work –
would I just answer them that? And the whole *mafraj* waited for
my decisive statement. A few bushels away lounged the Dean of
the University, a man I had endlessly sought interviews with.
Qassem al-Wazir, tipped by some to be North Yemen's next and
first elected president, entered the *mafraj*, threw me a smile of
welcome, and settled onto his cushion to arrange and prepare his
qat kit.

Abbas al-Wazir pushed more *qat* towards me, suggesting
politely that I was not chewing fast enough to get high enough
quick enough. As I chewed, my mind became crisp and minutely
alert to detail and the long room with its wild-eyed tribesmen
mingled in a half sleep became increasingly bizarre. Communities
of tribesmen got up to leave in silence and new communities
settled down in their places. I glanced among the eighty sleepy
eyes and wondered what daggers lurked beneath them, for Sanaa
is a village of much mischief and political violence bursts
spasmodically from within its medieval flux.

Forty cheeks expanded and contracted like tennis-balls. The
tribesman beside me jogged awake and offered me a cigarette.
He looked so astonished when I tried to refuse that I accepted it.
A cigarette is as much *de rigueur* after *qat* as brandy or After Eight
after dinner in Fulham. As I was eventually about to leave a

slightly balding, middle-aged man in a dark suit appeared. Everyone, even the spaced-out tribesmen, stirred a little to welcome him before slumbering off again. He brushed aside the honours, took off his shoes, and settled down to arrange his *qat*. He was one of North Yemen's best-loved ex-Prime Ministers, Hassan al-Makki. I shook his hand before saying good-bye to the now drooping salon, to a ripple of invitations from the al-Wazir brothers before they returned to chew over affairs of state.

10

Through the singing valleys of Yemen

When we saw the colony of baboons shrieking across our path in the rocky river-bed that falls between the misty castle-villages of central Yemen, the voice of the old lady, now a tiny yellow dot three hours' walk up into the mountain, was still calling our route instructions. Journeys through the rocky goat-tracks and tumbling terraces between villages are counted by the mountain tribes in hours not kilometres. 'As the eagle flies it is half an hour,' I was once told, 'but the way you must go is three hours.' Three hours through precipitous descents of knife-sharp rock, interminable hold-ups to watch bucket-blue lizards and silk-green parakeets or to gaze up at the arc of castle villages on every mountain-top or down into the gleaming valleys full of banana trees, brilliant flowers and the promise of streams.

And when it becomes five hours and you wonder whether you are wrong, you arrive, aware of only your clumsy, burnt body, and watch human and animal life moving up and down the mountains, conversing in shouts across the valley, arriving at perched destinations as if they had driven by car. But no cars, no roads, no electricity. In place of that you hear the soft and sharp babblings, shrieks and whistles of life, and experience the individuality that makes each village distinct from the next in personality, the cultural richness of a people whose imaginations feed off the living paradise around them and the clean demands of Islam that call them to involvement in it rather than to withdrawal from it.

Because of the contrast between its soaring mountains and lush green valleys and the endless deserts of the rest of the peninsula, Yemen was rightly called Arabia Felix – Happy

Arabia – by the Classical writers. The spice trade that passed from India and the legend of the Queen of Sheba are symbols of this romantic appeal. Politically, however, Yemen has also been the victim of war, disease, and tribal anarchy, characteristics which are alive today.

I had arranged to travel through the mountains with Charlie, a girl-friend, but we missed each others' connections and I spent three days searching the nooks and crannies of Sanaa for her, dreaming up all the ghastly fates that could have befallen her. Although foreign girls can usually roam the streets of Sanaa without fear of being molested, the danger always exists that they will be confused with the handful of European prostitutes who grace the beds of the rulers. The British Ambassador, standing before the thick-walled castle Embassy, coolly told me he had seen her and described her movements. She had called the previous day. My search took me among the charity organisations that clutter Sanaa and when two days later I reached the house of some sweet-natured Irish girls working with the Save the Children Fund I discovered that I had been on the tracks of somebody altogether different. I was on the point of panic when I suddenly discovered her staying with friends in a villa which overlooked President Ghashemi's semi-detached villa, made all the less imposing by the two tanks standing outside it. Our first meeting was less than romantic. She appeared completely unaware of my terrible anxieties on her behalf.

To pretend that we had any idea where our adventures were to take us would be fraudulent. I had spoken in Cairo of 'taking her to the wilds'. We had to visit a friendly British botanist to get instructions on how to get to those wilds. His only criterion for going anywhere was flowers – wild tribes, castle-villages, plummetting valleys were merely necessary adjuncts to his study of flowers. I envied his dedication but we were to discover that the most interesting flowers appear in the wildest places. He would cross battle-lines to find a rare orchid. Our goal was adventure and if some pretty flower appeared it would merely add to the romance of the general scene. The botanist, after some thought, scribbled eight names of villages on the back of an envelope and our expedition was arranged.

We wandered through the old town to buy odds and ends

before picking up a communal, tribal taxi at the Bab al-Yemen on the other side of the old city of Sanaa. It was abustle with Friday, Holy Day. On earth escarpments before the panorama of tall, stone, huddled castle-houses stood the little fruit markets with parasols, crowded with women in their brilliantly coloured cover-alls. Pretty little girls in sequinned bonnets rolled bicycle wheels with sticks through the dust. We moved through the tiny streets salaaming as we skirted rotting corpses of cats and dogs. The city was full of scents and stenches. Wandering through the plethora of medieval houses with their half-moon stained lunettes, wrought wood balustrades and white-wash patterns about the windows, inevitable children fell into crowds behind us, too charming to irritate. The most persistent were those in tatty Western dress. My main prize, the little girls in bright village frocks, shied away giggling when I raised my camera and renewed their pleas when I lowered it. They had not realised their puberty – when they did they would disappear forever into the flowery table-cloths – but they knew that they were on the cusp.

As elsewhere in the Middle East pre-pubescent girls demonstrate both a greater degree of maturity and a greater leaning towards frivolity than their brothers. As soon as they menstruate, or sooner if they marry before, they take on the heavy Yemeni veil never to discard it. As children they will flirt like adults, perhaps aware that the time for showing off their charms is limited. A much sadder image is that of little girls who take on the veil long before their time because, like children in the West who put on make-up to play the adult role, they want to emulate the sophistication of their sisters. In Sanaa you sometimes see tiny girls floating past like boats so enveloping is the trailing black shroud that covers them. Some such children have been married off at the age of ten or eleven although they are not expected to share their husband's bed until they have reached puberty.

Through the Bab al-Yemen among the Alice in Wonderland shops piled high with lucerne we came among the taxis, battered shooting-wagons whose drivers shouted destinations, 'Hodeyda, Taiz, Sa'ada!' while passengers slowly filled in. Our first village, Maghreba, is on the road to Hodeyda. Although it was only half way, some 200 kilometres, we had to pay the full YR 10

(£6). Finally we were a full complement of ten and rattled out through the dusty streets of Sanaa.

As we came into the mountains we stopped for tea in the little stone village of Souq al-Aman where everyone went off to pray in a mosque the size of a doll's house. A young man who 'want pratess inglesh' invited us to the 'hotel', which we entered by a night-black stone staircase, single-file only, up and up and up into the dirtiest *mafraj* I had ever seen. The cushions were thick with black grease, the watering place of a million flies. Two tribesmen wearing elegant silver *gambias* lounged in the corner arguing about the price of *qat*. One asked me where I had come from and had I flown to Yemen? He told me with great excitement that he had once been in an aeroplane, 'And suddenly I was up, up in the sky and everything became tiny, just like this,' he pinched his fingers together. 'By God, I liked the aeroplane but I preferred it when it went along the ground.' His companion was ill and pointed in despair to his lower abdomen. Had he not been to a doctor? 'All doctors are liars,' he told me with assurance and his companion nodded, frowning with agreement. A little boy brought in a big bowl of *hulba*, a white spicy froth, and bowls of spiced chunks of mutton fat. But the taxi was honking and we ran back to continue our journey.

The journey into the mountains started at Maghreba, 60 kilometres down the Hodeyda road from Sanaa, passing through astonishing mountain panoramas and that plethora of hill-top villages that says so much about Yemen's population potential. After the silent deserts of Arabia, Yemen is seething with people. Maghreba is a scruffy little place with army checkpoints. Even the truck driver carried a rifle on his back. But it was good for the last milky tea and flat bread before the ascent. We climbed up among terraces that may be four thousand years old until we met two child goat-herders who led us up through neat, steep tracks to a hill-top that dominated mountains and valleys that seemed to melt into eternity. On a little plain above stood their mortarless stone house, almost a fortress village in itself. The terraces were filled with what looked like privet hedges. 'Qat,' the children told us with pride. An old man wearing an expensive antique *gambia* came out and sat with us on the stony ground.

The people spoke impeccable Arabic, much closer to Classical than Sana'i Arabic, and treated us with courtesy, speaking directly to me until I made it clear that there was no taboo in speaking with my girl-friend too. An old lady brought us tea and hot, grainy bread. As we glanced up at the five tiny windows we saw that heads were peering out of each – a pretty girl, a young man, an old man, and in the fifth a black cat with a wagging tail nearly hiding the head of an old lady in black. The old man explained that he thought we were Egyptians. 'We liked the Egyptians. They used to camp just below us during the civil war. We would make them tea and bread and they brought us tinned food.' The poor Egyptians. They had swaggered into Yemen to support the Republic and had quickly found themselves fighting in these wild peaks among allies for whom they felt fear and urbane contempt. Few had ever seen a mountain. Most were *fellahin* who knew only the soft greenery of the Nile Delta. Driving to Hodeyda during the civil war the late David Holden was stopped by an Egyptian colonel leading a convoy of armoured cars. He asked if he was near the top. Holden told him he was only half-way. He was dejected. 'I never expected anything like this,' the colonel remarked. 'You see, I have no map.'

Civil war loyalties were to become a cautionary tale for us. 'The Imam Yahya visited us here once,' we were proudly told in one village. I wondered whether the speaker had been old enough to remember the medieval cruelties, the poverty and the disease of Yahya's day. During the ascent to a village later on a little boy would say, 'Hamdi very, very good. Ghashemi no good at all . . . well, quite good, but Hamdi much better.' There was no way of knowing which loyalty we were coming among, hill divided against hill and divisions existing even within the villages themselves.

We walked on above the rich *qat* plantations until we came in sight of the beautiful tall houses of Manakha clustered in the lap of the mountain. Similar villages were scattered down the mountainside and into the huge valley far below us. Suddenly the call to prayer came loudly from the mosque in Manakha and the entire valley echoed with the beautiful sound. It seemed to add unity to nature rather than, as a man-made discipline, to detract from the luxuriant freedom of the valley. Charlie said, 'Maybe mosques in the little villages below will follow.' We waited and suddenly heard the muffled '*Allahu akbar*' from a village far below, followed by another beyond. The whole valley was being called to submission – indeed Islam means 'submission' in Arabic. We, too, felt like going down on the ground, for the scenery was transcendent.

As we rounded a rock we saw Manakha. Standing on a mountain-top some 8,000 feet above sea-level and dominated by the imposing Jebel Shibam, Manakha is an example of stone architecture of such skill that it appears literally to grow out of the rock. The fact that the lower floors have no windows adds to this effect. The English traveller Walter Harris visited Manakha in 1892. 'Wonderful, stupendous it was,' he writes. 'Around us on all sides the bare fantastic peaks and perpendicular precipices, on the edge of one of which we perched, and up the face of which we could see the path we had climbed winding in and out. Below us, far below like ants, we could see our mules and men toiling up. . . . Of all the places that it has ever been my lot to see, Manakha is the most wonderfully situated.' Manakha was the home of the Ismaili sect, a communalist Shia sect which took its name from Ismail, the seventh descendant of Ali, the Prophet's son-in-law, and whose missionaries worked through a system of secret cells spread throughout the lands of Islam in the ninth century, preaching the return of Ismail's son Muhammad as the Mahdi or Messiah and eventually winning over the rulers of Yemen. Today the region of Jabal Haraz which overlooks Manakha is a centre for Ismaili pilgrims from as far afield as India.

As we entered Manakha, children in bright bonnets with earflaps came about us. '*Atini galam*' ('Give me a pen').

'We have no pens.'

'*Atini bakshish.*'

'Our pockets are empty.'

The children ran through the litany of things they wanted, moving on without pause to the second if we didn't have the first. But wherever we went the emphasis was on pens. Given the innate intelligence of the Yemenis, I wondered whether every Yemeni child was not an instinctive, atavistic intellectual.

Charlie sat to draw the tall buildings growing out of the cliff-face while I moved into the village. I spoke to a beautiful peasant woman who was scolding a child.

'Are you alone?'

'No, my wife [girl-friends don't exist in Arabia] is drawing the village.'

'Oh, but you must go back and fetch her. You musn't leave her alone.'

I went back, meekly, ashamed somehow. It was difficult to point out the independence of European women.

When we went in among the buildings of Manakha the calls for *bakshish* and '*B'jour, m'sieur*' became a babble and we began, disillusioned, to realise that we had hit the French tourist route, the Djibouti run. There are cheap flights from Paris to Djibouti and thence to Sanaa. The children, some forty of them, took us to a tall, handsome building in the centre and asked us to enter. Young women leaned out of every little window. 'A hotel?' I asked. 'A brothel?' I wondered. No, a private house, but we could go in. Would we go in? At that moment a large crowd of children emerged into the square, a group of Europeans in their midst. We made our *bonjours* and crept away, determined to disown Manakha for stranger places. When we asked for Hajra, a villager merely pointed across the valley to a village laced in mist on the opposite mountain. 'Two hours' walk,' they said. So we doubled the calculation and moved on around the mountain.

The air became cooler and we were walking through thin mist. When we reached Hajra at five o'clock it was Kafkaesque – tall square buildings rising from stone, mist, open areas of smooth flag-stones, and an air of desertion. It reminded me of Machu Picchu in the heights of the Peruvian Andes. I asked an old man, 'Is there a hotel, an inn?'

'No, there is nowhere to stay here,' he smiled. 'You must go on to Hujeila. Or you can go down to the café yonder.'

The village yonder was Masmara, a scattering of small stone houses. Mangy dogs snarled. We entered the café, a square, windowless shed half filled with branches and sacks of *bun*, Yemeni coffee, and half with the down-and-outs of the village squeezed along a ledge. They greeted us with curiosity but coldly. The café owner placed two soap boxes for us in the centre and lit a petrol lamp. The atmosphere was sinister and we were tired. We drank our tea and asked about lodgings. 'No, there is nowhere to stay here,' they assured us, 'the truck goes once a day to Manakha but it is too late now.' We had walked about three miles. 'You should go on to Hujeila but it is five hours' walk.' No way forward, no way back. Would a cosy peasant lady invite us to her house? Would the men compete to invite us to their houses?

No one made a move in that direction so we drank more tea and discussed *qat* – you can always discuss *qat* or the value of the men's *gambias* in Yemen without boring anyone; one *gambia* was worth YR 16,600 (£2,000). A pompous-looking man in gleaming white *futah* and beautiful *gambia* encrusted with gold entered. A shaikh said to me, 'Don't worry, you can stay in the café.' Charlie said, 'If we wait somebody will invite us to their house.' But it was dark and the night was turning cold, and howling dogs patrolled the lanes. We had no choice. Charlie wanted the loo – a predicament because we didn't want to leave the bags, but necessity overcame anxiety and a polite little boy led us out to a patch of wasteland gleaming in the moonlight which also flooded the valley. I kept the dogs at bay with a torch. Back in the café there was more tea and the publican, a laconic man with bulging, comic eyes like a frog's and a red turban was making us spiced *foul* (beans) on his midget stove. Suddenly a pair of long, naked bow-legs appeared in the doorway. They belonged to a crazy old man with a gaga-smile who had pulled his *futah* up about him as if it were underpants. He sat down beside us and gabbled at me with enough sense to warrant replies when I understood the questions. But whenever I spoke his neighbour screwed his finger against his temple with a grimace. A gentle old man came into the café with mattresses and later another came in with rough blankets. Time passed and drinkers left until the last, the gaga man, swayed out chattering to himself and we were alone with the publican.

The publican asked us meaningfully whether we would sleep '*sowa-sowa*' (together) or alone. '*Sowa-sowa*,' I said firmly to eliminate any doubts about our relationship. He placed sacks beside the ledge and with incredible – suggestive? – labours made a bed of the mattresses. Then he left and we locked ourselves in. A rat was scuttering on paper among the branches behind us. A loud banging on the door – I opened, the publican wandered in again casually and made tea, then *foul* (spiced beans) for himself and urged us to join him. We, seated inhibitedly on the ledge, refused. He looked up, amid gobbles, and said, 'Don't mind me, go to bed,' an eagerness in his voice.

'Not at all,' I said. 'We go in when you go out.' When I looked at him I saw that he had fixed a desperate stare on Charlie. But he had no *gambia* and I glanced around to see where he might have hidden one.

Did we want tea? 'No, thanks, we're tired.' He washed up and returned to his stool to continue his hideously crazed leer which I warded away with angry frowns, and when Charlie giggled I stopped her because he mistook it for sexual recognition. The night was silent about us and the door bolted and I wondered again about knives. The lamp hissed and flies pattered on paper bags. 'Are you married?' I asked.

'My wife lives in Hajra but we are very poor and we rent a single room. I have had the café for a month. But I have no money.' But was it money he was really after? He went back to his counter and took down an old cassette recorder which he placed on a stool between him and us and put on a piercing, wailing Yemeni song. He began wriggling in his stool, giggling.

'He thinks he's doing a Western dance,' Charlie said. 'Crumbs, he wants a party,' she groaned through her exhaustion.

'Where are you sleeping?' I asked.

'In Hajra.' He pointed to the bed. Why don't we go to it, he asked. We go when you go, we replied. He was getting very excited, although we couldn't see how we could be turning him on. Then he went to the centre of the room and, doing a ludicrous parody of the twist, began taking his clothes off. It was nearly more funny than alarming but the night was dark and I thought about the knives everybody wore and I knew would not hesitate to use if need be.

I leapt on the bed, grabbed our bags, and taking Charlie made for the door, telling him severely that he had broken the Arabian laws of hospitality. He was horrified and frightened and unlocked the door, sending up an inferno of barking from the dogs outside. Having explained how to extinguish the petrol lamp, he left. Leaving the door ajar for a while so that he couldn't lock us in – he could return with friends – we bolted it when the barking subsided and, turning out the lamp, were plunged into impenetrable darkness with only the pitter-patter of the rats and the sound of flies bashing their brains against the walls. We got to bed and slipped clumsily into sleep.

Suddenly Charlie woke me. 'It must be dawn; they are knocking.' There was a furious crashing at the steel door but it was pitch dark and my watch said midnight. Men were shouting and banging and we wondered whether they would break the door down. Imagination conjures up strange illusions and the darkness allowed it to phantasise about armed and ruthless mountain gangs.

'Who are you?' I shouted.

'Let us in, we want to sleep there.'

'Impossible,' I cried, 'come back in the morning.'

'Let us in or we'll break the door down.'

We searched in the darkness for our things and for each other and stood near the door so that we could escape in the *mêlée* if they succeeded in their threat. They shouted and banged and we heard them murmuring and creeping about the building as if in search of another entrance. Then we heard the sound of a truck with screaming music which roared to a halt outside and there was talking and the sound of steel being unloaded and soon there was silence. We went to bed again but heard the sound of footsteps creeping around the building and wondered whether they could possibly burn it down. But then we realised that the footsteps were rats, which was now a relief, and it dawned on us that the knockers were not bandits but wanderers in search of lodging as we ourselves were. But bandits or no bandits, we kept the door locked.

We were woken again but it was early dawn and the knocker was the senile old man with naked legs. He came in squeaking his phantasies and I wandered out into the crisp cool of the dawn. Mountains soared above me to the left. Ahead the valley wound down into the mist and to my right it curled up through lower mountains rising from a deep valley. A pink haze from the rising sun was appearing at the end of the valley. Looking up to the mountain high above me on my far right I could see the huddled villages emerging through circles of mist like fairy-tale castles. I stood, fascinated, between the rows of stone village houses. An old man was opening a tiny wooden shop front. Women were arguing over chickens and boys were galloping on donkeys down the hillside to the fields. Voices were clear and clean and full of plans for the day's work. This is Sabean agriculture, I thought. This is industry and dedication in a land which is man-made. But however sophisticated the technical knowledge of the mountain people and however efficient the terraces, these mountains would never again compete with the plains where modern equipment can so drastically increase output and decrease manpower needs.

I went back to find Charlie irritable because the madman had fondled her feet. We drank tea with the now icy publican, paid YR 20 for the night and moved away down the mountain.

We took the wrong track which inched around a precipice. Far below was a beautiful green valley, full of banana trees, palms and streams of flowers. Bright green plants grew in the clefts of the rock. Eagles hovering between us and the sun cast huge shadows over the valley. When we reached the village we were told to arc back and turn left at a white house. Here we approached a large castle. Before it was a paddock with five harnessed and hobbled camels. Several people stood among them including an extraordinarily beautiful girl of 16 in coloured silk and cotton clothing with an aristocratic air about her. I couldn't gather who she was but guessed that she had royal blood for the great house was called Dar al-Amir (House of the Prince) and had been one of the palaces of the Imams. When I asked the people how many lived in the house they said '*Wajid*' ('Many') for they have no idea of figures, whether in numbers or distances.

When we left we plummetted down jagged rocks into the brilliant valley, the villagers scattered above us in the rocks, forever guiding us and calling farewells. Below, the life of the land was converging on a little stream bridge. We could see women beating clothes against the rocks in the stream. Orange cows loitered along the edge. A boy led his donkey across the bridge. When we reached the bridge the women begged to be photographed and then there was the usual pathetic excitement as the little girls eagerly put their hands out for photographs and we had to explain that they couldn't have them 'for a long, but not a very long time'. Somebody, someday, had passed through with a Polaroid. When we stroked one of the healthy, silken cows they were very happy, very proud. 'These are the best cows in the world,' the lady said, for theirs was a very little world. We asked the way to Attara and they said 'a quarter of an hour' which was to mean that it was too far away to describe. They treated their cows with special care and love. They were their capital and symbol of wealth.

We walked on a little until we came to a stream in which the fertility of the valley seemed to have prismatically concentrated itself. We called it 'Paradise' and put our feet in the water. Bright red flowers grew from the rock and emerald green plants hung about us in confused profusion. Suddenly a brilliant blue lizard with orange paws and all of two foot long slapped itself onto the side of the huge boulder which overlooked the stream and began doing nervous press-ups. Then it whooshed behind a plant and peered out at us with a knowing grin. Sometimes its press-ups appeared to mean that it was howling with laughter at us, at other times to mean, 'Yes, just the sort of thing I like to do. Stick your paws into the stream and think of dinner.' A beautiful village woman came down to the stream and filled her tin can from below the point at which we had placed our feet. I wondered whether we were soiling her water. Some villagers came and we told them how beautiful their land was and they were pleased and agreed that it was the most beautiful land in the world and that our land must be horrible because of all the fog and machinery.

I lay back to absorb the sun, which was dangerously hot, and a precocious 12-year-old immediately said, 'Come, you must go on.' He insisted I go into the shade and I realised that they imagined I had lain back with the early signs of sun-stroke. The old men led me to a knoll and pointed to the prolific terraces of *qat* and said that *qat* was the best thing in the world because it made them happy, and when I said that wheat was better because you eat wheat they said that they had lots of wheat so that they could eat *and* be happy. You had to have *qat*, anyway, they said, because otherwise how could you have afternoon *qat* sessions? In discussing *qat* it never occurs to Yemenis that *qat* sessions could be abandoned any more than it occurs to them that clothes could, or dinner or roofs or houses.

We continued walking around the mountain for three quarters of an hour until we saw Attara perched on a small mountain below us. We found a defile path that fell steep and sheer through the terraces and reached the base of the castle perched above. Walking around to the right a crowd of children greeted us and led us to a tiny shop where we sagged onto the carpeted dais. There was no tea, only tinned peaches and chunks of sticky sugar sweet, but someone brought us tea and we were given large chunks of sweet for a few piastres. The village children crowded in the doorway until the café was half dusk. Suddenly a very mature 14-year-old in a lizard-pattern pyjama suit, very elegant, handsome, authoritative and clean, came marching in. The children broke to let him through. He carried a stick. He greeted us and shook our hands with authority. The café owner, his brother, handed us a photograph of a young soldier. Suddenly we realised that it was this little boy. He was the 14-year-old soldier of the village, back on leave from Sanaa, and he clearly bore the mantle of leadership. The café owner muttered something about the children and the lizard leapt up waving his stick and shooing them away like a child Garibaldi. He then handed the stick to a tall, teenage girl who was given the job of policing the children while he entertained us. He told us about the army and about Ghashemi with pride. He clearly had the makings of a leader, a galviniser of men. I wondered whether in him we had found the child king, the charismatic leader who would lead Yemen from its humiliating clientage to the Gulf oil states and to *qat*. How such a man is needed. Yemen, potentially so great, is rotten today.

The children led us in a glorious crowd to the edge of the mountain and we stumbled down the by now familiar, agonising tracks in our broken urban shoes. A little boy followed us forever saying good-bye but never leaving us. We were guided down the precipitous short-cuts. The heat intensified and we cast covetous glances at the long cuts. We needed shade and spied a cave. Looking back the villagers were standing waving, sharply silhouetted on the tops of buildings. It was like a romantic farewell in a nostalgic film. We reached the cave, which was filled with thick straw. I climbed up and quickly fell asleep. Charlie slept on the ground in front because of the floating wheat dust inside. Peasant women wandered past, staring at Charlie in astonishment but, mercifully, moving on.

When I woke up Charlie was seated beside the lizard and explaining that I was tired. He repeated, '*Ya meskin, ya meskin*' ('Poor thing, poor thing'). He begged her to wake me up because it was bad where I was. I came down and asked why it was bad.

'There are snakes and treacherous creatures and, worst of all, there were jinn.'

'Do you believe in jinn?'

He didn't understand the scepticism in my question. 'In jinn. Of course I believe in jinn. There are jinn everywhere here. They can be very dangerous.' He was very serious indeed and it was clear that the jinn were more dangerous than the snakes. He led us on, insisting on taking my bag. Once he said good-bye and handed the bag back but he didn't leave us for a long while. He explained that he was going to a village above where somebody owed him money. What to us was a physical feat was for him a quiet social call. He finally left us, moving up the mountain while we moved down. But for the next hour we heard his calls of guidance and greeting even when we could scarcely see him, high up, minute among the rocks.

As we turned the corner we gazed with some disappointment on Usil, a little village of smoky stone houses surrounded by a spinney of cacti. In its midst was one tall, pretty building that utterly dominated the others in size and splendour. We were greeted by the usual party of villagers. They were dirty and exhausted by poverty – very different from those of Attara. We asked for lodging but they said there was none and we were tempted to continue to Hujeila but they added the proviso that there was a *mahala* (residence – it had the connotation of manor-house where visitors may be allowed to stay). The entire village led us to the big building and we were lead up through five storeys of dark mud stairs. It reminded me of my uncle's manor-house in Oxfordshire.

The *mahala* had massively thick walls because like all Yemeni houses its rough-hewn basalt foundations were shallow. We entered a narrow mud staircase which was almost completely dark with only tiny slits for security against attack, and climbed up through five floors. As in most Yemeni houses the first floor contained the lavatory and wash-room, the second the kitchen with its large brick fire-place and the women's and children's rooms, the third bedrooms and the fourth the *diwan* or *makan al-kebir* which is a common living-room where meals are taken and relations or close acquaintances received. Another room for the exclusive use of the head of the house housed objects and furnishings of value, particularly the manuscripts and documents which are the pride of possession of every great Yemeni family. When you visit a Yemeni house its head will often bring you a beautiful decaying book filled with illuminated pages which has been in the family's possession for generations.

We were led into a beautiful airy *mafraj* on the roof whose tiny windows dominated the mountain ranges and deep valleys below. Silken cushions lay around the room and sepia photographs of the family lined the walls. Almost as soon as we entered some thirty-five women followed us in. All wore lovely, silk Yemeni dresses and the more sophisticated questioned us on every kind of subject while the rest peered over with fascinated curiosity. We were sunburnt, dirty and tired but the women were fascinated with their first contact with a European woman. A lovely little girl of 12 quickly had a crush on Charlie and began pouring out her life story in a dialect of Arabic neither of us could understand, but the child was quite unperturbed and really only wanted the music of communication. Soon the women began to sit along the edges of the *mafraj* and tea and enormous *narguileh* pipes, whose coils extended across the room, were brought in. The girls in their baggy silken pantaloons coaxed the pipes with charcoal and then sat cross-legged smoking as they stared at us with intelligent fascination. They reminded me of the painting of Turkish *hareem* women by Delacroix. Soon a middle-aged man came in, with blackened teeth and a villainous air which slightly poisoned the almost euphoric atmosphere, and we sighed in despair that such perfection might turn out to be a mirage. In travel one is always suspicious of things too beautiful – the pretty girl sitting Turkish style, cross-legged in silk pantaloons before her bubbling *narguileh*, the lovely little girl clutching Charlie with passion and indifferent to all around her, and the women smiling, talking to me without inhibition or hesitation.

The man had a cynical smile, but appeared to enjoy total authority over the women and I was soon to realise that he was the father of half of them and the husband of one. He began by plying me with questions about England, politics and the route we were taking. While his basic ignorance of world affairs made me slack in repartee at first, his quick-witted intelligence soon put me on my guard. I realised, too, that he was no rake but very much of a seigneur in the region. I longed to gaze at the women, who were wildly sensual, but he soon brought out his scruffy Egyptian Learn-English manual and asked me to test him. I took the book and read in English, 'The main street, where he is?' But one look at his bemused enthusiasm and I forbore to explain what was wrong with this little link with the Western intellect. I tested him in English, then he tested me in Arabic. He never knew the answers so I gave them to him. When I answered correctly, which was nearly always the case because the questions were easy, he would immediately look to the women with a patronising smile of, 'Look, I told you so; he speaks Arabic.' He did this every time, never listening to my replies. As long as what I said was vaguely Arabic, he gave me the benefit of the doubt. The women paid absolutely no attention to the game and I felt infuriated to be so cut off from their company by such tedious conversation. I began to feel like the man in Waugh's *A Handful of Dust*, who had to read Dickens for the rest of his life to the old man in the jungle.

A girl brought us huge bowls of food and I told Charlie, knowingly, that we should eat much for that was the custom. It was too much and we left half. The dishes were then taken to the other side of the room and the women crowded around them, eating healthily. We felt hopelessly ashamed. Acting according to Arab standards, one always goes wrong in Yemen. Things are different, uncertain. The rules are fickle – only the gods know them. That is the danger of this land.

After the meal the women brought us tea and *narguileh* pipes that tasted of smoky honey. Then one of the women asked us to sing and we found ourselves bursting with inhibition. I thought of a song that Charlie didn't know. Charlie thought of a song that I didn't know. She knew a few words of 'She Loves You' and I a few of 'I Could Have Danced All Night'. But the women were silent, waiting, and we knew we had to satisfy them and we knew we had to act quickly for their smiles did not hide their impatience. So we sang, two croaking voices and a jumble of meaningless words. They clapped politely but they had clearly expected more from us.

By midnight when all but Mohammed, his pretty wife, his equally pretty teenage daughter and the little girl in love with Charlie had left, I made for the loo, five winding, mud storeys down by candle-light. The loo was filled with beautifully chiselled objects of stone; basins, humps, mini-aqueducts. It took a while to understand their use. On what did one pee and into what? In what did one wash? I gazed around desperately trying to avoid peeing where they washed or washing where they peed. Where to place the candle? I squatted in various positions, clutching the quivering, dripping candle, until the position seemed right. Then I nearly despaired when I discovered how little water the can contained. Finally I re-emerged and chose my steps warily up the baked mud-straw stairs until I reached the glimmering *mafraj*. Charlie looked worried and tired. 'I'm afraid it's the old problem. Mohammed wants us all to sleep together and his wife seems keen too.' I laughed. I couldn't help it. For once the cards seemed decadently stacked in my favour. Arabian tales, I dreamed. I was a little disturbed that Charlie was so shocked. The little girl was fondling her knees, staring up into her eyes with real love. Mohammed's wife was peering at me from behind him with a knowing smile.

Charlie decided to go to the loo. 'How can I stop the little girl coming with me?' she asked. 'It's so inhibiting. She comes and stands there peering at me as she holds the candle. I think she wants to know what every part of my body looks like.' I really couldn't help laughing. Charlie disappeared in trembling candle-light.

Mohammed turned to me quizzically. 'Your wife doesn't like the idea of us all sleeping together. She says she only wants to sleep with you.'

'Yes. She's very conservative. We've only been married a short time. She doesn't understand your customs yet.' I felt a little disloyal. The apparent offer of a celebration with the many women seemed to be on the cards and in this wonderful wilderness seemed a gorgeous way to burn with this transcendent culture. Mohammed looked at me eagerly – for my acceptance – through his broken teeth. His wife gazed at me with what I understood for real excitement. But I said no – no, we didn't understand their society, we would rather sleep alone. Mohammed smiled sheepishly, his wife looked away, sullen. The daughter left the *mafraj*, bored. The little girl gazed oblivious, probably dreaming of Charlie, unaware of the adult games about her. When Charlie returned they got up and left and we locked ourselves in. Ironically, our relationship was still platonic.

When we awoke to a knock at the *mafraj* door light was streaming from the encircling mountains through the coloured crystal windows. Charlie couldn't find her skirt so draped a scarf about her. I opened to Mohammed who entered, English manual in hand as if the night were but an interlude between lessons. I nearly groaned. Soon the little girls came flocking in in their spangled dresses, then the elder girls with coffee. Then came a rough trio of men and all the girls melted away like magic. The little girl with a crush on Charlie led her down and away to the *hareem*. For me the whole pretty scene was within moments transformed to one of a dingy sub-class café. Mohammed tried the dictionary game but I more or less ignored him. Then he asked for money for the night – YR 100 – about £12, which was clearly extortionate, but I paid at once, terrified of making ugly the memories of so strange a house.

The men left and soon all the women re-emerged with Charlie and we tried to return to our former joviality. We were given spiced *foul* (beans) before leaving and we photographed the girls on the rampart of the *mahala*. Someone suggested Charlie took a donkey and crowds formed about us as the negotiations began. The donkey was tiny. When Charlie got on it began cantering off between the cacti. When it was brought to a halt everyone was laughing and the atmosphere was full of cheer. But then the donkey suddenly buckled under and Charlie had to get off. Its owner turned suddenly from laughter to fury and grabbing the harness led the creature away to the protests and heavings of the throng. But nothing would hold him and away he went. In true Yemeni style the good things were turning sour. We felt humiliated and wanted to depart quickly.

Then we noticed that an old lady with a scythe was walking briskly beside us and we saw that she was Mohammed's mother. The crowd called to her, 'Where are you going?' 'I'm cutting the hay on the other mountain,' she said, 'and I'm going with these people because you haven't treated them properly,' or words to that effect. I heard Mohammed snigger sheepishly. This was a lady of rock. We kept saying, 'Please don't bother. We are perfectly OK.' She laughed a lovely intelligent laugh and walked on unhesitatingly, guiding us along the easier paths. Then she turned, laughing, and took the rucksack that I was carrying. 'No, no, impossible,' I begged. But she just laughed quietly and tugged it off me and she carried it on her head as lightly as if it were a handkerchief. She moved down among the sharp rocks like a viper and we could barely keep up. She kept up a running commentary in a dialect that became less and less comprehensible, but we understood enough to know that she was apologising for the un-nice farewell of her people. Again, true to Yemeni type, she spoke with a communicative intelligence where we had expected the inhibition of a simple peasant woman. She was one of the most beautiful women I have ever met.

Down, down we went, down towards the belly of the valley and as we went down so the mountains rose about us like shimmering curtains. Then, suddenly, the lady handed me my bag and, saying she must go, smiled tenderly, pointed our route down, and moved swiftly up the steep other side of the mountain. Looking up the mountain-side we saw groups of people and hamlets as far as the eye could see. The mountains were full of jabber and it seemed that simple conversations were being held between one mountain-side and the other. It was more effective and much prettier than any telephone system. Finally we reached the bottom, a river-bed of large, jagged rocks that were painful to walk on. Then we heard the old lady's voice, tiny but clear, coming from high up in the mountain. At first we couldn't see her but then we did. She was a tiny yellow dot, but

her voice was clear and by gauging her tone we managed to
orient ourselves along an easier way.

Suddenly ahead of us leapt a huge baboon with a repulsive
red bottom, then another and another and finally fifteen leaping
across together in an acrobatic procession. We stood, *bouche bée*.
They galloped across to the other slope and we quickly saw that
it was literally teeming with baboons, leaping and squealing and
hanging from trees and odd ones sitting for pensive moments on
rocks. The atmosphere was magical. White light filled the now
burning air, enclosed in the tight valley. Looking among the
rocks of the immense mountain slope to the right we now saw
that there were at least fifty baboons moving in a line across the
mountainside. Beautiful birds came down sleepily among the
shrub trees about us – big-winged brown birds with white
stripes and long beaks hovered above the baboons; little birds
with green, silken wings stood on stones and brilliant flowers
grew profusely among them. Children were calling across the
valley, creating cycles of shrill echoes that never ceased. The
yellow lady was still calling to us from somewhere high above,
nearly in Paradise. It was as if the entire world was scattered in
nooks secreted in the mountainside. We came to a defile whose
rocks were as high as a cathedral. We entered nearly in reverence.
Emerging we saw another colony of baboons shrieking and
gibbering across the mountain.

Then we entered something of death – a huge, sterile,
gleaming valley-plain of broken boulders. Each step was an
agony. We tried to walk through, along and steeply down the
antique terraces alongside but in the searing heat it was too
tiring. Hot, heavy. Charlie was crying suddenly. Frightened,
because she was the toughest woman I had ever met, I held her.
She felt terribly ill. I was afraid that she had sun-stroke. We were
now days from the nearest doctor. The shrubs were sparse of
protective branches.

I laid her under a tree and tied my shirt about her head. She
lay quietly and I roamed a little through the valley to see if there
was a village or hovel or even bigger tree in sight. The heat was
throttling and the burning air was entirely still. Nothing. When I
returned she had recovered. She lay for nearly an hour and then
we continued but I made a much slower pace so that her body

could absorb the strain of exhaustion and heat. We seemed to be walking through a gleaming white valley of death. It was an interminable crisis walk as if we were overshadowed by the wings of death.

Once the valley became narrow and small trees appeared. Camels came into sight through the dust. Fine bedouin girls were exhorting them along but they loped idly, as always bored, dreamy, wondering perhaps when man's dreary tyranny would end. The girls wore wide-brimmed straw hats. I photographed them and they looked angry. As we passed I asked them for water as ours was finished and we were parched with thirst. They moved by, sullen and indifferent. Suddenly I felt a stone hit me in the back. I turned back and the girls were stooping in the rising dust picking up stones to throw. I cursed them loudly, but deep down I found their anger sensual and impenetrable and I suffered, knowing how badly I had failed to communicate with the culture of this gleaming world by trying to photograph them, drawing away their spirits into my machine world.

We emerged from the pass into another valley exactly like the first and we saw before us a vision of the myth of Sisyphus, the eternal passage through burning valleys until they conquered us. But to the right we saw a shepherd and a herd of sheep and to the right again a little village of spilling stones.

I left Charlie in the shadow of a rock and climbed up to the first stone hovel. Gazing in I saw that a young woman had lifted up her chiffon entirely exposing herself so I withdrew a little and called from out of sight. She re-appeared, a rather demented woman of 30 or so. I asked for water. She invited me in to the darkest corner and showed me a rough earthenware pot. I raised the lid and, filling the water jar, took it down to Charlie. I returned twice for more. We lay for a while in the shade. A woman in a bright dress and leading two camels, two children and a donkey stopped and immediately gave us water from her earthenware jug. She kept repeating, '*Ruh dela, dela,*' 'Go slow, always slowly.' They were as much conscious of the deadly heat as we are of the danger of city traffic.

We walked on for about an hour to a village on our left. The villagers bustled down among the rocks to greet us. One brought us water and we drank and drank and they tried to restrain us because they were very sensitive to the real influence of the heat. A man came up and asked me to extract his tooth. 'But I'm not a dentist.' He couldn't see the significance of my remark and repeated his request. In the mountains the people assume that all Westerners are doctors or dentists. Once a doctor must have passed this way from Sanaa. Ashamed of our failure in the medical profession we walked on, expecting more burning valleys for they had told us that there was twenty minutes to Hujeila, our new 'Mecca'. But within twenty minutes, indeed, we reached a well surrounded by little Abyssinian women pulling up buckets. A very black, handsome woman looked up and told me that we would be welcome in Hujeila.

We walked up through rotting houses into the village, which became increasingly squalid. Everyone was deep black but Abyssinian rather than negroid. People surrounded us petitioning as if we were visiting judges, but we misunderstood their dialect. We were taken to a sort of rest-house, a huge room of mud supported by wooden pillars and open on two sides, like a tent. It was packed with people, mostly women, and it reeked of decay. They lay in bundled groups on rope beds. They clung to us, petitioning incessantly, and we tried to edge away because the air appeared full of disease. Across the room lay an old woman slumped and moaning on a bed. Her withered breasts lay loose and naked. They ignored her and kept their distance. She was dying and they shied away from death. It was death village and we yearned to move on. A woman grasped me and pulled my hand to her heart crying, 'Qalbi, qalbi,' 'My heart, my heart.' She wanted medicine. Charlie fished for her Panadol but I restrained her. I feared that such a drug might do more harm than good, might even kill.

We asked how far it was to the Hodeyda Valley. They explained that we were on the track again and that a van stood outside. When did it leave? Soon. How soon? we asked in real desperation. A disgusting man approached us telling us the van was his. He asked an exorbitant price and shrugged away when we complained. We would have paid a hundred pounds to escape from Hujeila. We accepted his fee.

Soon we were plummetting down among knife-sharp boulders towards Hodeyda, sometimes driving over solid rock and jagged river beds where young girls were leading their goats through the dust. As we came down onto the plain of the Tihama, African thatched rondavels appeared amid extremely fertile cultivation. Hodeyda was dark when we reached it. The air was the most muggy I had known and we gasped for breath. The city was filled with exhaustion and decay. We found a hotel and took a tiny windowless room. Even with the huge fan turning we dribbled with sweat.

At dawn we went to the lorry compound. Before it lay an open-air dormitory of rope beds for the drivers. We found a service taxi for Zabid. People poured in grasping chickens and bundles until we could hardly breathe. We drove through beautiful African-type landscape until we reached Zabid. It was full of Ottoman stucco half obscured by washing lines. The dingiest slums had beautiful calligraphy in plaster on the walls. Children led us to the deserted synagogue, beautifully swept – by whom we could not tell as most Yemeni Jews have migrated to Israel. From there we went to Taiz, a now modern city enclosed by fertile mountains. From the main hotel which dominates the town we phoned the mayor whom a friend had put us in touch with. We went to his house where he plied us with whisky, organised our hotel accommodation and arranged for his driver to take us to Jibla the following day. It was to be the most comfortable journey we had had.

From Ibb, a lovely fortress town on the Sanaa road, we turned off along rocky tracks for about five miles. Jibla is one of the prettiest towns in Yemen. The cleanly preserved battlement houses straddle the rock and as elsewhere appear to grow out of the rock which sweeps down to the valleys far below. Charlie drew the buildings while I explored. Nowhere had photography been so popular and delighted crowds formed about me. But soon I saw the tourists appear and we realised that we had come away from the wild places. We were back on the Djibouti run.

11

Beirut's death ring tightens

I returned to Beirut in April 1979. This time I stayed with Charles-Henri and his delightful wife Catherine in their French Embassy flat near the Gefinor Building in Al-Hamra. On my first day we were invited to lunch by a Maronite family in Ashrafiyah. We decided to go there by the Death Ring flyover, the chilling dividing line.

Driving over Death Ring on that day was a strange experience, more spiritual than frightening. As you drove towards the tunnel you saw portraits of Nasser and Arafat and hammers and sickles crossed with machine-guns, huge, grainy pictures of Palestinian martyrs or pictures of the disappeared Imam Sadr, the Lebanese Shia leader.

From the end of the tunnel that leads onto the flyover takes about ten, silent seconds with your foot firmly on the accelerator, the last place in the world you want to have a breakdown. For ten seconds you watch the empty buildings on both sides of the flyover from which cool sharp-shooters with telescopic sights aim for the temple, not the man. You hold your breath, mesmerised by the silence and the emptiness and the stillness for fifteen seconds. And then you are suddenly in elegant Christian Ashrafiyah. There were a few gigantic shell-holes in the buildings surrounding the Phalangist barracks, but the damage from the recent heavy Syrian artillery attack had been almost entirely repaired over the past two months.

Some years later I heard that an innocent pedestrian was shot on Death Ring and fell to a seated position against a wall. Nobody ever dared slow down to remove the body and as the weeks went by the traffic watched the corpse decompose before its eyes. People even gave him comic names.

In Ashrafiyah glamorous photographs of the Gemayel brothers in elegant Italian suits contrasted with those of the wild-eyed Palestinian martyrs in Al-Hamra. Instead of hammer and sickles and Islamic Crescents there were Cedars of Lebanon and Virgin Marys. Lebanese soldiers trotted side by side with Maronite commandos in Cardin fatigues and sten-guns. We saw a ladies' hairdresser called Godiva. It had a sign with a picture of the naked lady on her horse.

Within three minutes of the Ring we entered a smart restaurant where waiters in dinner jackets led us to the table of the sophisticated Maronite family with whom we were lunching. The food was exquisite and the wines the very best French clarets. We discussed Margaret Thatcher, the latest plays on Broadway and the re-emergence of the mini skirt in Paris. The family had recently come from Paris. 'We go to Paris for the bombardments,' said the lady as if she meant the 'hot weather' – 'we go to Simla for the hot weather.' They had come back to check their flat during the lull. 'In the early days of the Syrian bombardments we didn't go out. We were frightened. Now the situation is worse because the future is so uncertain [within the year Ashrafiyah was evacuated for a period, so ferocious were the Syrian attacks]. But you get bored. You can't stay at home for ever. So now we go out again as we used to. You have to get used to the war.' The waiters wore velvet bow ties and velvet lapels. The snails in butter and garlic were delicious.

Daring inhabitants of Al-Hamra, only Christians, of course, braved the Ring to buy their caviar from Ashrafiyah's Armenian shops. The family with whom we lunched was not particularly partisan. They spoke with a kind of grudging respect for Arafat as if he were one of the local naughty boys. The lady's husband echoed the feelings of friends on the Muslim side: 'The situation is worse today than just after the civil war. Then and just after Sadat's trip to Jerusalem we believed, Christians and Muslims, that a solution was in sight. Now we all, Christians, Muslims, Druzes, feel forgotten and deceived. Now it is not open war. Inner forces are unleashed. It is the hour of the kidnappers, the killers, the brute in man. Gang law rules. No one stops anyone.

No one can. Only their own organisations can stop them.'

Over the crêpes suzettes the last lines of Yeats's poem flooded my brain: 'And what rough beast, its hour come round at last, Slouches towards Bethlehem to be born?' I thought of an Iranian friend of mine who had recently visited an Iranian writer in Al-Hamra. They were invited to visit a man in a tall, neat building. But as they reached his tidy office the friend suddenly remembered that the group that owned the building was fighting a deadly feud with Amal, the Shia militia. 'For God's sake don't speak Persian,' he said. They politely declined tea and made a hurried, but gushing farewell and ran down the stairs and out of the building. His friend said when they were out: 'If they'd discovered you were Persian, they'd have taken you into the cellar and shot you.'

Charles-Henri, Catherine and I finished lunch and returned over the Ring at about 4.00. The previous day I had spoken to a Christian girl who was working in a bookshop in Al-Hamra and who had to cross the Ring each day. She told me that she worked from 8.30 in the morning until 2.30. 'I have to cross the Ring before 3.00 because that's when the snipers wake up and it becomes a bit dangerous,' she told me casually. But we crossed back without incident.

Charles-Henri went to his office and Catherine and I returned to the flat where she took a siesta and I washed some shirts. As I hung a shirt up to dry on the balcony which looked over towards the windows of the American Hospital, there was a massive explosion some streets beyond the hospital. I heard some distant screams, a little machine-gun fire, then silence. Catherine was asleep so I decided to go and find out what was happening. As I reached the door Charles-Henri came running in. 'Be careful in the streets,' he said. 'Abu-Hassan Salameh, Arafat's chief security officer, has been blown up in Snawbra with some others by a time-bomb in their jeep. There'll probably be some trouble.' The previous December the whole area had been ringed by machine-gun fire when Danny Chamoun, the impetuous young leader of the Chamounists, had visited the Saudi ambassador, who had been wounded in an attack on his helicopter, in the American Hospital.

I walked across a few streets to the Gefinor Building, that

great square structure of marble and stone owned by Kuwaitis. The building had never received a single bullet, so efficiently had payments to all groups been made. I entered La Librairie Internationale to visit Antoine Helvadjian. 'There's just been an explosion in Snawbra,' I said.

He went white. 'My wife was due to shop just now in a supermarket there,' he said quietly. He wanted to hide his anxiety and tried to talk business. I suggested I wander up and see what was happening but he refused to let me.

'It's too dangerous,' he said, 'there'll be trouble.'

A man came running into the shop. 'There's been a big explosion in Al-Laban Street in Snawbra. Fifty people are killed,' he said.

My friend nodded but did not reveal his trouble. The man went on and on elaborating the incident, the scattered bodies, the screams, the burning jeep. Then another man came in very excitedly. 'Have you heard, there's been a big explosion in Al-Laban Street in Snawbra. They say 100 people are killed.'

For about an hour the incident was discussed with increasing colour by people coming into the haven of the shop, and the deadly uncertainty about Antoine's wife built up in my mind until I was ready to crack. Then the phone rang: his wife's voice. She had had a bit of a headache and was terribly sorry, she hadn't made it to the supermarket. We almost wept for joy.

Soon, thanks to Beirut's ingeniously efficient grapevine, the story had been tilted into recognition. A time-bomb had gone off in the Volkswagen of Abu-Hassan Salameh, Al-Fateh's Security Chief, thought to be the architect of the Munich Olympic killings and Arafat's blue-eyed playboy who had been married to Georgina Rizq, a former Miss World. Nine people had been killed and eighteen were wounded.

It was later reported that the bomb had been detonated by an Englishwoman sitting in a room near the square. 'The Israelis did it,' my Armenian, therefore Christian, friend assured me. 'They want to destroy Lebanon. They can't bear to watch us successfully resurrect our country after the civil war.' The other people in the bookshop, Muslims and Christians, concurred. Perhaps it was wishful thinking. Nobody wanted to believe anything else. In any case few doubted the ability of Israel, which had devastated southern Lebanon, to destroy one of the harshest elements in the PLO.

But the Lebanese, who had by then seen some 60,000 countrymen killed since the beginning of the civil war, who had seen the heart of their capital blown to a charnel house, and had seen a jealous outside world competing to destroy them, took no chances when the signal was up. When I left the bookshop it was dark and the streets, usually throbbing with life, were deserted. I wandered to Charlie Brown's bar nearby for a drink to discuss the events. It was all but empty. During the lulls it was teeming. The few there were thrashing out the implications of the afternoon's event.

I had planned to see *Death on the Nile* with Charles-Henri and Catherine so returned to the flat through silent streets to see whether we were still to go. We set out, and as we were driving through Al-Hamra we were stopped three times by surprised but friendly wild-haired commandos of the Murabitoun with sten-guns. The cinema was almost empty. There were one or two commandos. I found it difficult to concentrate on the slow-moving film and longed to know what was happening outside. When we finally re-emerged the streets were totally dead. We drove home but there were no road blocks.

We had a whisky in the flat and then went our separate ways to bed. As I was doing my teeth I heard the rattle of machine-gun fire. For those many people who had lived through the horrors of Beirut my dramatising that one, noisy night is laughable. However, virgin fear is worth describing if only to show that the loss of sensitivity to fear and death is, perhaps, what has allowed the war to continue with almost increasing intensity without respite.

I had never witnessed war. As I returned to my room I heard distant cannon and a few rifle shots in neighbouring streets. 'Quite normal,' I felt, 'that's just Beirut.' I peered through the curtains but leapt back when a flare lit up the streets around me. I went to bed and began reading Jane Austen's *Sense and Sensibility*. There was heavy cannon fire from the hills, a bomb went off a few blocks away. Another flare lit up our district. Then the machine-gun fire started again, first in the distance, then in neighbouring streets, then quite suddenly in the street outside, just below my window. Now everything seemed to be happening at the same time: flares, bombs, cannons and machine-gun fire which seemed to be coming from all sides. Suddenly I decided that the building was under attack. It was only a few blocks from the Damascus Road. I began trembling and cursed myself for my cowardice. I turned the light out so as not to draw attention to my room and lay, listening. But I couldn't sleep. To my horror I found that I was quaking.

Soon the whole city was roaring and flickering with its grotesque arsenals. I understood that much of it was 'night-firing'; every comment in Beirut, whether of joy or protest, is demonstrated with gun-fire. But I also knew that some of it was hard killing.

I could not sleep. As my eyes closed I saw in my waking dream unlimbed bodies and decapitated heads, arms and legs swirling about, and I saw cars careering through the streets, dragging behind them bloody, half-shredded corpses. My dream reflected the picture book of the war I had been leafing through during a quiet period in the drawing-room earlier in the day.

I tossed and turned until four in the morning when a storm began and as the rains came smashing down the noise of the battle petered away as fighters took shelter. I fell pleasantly asleep to the din of thunder.

At breakfast I muttered over my croissant and *café crème*, 'Quite a battle last night!'

'Oh, we didn't hear anything,' replied Charles-Henri casually, 'we were so tired.'

When I reached La Librairie Internationale I said, 'Quite a battle last night, wasn't it?'

Antoine replied, 'Yes, it gets a bit noisy sometimes but you'll get used to it. We all do.'

I felt shut up again. I resolved not to confess that I had lain sick with fear in bed all night. I quickly learnt that many Beirutis had lost their fear over the years and could not sleep without a little shooting. My own personal drama began to seem sillier and sillier to me.

12

Entering the tempest

When I returned to my tiny Oxford house from my travels during the late 1970s it was filled with Iranian friends of one of my closest friends to this day, Baqer Moin, who was sharing my house. Baqer's father was a gentle and apolitical ayatollah living in Nishapur near Mashad and his grandfather had been one of Iran's 'grand ayatollahs'. As a publisher's rep I visited Iran about six times a year, returning between trips to my house where my political views would be moulded. As I walked along Princes Street on a Friday evening I could hear the sad wail of Gougoush, the singer who represented Iran's days of affluence as well as that morbid pessimism that underlies the Persian soul. And I could, as I approached my door, smell the piquant aromas of Iranian dishes such as Kouqu Sabzi and Korme Sabzi.

As I entered my drawing-room, from which there was nowhere to withdraw to but a scarcely bigger garden, the Iranians would leap politely to their feet and hand me delicious dishes and a glass of vodka spiced with lemon and salt. Then the political horror stories would begin: stories of student friends suddenly disappeared from the campus of Tehran University or returned as zombies from torture in Evin prison by the Shah's secret police, SAVAK; rumours of dungeons hollowed out in the rock near Tehran and rumours about the activities of the Shah's domineering elder sister, Princess Ashraf. The Iranians wanted a social-democratic system based on the constitution of 1906, but the Shah's army was spoilt and strong and nobody expected change for many years. No one whispered the name Khomeini and little was said of Islamic fundamentalism. Indeed, it was only during the last year before the revolution in 1979 that Islam as a

147

political force, a force to be exploited merely to rid the country
of the Shah's tyranny, was mentioned at all. The Shah had
emasculated the Tudeh (Communist) Party but despite his
attempts to bypass Islam with his pre-Islamic Pahlavi cultural
propaganda, he had completely failed to stifle the power of the
mosque whose overt 'cell' system was the Khutba or sermon
given in every mosque in the land.

On a cruelly cold Tehran Friday in November 1976 I made my
way from the lugubrious Park Hotel below Shahreza Avenue to
the slum streets of South Tehran from where the revolution was
later to breed. It was filled with weekending soldiers in uniform
clustering around cinema posters portraying grotesque caricatures
of pink-thighed heroines with huge breasts bursting from
plunging bodices, and splayed legs – violent substitutes, perhaps,
for the barely forbidden nude. Despite the Shah's grudging lip-
service to Islam, he had no truck with Muslim sensitivities.
Genitalia seemed to burst from these ripe, Aryan super-women.
The soldiers peered at the posters with an idiotic lust. It was
sinister, surrogate sex. When the cinemas opened the khaki mob
tumbled forward, gabbling furiously at the box office. Cakes for
the masses and uniforms and soft porn for the soldiery; such was
the Shah's short-term policy for steering his people from more
serious matters.
   A big group was clustered around something which I could
not see, nor could I initially break through. I could only hear the
tinkle of coins and the crying of an infant. Forcing my way
through I was quite suddenly released into the emptiness of the
circle. Before me, in the middle of the circle, lay a naked baby of
several months, crying and shimmering with hundreds of coins
which covered its famine-bloated belly. Beyond the soldiers on
the pavement beneath the poster of a fleshy odalisque sat a
woman nervously gripping her black *chador* in her lips and gazing
at her shimmering child. There was no laughter. The arms
belonging to those idiotic eyes cast coin upon coin as if at a
fairground. I wondered whether they flung them to still their
guilty revulsion as I walked away cursing the Empire under my
breath.

This was the great, short era of the oil boom when the West worshipped the Shah for dragging Iran from the medieval into the jet age, when Western businessmen grovelled to obtain immense contracts, sprawling on hotel sofas, even carpets, in their desperate eagerness to sell, sell, sell. It was a buyer's market, the too few hotels were always double- or treble-booked and service was abysmal. The businessmen did not visit South Tehran or the have-nots nor did they appreciate the wall of silence that greeted them from the gloomy mobs in Tehran's dull boulevards.

In 1975, during my brief career as a management consultant, I had been swept along in the rush. Only my knowledge of Persian and Iranian culture and a few well-placed contracts stood between me and the lonesome Western salesmen who sat in faded suits before unpleasant meals swilled down with rough Padkis wine in hotels which were among the gloomiest in the world. The Sheraton, owned by the Shah himself, boasted a trace of vulgar glamour when society couples in silks and furs poured in for their parties and weddings. But nothing could mask the general air of boredom, squalid materialism and suspicion that pervaded the spirit of Tehran.

Huge photographs of a magnificently decorated Shahanshah ('King of Kings') Aryamehr Pahlavi, Light of the Aryans and son of a peasant army officer, peered from the walls of the city's offices, of the hotels and of the glittering drawing-rooms of the North Tehran elite. Few discussed the man. The students and the poor would not, dared not mention his name. The upper middle classes restricted themselves to expressions such as 'His Imperial Majesty believes. . . . '

The attitude of the rich to terrorism, brushed off by the press as mere criminal violence, was quite simply 'Shoot them – they're dogs.' A charming man who insured arms for the Shah told me, 'Why should we care for terrorists? Why should we create prisons like hotels as you do in Europe? We haven't got time for that. We're a country in a hurry.' In a West German television interview the Shah had said coolly, 'We don't have internal problems. We have terrorist problems as you do in Germany.' Iranian television news would show endless footage of riots in Europe and America, to keep people's minds off the internal situation.

Tehran's tragedy was its obsession with wealth. Society at all levels mirrored itself in wealth, in the car you drove, the house you entertained in, the breast-pocket bulge of your jacket, the size of your gold cuff-links. A well-educated English girl whom I knew and who had lived in Tehran for many years told me, 'At first I was invited to society cocktails by the well-travelled, well-read Iranians. But they quickly discovered that I had neither status nor money and they soon stopped asking me.' If, as a visiting businessman, you were compelled to stay in a small hotel you pretended that you were staying in a big one. You never let anyone know that you were sleeping on the carpet!

One of my first introductions in Tehran was to a Pakistani girl called Setare, a woman with the plumpness of a Renoir model and a lyrical English voice. Setare was teaching English to the Iranian Air Force. I telephoned to invite her to dinner. She accepted a little reluctantly and when I arrived at her one-room flat in central Tehran she was still changing behind the screen. 'Go ahead and pour yourself a drink,' she shouted as bits of her clothing appeared on top of the screen and others were withdrawn from it one by one. It was erotic theatre and I sat drinking my Scotch and puzzling over what she might look like. After a few moments and much rustling of lingerie she called out to me, 'It's funny how modest you English are. If you'd been Iranian you'd have been behind the screen seducing me by now!' I replied rather lamely, uncertain whether this was taunt or eulogy, but I didn't, somehow couldn't, move. When she appeared she was dressed in a glimmering silk decolleté dress and wore thick red lipstick which made her look like a pretty courtesan, contrasting strongly with her murmuring Oxford English.

We took a taxi to the Sheraton where we had drinks with a business colleague of mine whom she treated with complete uninterest, even contempt. As the evening wore on she became increasingly maudlin. Finally I asked her why. 'I nearly cancelled the evening,' she said. 'It's Ashura. I'm not religious by nature but I'm Shia by birth and I should have been at home mourning all day. Instead, here I am drinking whisky, dressed up to the nines and out with a man.' The feast of Ashura, the tenth day of the month of Muharram, is mourned by the Shia to commemorate the death of the Prophet Muhammad's grandson Hussain who was killed in battle by the army of the Caliph Yazid at Kerbela in present-day Iraq. Two million Iranians were to march against the Shah in 1978 on this day of self-denial and even self-flagellation.

The next time I saw Setare was at a party she gave. The guests were almost all US Vietnam veterans, a breed of shell-shocked people I had also met in Riyadh. They were men who had been through a tempest, men devoured by hideous memories and guilt who had been unable to readjust to the neat American lives they had left behind. Despite this they were extremely friendly in a way that only Americans can be. One had a pretty Vietnamese wife who spoke with a repulsive half-American drawl. Her every second words was 'shit' and 'mother-fucker' as if she were trying to outcurse her war-traumatised husband. Everyone was drunk and I did my best to catch up and get into the spirit of things.

By the time that guests were preparing to leave I somehow found myself embracing Setare with passion on the sofa in what I thought was an empty room, although I had vaguely remembered seeing her in the company of a silent American. She was drunk and responding to me with some passion but I suddenly realised that three big men were standing silently about the sofa so I got up. One said to me so quietly that I almost thought he was being friendly, 'Do you want us to smash your f... face in?' They all stood staring at me with looks of chilling hatred and I struggled to withdraw without losing too much pride, but determined not to have my face smashed in by these terrible men. I turned to Setare intending to say that I was afraid it really was time to go and thank her for the party and so forth – but she was asleep. I nodded pleasantly at my opponents, explaining to them, too, that most unfortunately I had to go, and then made hastily for the door, utterly relieved to find myself leaving the flat without further challenge. As I stumbled through Tehran's silent streets I reflected on these men who were training the Iranian and Saudi air forces and wondered what cruelties they would instill in already temperamental troops.

Although Tehran's paraphernalia of glittering power and eminence contrasted so much with the superficial egalitarianism of Riyadh, I went armed with a deep self-confidence born of pure ignorance. I assumed that I would see the top people in those early days and I saw them – at least for long enough for them to realise how hopelessly unimportant I was.

One of Iran's key figures was Manuchehr Eqbal, the chairman of the National Iranian Oil Company. Eqbal was an ex-Prime Minister and his daughter had married the Shah's brother. I telephoned his secretary with complete authority and insisted on a meeting. The meeting was immediately arranged, and two days later I was climbing in the lift of the gleaming NIOC building. After a wait of about half an hour, I was ushered into a very small office and greeted with a warm handshake by a beaming man. I could scarcely believe that this was the prince of oil himself. I was overcome with panic.

Eqbal ordered tea, and the relaxed atmosphere suggested I was expected to stay quite some time. I explained my mission, which was to offer to fill in any gaps in the industry that might need filling. Eqbal very pleasantly explained that his subordinate might be a better man to see and within a minute I was politely escorted, teacup in hand, to another office. The subordinate greeted me with equal warmth and suggested that I see his director of sales. I was led to an office some floors below where the sales manager, a somewhat indifferent man, suggested I discuss the matter with his Pakistani clerk. I was taken to the basement where the clerk treated my mission with complete indifference and told me brusquely that he would 'be in touch'. Within about twelve minutes of my nice meeting with Eqbal, and in a kind of accelerating downward spiral, I was out in the street again, a sales rep with an uncertain product.

Persian splendour and its stark contrast with Saudi Arabia's egalitarianism was revealed to me again when I visited Mr Saghotelian, the Director General of the Foreign Trade of Bank of Iran on Ferdousi Avenue. After Eqbal I was expecting to meet a bank manager. When I reached the magnificent Rococo building I was ushered into a small waiting room by flunkeys in tail coats and gold braid. After an obligatory forty-five-minute wait the flunkeys led me to two immense, elaborately carved wooden doors, twice the height of a man. These opened to reveal an enormous drawing-room, the walls of which were covered with gilded mirrors and chiaroscuros of glittering, chipped mirror. I blinked in the dazzling light. I felt that I was entering some Baroque Paradise. In the middle of the room were some expensive armchairs and sofas in which smart Japanese bankers sat talking in quiet whispers. At the very end of the room behind an immense desk sat a small, bald man, almost submerged in his own glory.

Trembling, I made my way across the room. As I glanced in a mirror, I remembered the scene in Solzhenitsyn's *First Circle* when the prisoner, who has spent most of his life in a dungeon, has been called up to a similar room to see the governor of the Lubianka prison, a man who has signed the death warrant of thousands. At that moment I imagined myself the prisoner, who, upon catching sight of his face and ragged clothing for the first time in thirty years, beams into the mirror and makes faces, completely oblivious of the governor, who has the power of life and death over him. I arrived at the desk of the great, little man. He did not look up so I sat down and began the obligatory wait. I soon became amused by the situation as I glanced over the flickering walls amid the pompous silence. Finally Saghotelian looked up at me with an arrogant disdain. I explained my mission, reeling off my management consultant patter, and he replied indifferently as if to say, 'If you have nothing better to talk about, then the audience is over.' But then I spotted in a frame behind him a *ghazal* (love-poem) of the great Persian poet Hafez and I read in Persian the following lines:

> 'My soul is on my lips ready to fly,
> But grief beats in my heart and will not cease
> Because not once, not once before I die,
> Will her sweet lips give all my longing peace.'

Saghotelian gazed at me in wonder. 'You read Persian?' he asked, 'And you like Hafez?' He looked up at the ceiling and said: 'Ah Hafez, Hafez! When you read Hafez your soul is free from all cares like a petal floating in the wind.' Then he suddenly remembered who he was and looked busy. But, obviously yearning to break the barrier of his dreary world again, he said,

'Do you write poetry? I wrote love-poetry to my sweetheart when I was a young man, you know.' And he leant forward so that no one could hear him – the nearest person was at the other end of the hall – and added conspiratorially, 'If you come again I will show it to you.'

Saghotelian and I were soon bandying lines of Hafez and Sadi back and forth across his huge table. Then he interrupted himself to say; 'You see, I have so many troubles here. I have an English secretary who is hopeless but I don't dare sack her. Just look at this. There are spelling mistakes on every page. I sit here at my desk buzzing that bell on the wall to call her back every five minutes.' He was trapped in his splendid isolation, a lonely figure overwhelmed with the trappings of power. I saw him as a symbol of the Shah's Iran, an imperial distancing of the ruler from the masses in the classical style of the great empires before Islam. I promised to find him a new secretary through my company and, quite humble now, he begged me to return and talk whenever I liked. When I got up to leave he stood up, beaming, and we shook hands like old friends. I think I left behind a lonelier man than I had found.

When I returned to Tehran in March 1978 as a publisher's rep I had been heavily influenced by the articles of the intrepid *Guardian* correspondent, Liz Thurgood, who daily revealed how close to collapse the Shah's regime really was. My employers shared the general opinion in the West that all was well and that the army would always stand firm beside the Shah. Indeed, Tehran was as dull and quiet as I had ever known it although there had been various demonstrations over the preceding months. Each demonstration had its *raison d'être*. None declared themselves to be opposing the regime, let alone the Shah himself. The clergy had marched for greater Islam-isation, the bourgeoisie had marched over rising food prices, the students had marched over fees. But beneath everything, everyone was marching against a Shah whom they saw as a tyrannical foreign imposition.

Having done my round of bookshops in Shahreza, I approached the gates of the Tehran University campus. For three years it had been impossible for foreigners to enter the campus without a hard-to-obtain official letter and on each visit I would make my unending attempts to enter, only to be politely turned away by a policeman.

Today, however, riot police with visors casually pushed onto their foreheads and batons hanging idly by their sides stood before the gates. There had obviously been no allowance for the entry of foreigners and despite the lorries filled with riot police in the surrounding side streets and riot police at flash points on the campus, no one challenged my entry. All was quiet. Mothers and children played on the grass and students milled about with textbooks in their hands.

I walked up the campus hill and, as I walked, I could hear large crowds shouting further above. When I reached the Medical Faculty I asked a group of students in white coats the way to the Department of Physics, as I intended to visit the Professor of Physics. 'I wouldn't go up now,' they said. 'There's a little trouble.' What trouble, I asked. 'Oh, nothing serious,' they smiled. 'The students are complaining about the new rule that they cannot go mountaineering in groups.' I was keen to go up anyway, I said, and they shrugged and pointed the way. 'Be careful, the police have the whole building under siege.'

I came up past the medical buildings into a square dominated by the huge sciences block, every window crammed with jeering students. The riot police wandered about indifferently in quiet groups. Any possible confrontation seemed a long way off.

As I made to cross the square, a girl joined me, probably assuming that association with a foreigner would protect her or else that a well-dressed foreigner's judgment that there was no danger must be sound. As we reached the middle of the square I glanced at some hundred students to my right who were edging away to the wall. Suddenly they let out a long hiss before running and tumbling backwards. Some began running for the walls. I turned round but the girl, as if by magic, had disappeared. I was left standing alone, feeling out of my depth in the middle of the square.

As I quietly turned to my left, I saw, to my sheer horror, that the riot police had formed six tidy columns. Their shining Perspex visors were down and their batons up. I had little time to admire this martial scene for a second later the phalanx let out a terrific war-cry and charged as if I was the sole target of their fury. There was a noisy retreat from behind as the whole corner of the campus dispersed in howls of panic. Clutching my heavy black Samsonite full of Macmillan textbooks I fled right across the path of the horrible pack with a speed that I had never before – and have never since! – attained. I must have virtually brushed past the last baton as I dived for a ditch and covered my head. I could hear the screams, the clatter of batons on heads, the curses of the butchering riot police and then the wail of sirens. Peering up I saw students clambering desperately up the walls, only to be knocked down by the Perspex thugs.

I crept out of my hole and made my way, nursing a bruised knee, down the campus which had virtually emptied into the buildings. A car came past. The laughing men inside shouted, 'Don't worry, you won't get hurt!' I assumed they were SAVAK. When I reached the main gates, they were unmanned – the riot police were all battling away at the north face of the campus. I crossed the road to a book publishers where I met the director, an arrogant man, to whom I told my tale. He smiled and replied in the euphemistic way that Persians have – perhaps he was showing sympathy with the students when he said, 'The new Chancellor of the Aryamehr University is like Idi Amin. He's blocked the budget for all books. We're in a mad world. They send students to study, but they have no books to read.' Not understanding what this had to do with the riot, I asked him to explain, but he smiled and changed the conversation.

The riot had made me late for an appointment with the man who ran a well-known bookstore high up on Pahlavi Avenue. His uncle was a SAVAK chief. Two colleagues from Macmillan were with him, waiting for me. I came in breathless and told them that I had almost been trapped by the riot police. My friends laughed and ignored my comments. We discussed books for about twenty minutes and the bookseller turned to me and asked simply, 'How many riot police were there?' We never alluded to the subject again.

When I returned to Iran in November 1978, I was a confirmed opponent of the Shah. I had for a long time interpreted the superficial peace – contrasting so much with the turmoil in the

Arab world – and the silence that met my political questions as signs of a wall of fear. That November the British press had lulled the public into rejecting any idea of revolution. When I told my managing director that 'Tehran was going to explode', he simply remarked that the army would never forsake the Shah. I didn't push the point – I didn't want the market to collapse before I had seen for myself.

I was accompanied on this trip by my new assistant, a sober, pleasant person just out of university, named Jack. I was taking him on a round of Middle East countries to teach him to sell books, a job I hated. We yawned our way through the bookshops of Cairo, reading out our lists of books like vegetables and trying to ward off the eternal questions about 'returns', lost invoices and the 'Beasts of Basingstoke' credit controllers and, finally, flew off to Muscat. Sitting on the plush sofas of the huge, open-plan Oman Inter-Continental, with its pools of water reflecting the progress of the glass lift, I submerged myself in the daily headlines of massive processions, burnings of cars and martial law that was becoming normal life in Tehran. We were leaving for Shiraz in two days and, feeling in a dramatic and protective mood, I told Jack, 'We are entering a tempest!' I assured him that he could return home with no honour lost, indeed, he would be praised by the company for sobriety, but he insisted on coming.

The day before we were to fly, we visited the Iranian Embassy for information. It was closed but we asked two well dressed Iranians outside for news. They assured us in a paternal way that all was well, that the army had everything under control, and that the press had blown out of all proportion what were, in reality, merely the games of a few religious fanatics. The local Omani press published a two-page spread of pictures of a smiling Shah with his family at his weekend retreat on the beaches of the Caspian.

When we flew into Shiraz Airport, I wondered whether anything was wrong. The air was fresh and the trees green and leafy. The customs officials were inordinately polite in their well-pressed blue uniforms. Only one detail at the airport struck me as unusual. I had met little religious fervour in the past in Iran yet, when one policeman saw the Muslim Profession of

Faith – 'There is no God but God: Muhammad is the Prophet of God' – inside my briefcase he became wildly excited and called his friends, who proceeded to flock around to exchange lines from Qur'anic suras and the Hadith (Sayings of the Prophet).

Nothing during our first evening in Shiraz, except for some army lorries and dull-looking soldiers at street corners, gave any indication of revolt. We sat in the gloomy hotel eating dried-up chicken and drinking rasping Padkis wine served by typically grumpy waiters. On the television we watched scenes of arguing members of the Majlis (Parliament), an attempt to persuade the Iranians that the problems of the people were being thrashed out openly and democratically.

The following morning we were wandering up Vakil Avenue when we were suddenly jostled by a group of youths running past us in consternation. We turned round to see three soldiers pointing their bayonets at us so we quickly side-stepped into the recess of a shop. We decided to make for the British Council, a walk of about half a kilometre, to discuss English language courses. We found the main gate to the cypress-edged lane locked and had to ring several times before a gate-keeper ran to open it. He re-locked it immediately.

The Council representative was one of those prim-looking men, the type that one imagines would be unable to leave the security of his prep school, who would return as a teacher, never re-emerging into the real world. However, there are such Englishmen scattered through strange corners of the world who actually know their regions well and are completely fearless. 'We've closed the gates,' he said airily, 'because a lot of them are on their way down and there's been talk of burning down the Council.' We then had to move on to English as a Foreign Language and we almost pleaded for the sound of the rabble to deflect us from the tedium of sales.

When we managed to escape we visited the language school further down the road which belonged to a British company operating in Shiraz. We knocked several times on the steel gates and, as we were about to leave, a timid voice called from behind, asking, 'Who is it?' 'We're publishing reps,' we explained, 'and we would like to discuss the use of EFL books in your school.' The locks slid open heavily, a very quiet Iranian let us in and

quickly pushed the locks closed again. We were led to the office
of the school's director. He greeted us hurriedly and explained
that he was arranging for all the women and children to leave.
'We're a target,' he informed me as he dashed from room to
room like the March Hare. 'We've been warned that a large mob
is moving up the street and intends to burn us down.'

We were relieved that on no account would we have to sell
our Active Context English Course. However, we were a little
startled when the shouts of people could be heard in the distance,
and when the shouts merged into an uproar, and the tread of
some thousand feet became audible, we thought our friend less
eccentric. Indeed, we too began glancing around for various
means of escape. The noise of the crowd became deafening, with
chants of '*Zindebad Khomeini*' and '*Marg bar-Shah-e khain*' ('Death
to the Shah, traitor') as it reached the gates. We held our breath
for some moments until we realised that, target or no target, we
had been let off – the crowd had moved on.

Our exit from Shiraz was chaotic. Most flights had been
cancelled due to strikes (unheard of, before!) and the airport was
filled with Americans evacuating the oil towns of the south.
They seemed very frightened. One told us he had decided to
make a run for it when he had seen a poster in Bandar Abbas on
which was written: 'What shall we give the Shah for his
birthday? Twenty dead Americans!' One sad American sat
patiently in front of us, wearing his wide-brimmed cowboy hat
and leather-laced neckpiece. I guessed that this was the first time
he had left his 'Little America' oil camp in the sticks. The
Americans cheered up in the plane, probably assuming that they
would get connecting flights out immediately. For us it was the
contrary – we saw ourselves moving into the epicentre of
something macabre.

When we reached Tehran, all seemed astonishingly peaceful,
the same dull city of regimented boulevards and bored, ill-
dressed youths loitering outside corner cafés. We reached the
President Hotel, which was set back behind a courtyard fronted
by shops. We hadn't booked, but for once there was no lack of
rooms. As we waited for our keys, I asked the concierge for
news about what was going to happen. He was non-committal.
This was the Iran I knew so well. Then, suddenly, without

prompting and as if he had been seized by a desire to open his long-sealed heart to me, he leant forward and said, 'Terrible violence is approaching here. Soon we will be like Beirut.' I smiled – given Tehran as it was then, even with protest crowds becoming 'in vogue', the greatest pessimist could not have foreseen what was really about to take place. The foyer was filled with American families working with the Bell Helicopter Company, billed by many Iranians as an extension of the CIA.

Tehran seemed calm that morning but by lunchtime there was the sound of shouting from further up Takhte Jamshid. I entered the street and saw a crowd of several hundred youths and girls in *chadors*. Their leader was waving a blood-stained shirt. I walked towards them and asked a passerby what the shirt was. 'The police opened fire on them yesterday,' he told me. 'They killed one student.' The bank staff were pulling down their steel gates and laughing. There was still an air of carnival. The crowd did not get any bigger and soon turned away down a side street.

Late in the morning we took a taxi up to the corner of Khiaban Takhte Tavus (Peacock Throne Street) and Roosevelt Avenue to visit the Tehran Bookshop. This was run by a good-looking and industrious young Iranian, Hussain. Albeit reticent about politics, he had always appeared a pillar of the political establishment. I approached him almost tongue-in-cheek with my publishers' suggestions for a book by a well-known British writer on Princess Ashraf. I was astonished when he immediately asked whether it would include descriptions of the flamboyant lifestyle she had pursued on her numerous trips to Europe. 'No,' I smiled, 'that is not at all the sort of book they are looking for.' So we dropped the subject.

Hussain and his friend took us to lunch, where the conversation was entirely political. I was amazed at the openness of the discussion. The friend made it quite clear that he foresaw, and hoped for, a full-scale revolution. The people would never forgive the Shah for the killing of 3,000 – some said 15,000 – at Jaleh Square the previous September. Hussain believed the Shah should resign in favour of his son. I asked him how he thought the Shah could save himself at this stage. He answered chillingly, 'Either he must abdicate or be prepared to kill up to two million demonstrators. There's no longer any other way.'

When we returned to his office, I telephoned friends who ran the bookshop opposite the gates of the Tehran University campus. I could hardly hear the woman speak, there was so much noise on the line. 'No, don't come now,' she said. 'Things are very bad here. Two soldiers have just shot themselves in front of the bookshop because they refused to obey their officers' command to fire on the crowd. There are about half a million people here, and, Christ, they're angry!' I couldn't hear any more amid the uproar so I put the receiver down.

When we got back to the hotel, the staff were in a flurry. 'A big crowd is moving up this way!' cried one as he rushed away. In the distance, emanating from somewhere in the hovels of South Tehran, I could hear the now familiar sound of a big crowd shouting. We took our bags to our third-floor adjoining rooms and looked out over the courtyard and at the buildings around the crossroads of Pahlavi and Takhte Jamshid, over the cinema which stood next to us on our right. 'The cinema's sure to be a target,' I said. The noise of thousands shouting, the trudge of feet and the occasional shattering of windows increased. Soon windows were breaking a few blocks away. Within five minutes the crowds were surging through the crossroads and spreading out. The sounds of smashing glass were followed by cheers.

We decided it was time to get downstairs in case they set fire to the hotel. The lobby was now full of American families, the women looking white with fear, the children romping on the carpets. The men tried to retain their machismo by sitting with vacant looks. By now the noise outside was that of a full-scale riot – the crashing of glass was more disturbing than the shouting and the chanting. The crowd had by now spilled into all the streets about us and we were beseiged.

I calmly asked the manager – mainly to still my own anxiety – whether his fire equipment was in order. 'Yes, yes,' he replied desperately. 'We've taken care of all that. It's working and it's all ready. Please don't panic!' He rushed out into the courtyard to order the staff to bring out the hoses. At first no one seemed to know where they were, then at last they emerged from a trap door in the courtyard. The taps were turned on but the water came out in a trickle, then dried up completely. The manager glanced at me with embarrassment, then hurried back into the foyer.

Two of the hotel staff were pushing two cars up against the steel gates giving out onto the street from the covered entrance which linked shops on both sides. Looking through the windows in the backs and road fronts of the shops we could see scrums of yelling women in black *chadors* beating their fists against the glass. In those days it was an extraordinary sight to see Muslim women showing such emotion.

But our time had not come. Indeed, this was the first time the crowds had reached so far north in Tehran and they were still mildly diffident about entering the bourgeois side of the city. As they began spilling up Pahlavi, we realised their concentration was moving away from us – the rabble and breaking glass was now heard from behind us. Within twenty minutes our immediate vicinity had quietened. There was no traffic and a strange silence fell upon the streets about us. When I came out into the street I surveyed the broken glass sprinkled about.

The hotel restaurant was crowded at dinner that evening and buzzing with excitement. The management cannot have rejoiced in having such a full house; it was to be a short-lived experience. From all the regions of Iran, expatriates were flooding into the capital to prepare for evacuation. There had, we gathered, been a lot of shooting near the university. Sixty-three students had been killed in the surrounding streets.

After dinner we watched television. This government mouth-piece, accustomed to filming ministers and courtiers in resplen-dent court dress bowing before an even more glamourous Shah, now showed the Majlis in an uproar. Although every member was traditionally hand-picked by the regime, there was now a genuine atmosphere of hot and sometimes bitter debate. The then Prime Minister, Sharif Emami, was speaking at length about the government's determination to root out corruption. This evening we were amazed when the entire hotel staff roared with laughter. When the deputy from Karaj, Akhbari, embarked on a two-hour speech in which he denounced several ministers for amassing and exporting large sums of money, they laughed even louder.

'But isn't this democracy?' I asked.

'Democracy?' replied the wine-waiter. 'It's just an amphitheatre. They just talk and talk while people go hungry and thousands die in prisons.'

The desk manager explained that these inordinately long speeches had been 'set up' so that the Prime Minister would not have to answer 142 'sensitive' questions about people close to the Monarch.

That night I could hardly sleep for the noise of troop carriers landing and taking off from Mehrabad Airport. Behind these movements lay the government's policy of stationing ethnic groups outside their native areas, sending Turkish-speaking Azerbaijanis to Tehran and troops from Tehran to Azerbaijan, Shirazi soldiers to Mashad and Baluch to Hamadan.

The morning of Sunday 5 November was a quiet, crisp, bright winter morning. It was impossible to foresee the explosion that was now to rock the city and, with it, the dynasty of the Pahlavi King of Kings, Light of the Aryans, descendant of Cyrus and Xerxes, or, more correctly, son of a wily army officer who had seen the rationale of selecting the trappings of a dynasty which bypassed the very roots of his people, Islam.

We decided to head for the bookshop opposite the university before the day's rioting began, before our access was blocked by the crowds which would emerge. Walking down Takhte Jamshid, we saw the windowless Golden City Cinema and the burnt-out hulk of the Bank Saderat, victims of the previous day. Along the streets broken glass had been swept into neat piles. Civic sense had not yet been cast aside. At the Anatole France intersection, the wrecks of eight cars and a lorry lay still smouldering and glinting. The square was filled with armed lorries crammed with miserable, shivering soldiers, huddled like owls about their rifles. On top sat soldiers before big machine-guns, which faced down the streets. When we reached Anatole France Street adjoining the university we could hear the campus loudspeakers carrying the booming voices of professors denouncing the regime, and the cheering of thousands of students.

We decided to pay a short courtesy visit to the Kharazmi Language Centre in the street. It was run by an extremely timid, prim and tediously nagging man, a Mr Abolhassani. We were led to his office. He looked ill with nerves but greeted us warmly. Tea was brought. Above we could hear the clatter of helicopters and across the road the turmoil of the campus. Mr Abolhassani began complaining about books that had not arrived. He began explaining the promised dates of their arrival, the method by which they should have come but hadn't, the invoice numbers, and so on. We tried to interrupt, but as the noise outside got louder, his complaints became fiercer. He would cancel all orders! The books would arrive too late for the year. The students (the students? – we glanced nervously out) had no textbooks.

After a while I simply asked, 'How is everything here?'

'Everything's all right,' he said, 'but we need the books for our course.'

'Yes, but how's everything in Tehran? You know, all that noise outside?'

'Noise? I don't hear any noise!'

'Yes, well, maybe the books have been held up by the disturbances.'

'What disturbances? There are no disturbances.'

'All that shouting,' I said.

'What shouting?' he said. 'There's no shouting,' he repeated irritably. 'Look, here I have the invoice numbers, they should have been sent on. . . . '

'Yes, I will check with our export department today, Mr Abolhassani, now we must go.' We got up. The noise outside was deafening.

'We'll cancel the order!' said Mr Abolhassani, 'Unless we get the books by next week!'

'Yes, good-bye, Mr Abolhassani!'

We left Mr Abolhassani and walked the few yards down to Shahreza Avenue, the meeting-point of students from several campuses and of the huge crowds of 'have-not, shirtless ones' that daily moved up from the bazaar in lower South Tehran on the other side of Shahreza Avenue. By now the traffic, which only ever disappeared when firing actually broke out, was edging through fairly thick crowds of students making for the campus.

Students, intermingled with ordinary housewives and passersby, were moving quietly together from every direction.

When the shooting had broken out on the previous day, housewives, far from fleeing, automatically joined the demonstrators in active support. As we came into Shahreza Avenue I noticed, with pleasure, across the road, talking with arms folded before a bookshop, a beautiful young woman I had known and much admired when I had met her working at Amir Kabir publishing company. She was a tall girl of about 23 with high cheek-bones, an extraordinarily handsome face and large, intelligent, decisive eyes. We used to sit discussing English and schools she might go to in England. Once I had overslept for a very important meeting with the director of Amir Kabir and she had politely phoned half an hour after the appointment. I had thrown my clothes together in despair and taken a taxi to the company, arriving in great embarrassment. That was the last I had seen of her.

'What are you doing here?' I asked.

'I've come to be with the People,' she replied simply.

'Aren't you afraid of what will happen here?'

'No,' she smiled. 'During these days we must remain together.'

'I hope I'll see you later,' I said.

'Yes, I hope so,' she replied.

I walked on towards the bookshop. I was not to see her again.

By now the shouts of 'Death to the Shah, traitor!' and 'Death to the American Shah!' had sporadically begun within the campus and were being echoed outside. I was surprised by the mixture of people within the crowds – housewives, prim girls, students with textbooks under their arms. When we reached the bookshop, the place was chaotic. For long it had been the refuge of radical students – indeed, its American managers were wont to employ students baffled from years of prison to work in the shop. As it almost faced the gates of the campus, it had now become a meeting-place for young dreamers. The American couple welcomed us, the only publishing reps in Tehran, with some astonishment. Seated with them was the very neat and bookish, middle-aged Iranian who ran the science books section in the basement. Revolution seemed the farthest thing away from his life – his greatest drama until then had been a cold.

We drank tea and tried to foresee how the day would develop. We didn't have long to wait. It began with the clattering of choppers above, swooping so low that through the back window we could see the gunners crouching. There was more shouting in the street and the ground floor on to which we looked from the galleried office began to fill up with students running in in some consternation. We asked what was happening. 'The soldiers are pointing their guns down the street!' they cried. Then we heard a cheer. I forced myself through the crowded street. A cheering procession came past led by a young European with a TV camera on his shoulder. They shouted. This was the BBC correspondent in Tehran. The walls across the road were packed with rows of students. Lorries crammed with soldiers peeped out of the side streets. For the next five hours, while the turning point of the Iranian uprising and the end of the chances for the dynasty's survival built up around us, our telephone buzzed endlessly with reports of banks and cinemas burning down all over the centre of the city. Then the cars in the streets began flashing their lights and a cry went up: 'Uvaisi is dead!' The rumour that Uvaisi, the martial law administrator, had died of a heart attack, later proved to be false. Indeed, Uvaisi was not even to face the firing squad after the revolution the following February. He managed to find exile in the West and died from an assassin's bullet in Paris in February 1984.

No sooner had I re-entered the bookshop, now crammed with fugitives from the tear gas being lobbed from low-flying choppers, than a crowd of youths burst in, announcing that the Capri Cinema across the road was burning. We pushed our way out to watch the flames and smoke billowing out of the cinema, next to Bisto-Chahar-e-Esfand Square, in which troops filling the trucks watched idly. One young man turned to me and said, 'We are not burning the cinemas – the Shah's agents provocateurs are. That's why the soldiers aren't responding.' But the general feeling was that the Shah wanted to show the city what anarchy really meant and thereby force the army to clamp down violently before the day's end. Everyone assumed that the day would end in much blood.

Another ripple of excitement ran through the orgiastic crowds, moving like waves this way and that, oscillating between hilarity and terror. A student rushed up to tell us that the officer in charge of the Shareza section of the army had mutinied and joined the students. He could be seen, they said, amid students waving pictures of Khomeini, borne shoulder high through the campus. We were later to hear that he had been summarily shot. One journalist who had seen him claimed that his defection had been less than voluntary – cornered by the students, he had decided to smile his way from death. The belief that the army was now mutinous added hysteria to the crowds, and demonstrators were urging their friends with, 'Say, Shah, we will kill you!' 'Listen to that,' said my neighbour with sinister sentimentality. 'I've waited all my life to hear that!' I winced. Then came another cheer to our right and the cry, 'The Bank Omran is burning!' A sheet of flame shot up the face of the building, turning the carnival reels of ticker tape that flew way above the buildings to floating bits of carbon.

Then another shout (hardly a moment passed without a dramatic incident) that 1,000 zealously Islamic demonstrators were approaching from the slums around the bazaar area of South Tehran to link up with the crowds. At about 4.20 a huge, orderly procession bearing hundreds of portraits of Khomeini appeared through the smoke on our left, implying that the army had evacuated the square. The two masses gradually approached each other. Meanwhile, students were running past the shops, pinning photographs of Khomeini to the walls. A conscript soldier beside me – 'I'm a soldier in the morning; I join the People in the afternoon' – was helping a student pin one up properly. When the two crowds came together, their very mass in unity was frightening. They spread through each other with huge cheers, and a ripple of embraces.

Then a shudder went through the crowd and it suddenly rolled to and fro in slow panic as the word went round: 'Tanks are coming!' followed by, 'They're coming from both directions!' But first a fire engine emerged and a cheering passage was made for it. Then, through the mist of smoke, appeared the gun of a Chieftain tank and the crowd of some half a million fell deathly silent. The tank rolled into full view and the crowd began to edge away, as if from some hellish beast. For one moment the silence was terrible, biblically terrible. We held our million breaths. Was this, I wondered, our apocalypse, our Gehenna? But then, but then – was that a flicker of a smile on a pale soldier's face? – a thunderous roar of joy burst from the crowd as if an emperor had been crowned and 100,000 olive branches were thrown simultaneously into the air (I lifted my camera – click! – no film!) in one of the most dramatic pieces of theatre I have ever seen. Demonstrators leapt on to the tank, hugging and kissing the soldiers until it became a moving bundle of cloth and flesh and pretty girls – with the gun protruding among them with phallic incongruity. The now familiar cry of 'Soldiers, you are our brothers' filled the air and lily-white flowers seemed to bloom from their rifles. The tank moved through the crowd like a conquering hero of peace and the soldiers (was this their swan-song?) smiled diffidently like martyrs rumbling in tumbrils to the slaughter.

By now it appeared that the whole city was burning. In the early part of the day considerable friendship had been shown to myself and the three other foreigners – my rather awe-struck assistant and the couple who ran the bookshop. We seemed to be the only non-Iranians in the inner circle of revolt. A television team had scrambled in briefly when the Bank Omran burned, but by the time of peak commotion no journalists were to be seen. Every time I appeared in the street, people would turn and say, 'Look what we're doing – the People have had enough!'

An old lady, one passionate eye peering through her black *chador*, grabbed me with more excitement than anger and said, 'Yankee, go home!'

'*Man yankee neestam*,' I replied defensively, '*man inglisi hastam!*'

'*Inglisi khaili bad ast* – David Owen! David Owen!' she retorted.

I explained that I was *not* England, *not* the English government, and certainly *not* David Owen! His remark the previous day – broadcast on the BBC Persian service, to which everyone listened constantly – that the Shah was a friend of the West and should be supported, and that the human rights record (what record?) of the religious was no better than the Shah's, had already given the expression 'David Owen' the meaning of 'Bugger off!' But the old lady, reflecting the mood of Iranians throughout our visit, released me and patted me maternally instead. 'Yes, yes, you are a very good Englishman. But England very bad, David Owen very bad!'

'Yes, yes,' I intoned. 'England very bad, David Owen very bad.'

The crowd around us laughed and a group asked me whether, since I had a camera, I was from the BBC. I had no time to reply. They began dragging me through the crowd to what was the front line, the front of the crowd by the university gates that was peering down the bayonets of rows of nervous soldiers. Deciding to laugh my way out of the heroic death now on offer, I scrambled away.

We had joined in the cheering when the tank had mutinied, partly through genuine sympathy for the revolution and partly through sheer relief. But when joy gave way to anarchy, we began to feel isolated. The crowds were rampaging, fearless and boisterous now, through the streets, and for the first time it occurred to us that some might vent their anger on the few representatives of the Western values that they detested. The crowds flooded into the campus as dusk fell and began heaving down the huge, bronze statue of the King of Kings. The booksellers decided to make a run for their flat, which meant passing through the area which had until recently been held by the army. But the army had gone. One million young people now ruled the heart of the city. A rumour spread through the crowd that the curfew had been put back to 4.30. It was now 5.30. Laughter spread among the crowd. We turned on the radio and listened to the announcement that Sharif Emami's government had fallen and that the military had taken over. Martial law had been declared. All meetings of more than three people were forbidden. That night the Shah was nearly weeping on television when he said, 'I have understood the message of your revolution.'

In their panic the booksellers forgot about Jack and me. We joined them all the same and crept along the edges of Shahreza and down the side street facing the university. Their flat lay in a cul-de-sac behind the bookshop and once inside we drank large whiskys. We could hear cheering in Shahreza. People were leaping over the walls around us. Our reluctant hosts were discussing how soon they could evacuate. We soon realised that we were outstaying our welcome and decided to make our way back to the President Hotel via a maze of side streets. We got back to Shahreza, having to keep our distance from cars that were still smouldering. Rough youths shouted 'Go home, Yankee!' Although throughout the day there had been no personal violence and no looting, the destruction everywhere was indescribable – the blackened hulks of burnt-out buildings, burning cars, glass, paper and furniture scattered across the street. The scene was the same all the way to Takhte Jamshid.

We were shocked to find that the cinema adjoining our hotel had been virtually burned to the ground. Six or seven hotels had suffered the same fate, but ours – God knows why – had been spared. Everyone looked frightened out of their wits. 'They surrounded the hotel again, just like yesterday,' a young American girl told me, 'and this time they nearly broke through. Then we suddenly realised that the cinema was on fire. There was cheering in the streets. It got so hot in here that we thought we were burning, too.' The restaurant was packed that night and full of nervous jabber. The waiters hardly listened to orders, merely plonking anything they could think of before the diners. One was so nervous that his tray shook, glasses tinkling as he walked.

We decided to evacuate to northern Tehran and phoned a girl we knew about one kilometre away in Roosevelt Avenue. We were anxious not so much about self-preservation as about losing all our documents and files. We had been told that no one in any hotel had been hurt. The appearance of anarchy was deceptive. The arsonists had been sure to evacuate the hotels before setting them on fire. Indeed, an old friend of mine, Nick Cumming-Bruce, the *Guardian* correspondent, had told me that on the previous day the British Embassy staff had been led out of the office, which had been earmarked for burning, with apologies! When it was realised that some staff in a neighbouring building might be threatened, ropes were quickly thrown up so that they could make their way out.

Our lady friend seemed oblivious of our dilemma. She had heard about the rioting but did not realise, at that stage, how serious it had been. 'Why should they burn down the President?' she asked.

'Because it houses the Bell Helicopter people – they've been trying to burn it down for two days,' I replied in exasperation.

She seemed reluctant to share her minute flat with two others for an indefinite period. 'Let's see what happens. If things get too bad, then move in.' She phoned back five minutes later. 'You're right. You're a target. I've phoned friends among the radicals and they confirm it,' she assured us. It was agreed that we would move up there the following morning. A few minutes later she phoned again to invite us to have a drink with some communist friends in North Tehran.

We made our way up to her flat, then took a taxi out to theirs. They gave Sandra a warm welcome – from which I learnt something more about her. Towards us, they were icy. They brought us a whisky and began discussing the revolt with Sandra. One turned to me, almost accusingly, and said, 'Yesterday, one of our friends was shot dead.'

'It's a fine revolution,' I replied.

'The Shah is a swine, he's sold our country to the Americans. He tortures our friends and kills them.'

We nodded, told them that we had been at the university all day. They began to trust us more and told us they were unhappy about the day's events. The religious fanatics were getting too involved and the anarchy stemmed from agents provocateurs who wanted to force the army's hand. 'We didn't burn the banks and cinemas – the Shah's men did.'

When we returned to Sandra's flat we discovered through friends that there was now a severe shortage of petrol and that early the next morning but one British Airways was running an 'evacuation flight' to London. We spent the next day in the flat and had one visitor, Nick Cumming-Bruce. Nick was one of those fearless young journalists who was so dedicated to accuracy that he would only file a story when he had checked the facts minutely. During one of the later gun battles he had found himself on a roof in the middle of the cross-fire and it had fallen to a colleague to file the story whose most colourful element was the courage of a British journalist caught in the middle of a battle.

Nick covered the whole revolution and the early part of the new rule of the Ayatollahs, but in the first year of the new regime he was arrested and locked up in the Central Komiteh building, part of Tehran's old Majlis or Parliament building, for two weeks because his papers were not in order. Nick worked from the Reuters office in Tehran but his interrogators were not genned up on the Western media. 'Who is this Mr Reuter you are working for?' they asked him repeatedly. He had great difficulty in explaining that Reuters was a worldwide institution rather than some mysterious 'Godfather'.

Nick's companion in gaol was one of the Shah's generals, a sympathetic man who was prepared for the almost certain death that awaited him. Eventually Nick was told by his guards that he was to be flown home but when he reached the airport and its confusing series of checks by the Pasdaran and the Komitehs his papers were questioned and he was driven away along the road towards Evin, Iran's 'Lubianka', the political prison whose very name sends a shudder through any Iranian. 'That was the first time that I ever became really frightened,' he told me. 'I asked them where we were going but they refused to tell me. For about twenty minutes I was convinced that I was being sent to Evin but then, to my immense relief, they stopped at a special ice-cream shop and handed me an ice-cream, all smiles.' He spent a last night in the State Security building and, his papers now in order, he was flown back to England on the following day.

After Nick had left our flat we found a taxi driver who agreed to take us, for a very large sum, to our hotel to collect our suitcases. The driver was frightened and said he would wait outside the hotel for precisely three minutes. When we reached the hotel the streets were in chaos, with burnt-out cars and broken glass scattered along Takhte Jamshid. We raced in and were back in the taxi with our luggage within the agreed three minutes.

That night we debated whether to take the evacuation flight or stay put and risk trouble with Macmillan's in London. We were already a week late and hadn't sold a single book in Iran. I was keen to stay and file some stories but my colleague, who had until then shown no fear, said that he had had enough and wanted to go home. Strangely, the following morning a taxi appeared duly at our door. When we reached the airport it was bedlam, with Americans and British panicking that their names might not be on the manifest. It was a little like the last hours of the evacuation from Vietnam. Unfortunately our names were on the manifest so our last pretext for staying on a little to watch the revolution unfold was over.

When I reached London the following day I made straight for the *New Statesman* office in Holborn and the editor, Bruce Page, and his colleague Chris Hitchens gave me an office. I sat down for three hours and typed up my story furiously for a three-page article in that week's edition.

13

The tidy wives of the Gulf

'Phone for the fish knives, Norman
As Cook is a little unnerved'

(John Betjeman: 'How to get on in society')

Getting to understand Arabian culture is the main theme of any talk given by Arabists to businessmen keen to pick up contracts in the Gulf. But as one British businessman put it to me at question time after a talk I had given, the most difficult customs of all to come to terms with are those of the British expatriates, a race unto themselves. Oh, no worry about pointing the sole of the foot at the person you are talking to, or eating with the right hand, and no taboos about pork and alcohol. But the average 'expat' represents a caste that I have always found anthropologically the most bizarre and often the least attractive. Such is the come-uppance of this Godalming class that Indian friends of mine in the Gulf have found themselves ostracised on racial grounds.

In London the old Raj classes dream nostalgically of P. & O. and hill stations, pig-sticking and tiffin, tennis in pleated white dresses and gin slings on the tea plantation veranda. In the Gulf the British petit bourgeoisie have much of this. They've read books about the Raj and try to emulate it to musak in a shishi, tidy, faultless way. Arriving at Abu Dhabi Airport with its glimmering marble floors and neatly dressed policemen, you will see beautiful young English women in whites with tennis rackets, fair-haired, bronzed young men just off their yachts, grannies in expensive 1940s clothing and blond-haired, blue-eyed children playing tig. The nine to five struggle and heartache of Godalming is suddenly replaced with the ease and emulated aristocracy of the Gulf where career responsibility, servants, villas heavy with jasmine and wisteria and endless, exquisitely equipped clubs and beaches have given them a new, harsh, self-confidence. Little men become big men; healthy, handsome people become Waugh's 'bright young things' but in a mannered, classless way. Plastic Art Nouveau statues grace the coffee rooms of the cocooned, air-conditioned hotels and Mozart murmurs beyond the social persiflage. You dance Viennese waltzes in evening dresses; you dress up for the theatre and the opera. Young bachelors have endless affairs. Unlike in Saudi Arabia, they are not necessarily with their friends' wives, although that can be OK too.

Faced with the influx of expatriates whose social mores are alien to the old life-style of the Gulf, the Shaikhs have clung to tradition with a curious success. They never discard *dishdashes* or *ghutras*. Like the Saudis they have made no real compromise with the West. They have merely allowed it to survive intact in a free, segregated existence. The lifestyle of Shaikh Zayed's family in Abu Dhabi and the Boltons has remained Victorian in a pleasant Arabian way while Shaikh Rashid runs a *majlis* that is completely Dubaian. His laissez-faire policy allows the Dubaians a bemused view of the bustle of nostalgia and cheap wealth that Europe has emulated about him.

When I first visited Saudi Arabia during the Hajj I was whisked off by an adventurous friend into the Empty Quarter by tracks. When I visited Abu Dhabi for the first time in Ramadan in 1975 I was driven down the four-lane highway in an air-conditioned car to the Omani mountains by Ras al-Khaima. Nobody would even open the windows, let alone stop the car and get out. The Gulf is health and wealth and elegant hotel drawing-rooms and sporting clubs.

When I came back to the United Arab Emirates to research for yet another book on these massively over-written-about 'white elephant' villages in 1982, my hotel suites became my commissioning bases for expert writers. They also became a tuning-fork to the vicissitudes and smouldering resentments of the British expatriate community.

If I arranged meetings in quick succession and one writer was late I found myself in the awkward position of entertaining two deadly rivals. One of my correspondents was a disc jockey on Abu Dhabi's Capital Radio and when the day's work became over-strained I would phone her between records to put through my request for an early Noël Coward or a Cole Porter song. 'And now I want to introduce Trevor Mostyn who has reappeared in Abu Dhabi, hot-foot from the Liwa Sands and we all wish him the best of luck. . . . ' The wail of Neil Sedaka's 'On the Road' or Cole Porter's 'Night and Day' followed to relieve me from my mass of import-export statistics.

Abu Dhabi is a soulless city, the epitome of the new Arabian 'Perfect City' with its lifeless concrete blocks of flats and shops running along its endless and often unmarked grid-planned streets. Behind its pivotal clock-tower on the corniche stands the Mickey Mouse Mosque (in Arabic the Secret Mosque – Al-Masjid al-Sirri), which looks like a cardboard cut-out from an Aladdin pantomime with its coloured domes and minarets. At dusk the brilliant splashes of green lawns, watered round the clock by dead-eyed Baluchis, are filled with chattering saris, jodhpuris and Sikh turbans. Indians are scattered into the furthest corners of the UAE. Shops and *souqs* are mostly Indian. Indian grocers can be found in tiny shops on the edges of the desolate Liwa Sands.

A lady jazz singer is singing her sensual blues as I sit with the tall, elegant correspondent of *Gulf Commercial* in Abu Dhabi's Hilton. Once I had overcome my admiration for her beauty, I noted how easily she took offence and began to regret having commissioned her to write so much. I was a stranger in a town whose expatriates are so incestuously intertwined that everyone is the constant victim of gossip and vituperation. I watched the whole community paraded before me and became a go-between among the warring factions. The dapper Englishman from the Ministry of Information in coiffeured blond hair and colonial white suit was the ministry's window to the West and soon joined me to discuss censorship problems.

My local correspondent took me on a guided tour of Abu Dhabi, finding it almost as difficult as I to recognise streets by name. Many streets were known by buildings long since demolished. Zayed II Street was Electra Street (the Electra Cinema once stood there). Tourist Club Street is the street which passes the Tourist Club and the Meridien Hotel. I wanted to visit the virtually impregnable bastion of middle-class expatriate England, 'The Club'. My correspondent was reluctant and I soon saw why. Uniformed men guarded The Club from a pill-box at its entrance. 'No, we're not members but journalists and we'd like to see the Principal,' we explained.

The guards contacted the Principal who was reluctant to see 'journalists'. We insisted, explaining that we were not after a story but wanted to write the Club up for a book which would not see the light of day without the approval of the government censor. The Club was as difficult to penetrate as a Soviet missile site. Eventually we had the go-ahead to proceed to the Club building in the middle of the little peninsula with its two marinas. We sat in Mrs Alexander's office. After a long wait the powerful lady, who reminded me of my frightening Kindergarten head-mistress, appeared.

She was an honest but forbidding lady. 'Did we have ministry permission to produce a guide?' We assured her that the ministry were bending over backwards for us to produce it. Well, she'd give us the Club prospectus but nothing must be published without her written approval. We began to wonder whether there wasn't a real story here after all. It was explained that there was a two-year waiting list for entry to the Club and that every applicant was invited to a cocktail party at which he or she was vetted for suitability. For many expatriates the Club is the very key to social and sporting life. The charm one had to put on at this terrifying cocktail ordeal must have been terrible.

During my month in the UAE I interviewed some one hundred potential correspondents for my guide-book. I often fell into the danger of catching people's enthusiasm and commissioning them to write things before realising that they couldn't write, wouldn't write, wrote dangerously inaccurately or were just bullshitting. At other times I found that I had commissioned someone who had a smattering of knowledge on their subject, whether wildlife or crochet at the al-Ain Women's Institute, only to discover that they were experts on subjects which I had ignored.

One elegant Englishwoman visited me full of promises. She would write almost anything but she haggled and haggled for the right price and I received her two pages of copy some six months late. Another girl who never discussed money at all, who was diffident about her writing ability and who promised little, produced large, excellent sections in record time. It was a world of promises and counter promises, bluff and counter bluff. I arranged meetings tightly together to save time.

One lady correspondent turned up at the Abu Dhabi Sheraton half an hour late. When I mentioned the name of the correspondent who was to appear half an hour later she blanched and explained that for personal reasons they were not friends. I tried to speed up the first meeting to avoid the coming confrontation but the first correspondent was in no hurry to go and the second arrived early. Correspondent number two's smile vanished when she saw correspondent number one. When correspondent number one saw correspondent number two she got up abruptly, shook my hand, and walked out without a nod to the other woman. I realised that she had waited intentionally in order to have the pleasure of this dramatic snub. The intricate machinery of Gulf social life and its open secret scandals and jealousies were always to remain somewhat of a mystery to me. I was something between a voyeur and a go-between.

I took a taxi by night on the long road to Dubai. It was crammed with poor Indians and cackling chickens on the floor. We stopped at a soap-box tea-house on the road. There on the colour television screen was my most difficult and most beautiful lady correspondent reading in a stilted way the latest news from Belfast. When I arrived at the Dubai Sheraton a bottle of whisky and a bowl of fruit with a personal message for me, the VIP guest, stood in the centre of my magnificent suite. My magazine, *MEED*, was lavishly respected in the Gulf, particularly in the big hotels.

I visited the editor of Dubai's glossy *Khaleej Times* which had just re-emerged from a five-day ban for bravely publicising the fact that UAE federal civil servants had recently gone on strike for more pay. Everybody is well paid in the Gulf. Nobody goes on strike. So it was banned for a while to prove the government's point.

Father Eusebius Daveri, a jolly, hyper-active Italian priest, ran Dubai's St Mary's Catholic Church which, as he proudly boasts, he helped build with his own hands in 1967. Father Eusebius ran one of those old-fashioned, humane schools whose teachers were the local nuns. Educational standards were higher than at government schools, a factor that had aroused jealousies. Islamic fundamentalism after the revolution in Iran had led to a new ruling that all schools must be segregated. 'How can we segregate?' sighed Father Eusebius. 'How can we divide classrooms and corridors and lavatories? They know it is impossible. They know it'll mean we'll have to close down entirely.'

At church I met Pat Wright, the British coach to the Dubai football team, who almost crushed my hand with his handshake. The football pitch stands on Dubai's pleasure world Leisureland and both Wright and the team's manager, Don Revie, lived on the complex. Wright took me on a tour of the immense, empty stadium with its neat, plastic grass. From there I was taken on the Leisureland ghost-train, a wooden and brasswork dhow on rails which trundles through tunnels in which you are clawed in the dark by massive spiders. Cobras hiss from dark corners and goblins cackle and giggle from all sides.

Like the Ruler's palace in Bastakiyah the nearby Dubai Museum is one of the last of Dubai's lovely old buildings. When I sat in the cool of its wind-tower on a baking day I thought of the waste throughout the Middle East on complex air-conditioning units. Surely it would be healthier, cheaper and quieter to harness the natural breezes to flow through even the largest buildings than to cocoon oneself in glass and concrete and breathe chemical air.

I met Jack Briggs, a magnificently built man who had founded the Dubai police force. Although he had retired no one had had the heart to move him from the commandant's house. Jack Briggs was a warm Lancashire man. He was chilly at first when he gathered I was writing a book. Was I a businessman trying to fix a meeting with the Ruler? Was I going to 'do the dirty' like Linda Blandford, whose book *The Oil Shaikhs* aroused incredible emotion throughout the Gulf. It had mischievous anecdotes but sold like hot cakes to anyone who felt they might be mentioned. Or worse, would I write something like Robert Moore's *Dubai*, one long tale of orgy and oriental intrigue? No, I explained, I was writing a guide for a commercial magazine and the guide would, alas, have to be approved by the censor before publication. When Briggs was convinced of this he brightened up. After several beers he gave me a stream of anecdotes about the Ruler and even asked if I would like to produce a biography of Rashid with him after the Ruler's death.

I had not been to Shaikh Rashid's building in Bastakiyah for many years. The Ruler was sick and seemed to be on the point of death. But he would attend the *majlis*, arriving at 11.00 and leaving some two hours later. His sickness was a taboo subject. Discussed everywhere in drawing-rooms, it was never referred to in court circles. In the drawing-rooms even the best informed had widely differing theories. Some said it was heart, some said liver, others said brain cancer. It's amazing in the Arabian world how little truth finds its way down the grapevine, how closely guarded secrets remain.

When I reached the building, Rashid was in session. In theory I could have joined him, but in practice foreigners these days have to make appointments with key officials. I climbed the steps of the sprawling building. Nationals in *dishdashes* clustered about at the top. Many had Kalashnikovs slung lazily over their shoulders. I looked ahead between the glass windows of the two simple *majlis* rooms and beyond at the view of the dhows clustered along the Creek side through the shimmering arch that dominated the waters. Inside the building on the left Dubaians sat around the huge square room before Thermos flasks and paper tissues.

My eye fell immediately upon the Ruler with his strong eyes and hawk-like nose, althouth he wore nothing to distinguish him from the others. All the stories told about him flooded back to me. A man from the British construction company Halcrow had explained how he had watched Rashid run rings around those about him or around Lebanese businessmen who came to seek favours. He ruled not merely through the consent of his people but also through his complete ability to dominate by his astuteness, his tricks, by the psychological games he employed to sum up a man or a deal. He asked the Halcrow man, 'Can you build a harbour in so and so time?' offering a virtually impossible time limit. The man said they could despite the Herculean reality of the task. Immediately Rashid stood up in the *majlis*, ordered a helicopter and flew the man down the coast, pointing out the areas he wanted dredged. He had it right. He knew what he wanted done.

Jack Briggs had the love of a son for Rashid. Briggs speaks the Dubai dialect so impeccably that Rashid would turn to his friends and say, to taunt them: 'This Wejh al-Ahmar [red-face] knows Arabic better than you do.' But Briggs also knew the other side of Rashid. Rashid would not discuss. He had no idea of the Western concept of thrashing things out. He listened to views and made his decision. There was no more to be said. He would say of Briggs, 'Look, this Wejh al-Ahmar can pick ideas out of the air.'

Poor Briggs had fallen foul of the hard-liners who contrasted so much with Rashid but whose day had dawned. If we're going to have a foreign police chief, they said, let's at least have an Arab one. Briggs had to resign.

Bill Duff, another of the grand old expatriates of Imperial days, worked down the corridor from the Ruler, running Customs and Excise. He told me that Arabs were petrefied of Rashid. Rashid was gentle with foreigners but they did not see the other side of the man. The Arabs, he said, felt constantly humbled by him. Yet Rashid, like so many bedouin, had a bedouin humour. When Duff lunched with him one day, Rashid, deciding the meal was over, had leapt onto the table, run right down it among myriad guests, leapt off the end, out of the door, into a huge open Rolls Royce and sped away.

To meet Rashid – I never did – I had to see an adviser, Fulan Fulan, once a wild and pleasure-loving youth, today the tuning fork of Dubaian court circles. Waiting in the ante-room I watched a conversation between his assistant and some Pakistanis. The man was chatting quite casually in Urdu. When the phone rang he switched to Farsi and when a shaikh entered he switched again to Arabic before telling me in impeccable English that Fulan would see me.

Fulan's big smile did not mask the roughness of the youth that one British officer had told me he had wanted to 'bash up' to improve his manners. My meeting with him was hampered by the fact that the UAE correspondent of my magazine had quoted an off-the-cuff remark that 'Dubai would revert to the sand when the oil ran out.' So what was my business? I told him I wanted to learn how the *majlis* system worked for my book and wanted to meet Rashid. One of the problems with peninsula Arabs is that they are constantly losing concentration, or appearing to. In reality they miss nothing. Hours later they return to a remark that you thought they'd completely ignored. Usually someone enters the room and you have to begin all over again. That's the curse of the *majlis* system. There was no way Fulan was going to tell me how the system worked but his very evasiveness and mercurial attitude told me enough. 'The Ruler is very busy,' he began. But eventually he told me to return the following day.

When I returned to the steps of the *majlis*, the Ruler and his entourage burst out onto the steps like a flock of doves. Tumbling down in shimmering white around the charismatic old man were the grandees, the guards, the grovellers. As he stepped to his car, Rashid turned towards me and smiled, asking one of his aides who I was. I smiled back. But my meeting with Rashid never took place.

I hired a Suzuki jeep in Dubai and had to visit the driving section of the police station to take my test. To get your licence you take a sponsor's letter, a British licence and two passport photos and take an eye test that must be the simplest known to man. When the policeman pointed to the letters I tried to read them. 'No, no don't read them, please. Just say up or down.' So there I was for five minutes saying up, down, down, down, up, almost missing ups and downs with the speed of the stick. But after three minutes I had passed.

I visited a lawyer in Dubai who was close to my magazine. He told me a story which was doing the rounds of Dubai at the time. The previous week an important American senator who must remain nameless had dined with Shaikh Zayed, the UAE President, and the commercial elite of Dubai. At one moment he began losing his temper and sang the praises of Israel, to the embarrassment of the guests. One of the top people after Zayed – the lawyer would not say who – leapt up and stormed out of the room in protest. When the senator dined with Shaikh

Rashid some days later in Dubai he turned to a prominent Dubaian and said, 'You know, I think your *dishdashes* are marvellous. You can just pull them up and copulate without any fooling around.'

From Dubai I drove my Suzuki jeep to Fujeirah on the southern coast. So far I had been overwhelmed with contacts, each one leading to a self-perpetuating cycle of new people, new experts on new subjects who would inevitably make me regret having selected a previous expert. But in Fujeirah I knew nobody, so I drove to the Ministry of the Interior where I asked an official in my most impeccable Arabic where the Municipality was. A young Fujeiran merely said 'Follow me' and without more ado got into his car and I drove off after him.

He led me to a row of shops. When I got out I was angry and repeated in my purest Arabic my wish to visit the Municipality. The man smiled and led me into a fridge sales shop. I was clouded with annoyance as I entered. Once again I felt that my Arabic had been despised. Inside leaning against a fridge, was a smiling, blond-haired Fujeiran. 'Can I help?' he asked in rather funny but competent English.

'No, you can't,' I replied in Arabic. I now made sure of every vowel. 'I asked for the Municipality and he brings me to a fridge shop.'

'Why do you want the Municipality?' he asked in really very good English.

'Frankly, that's none of your business,' I replied. 'And where did you learn your English, for that matter?'

'I am English,' he replied quietly. 'I come from Northumberland.'

I pulled myself up sharp. It immediately dawned upon me that the nice government official had taken me to the fridge shop to meet Tom, now converted to Islam.

Tom had been in the Trucial Oman Scouts in 1970, he stayed on and now called himself Abdullah Mohammed. He had a friend from the TOS in Abu Dhabi called King who had done the same and called himself Hajji Abdullah Malek. Malek is Arabic for King.

After I had visited some jolly Pakistanis at the Municipality and scoured maps that covered a carpet, I returned to my hotel to make notes. There was a knock on my door. It was Abdullah. In the fridge shop he had been an imposing young shaikh surrounded by admiring Fujeirans whom he called 'his family'. But the man who sat drinking tea on my balcony was a sad, lonely person, ready to pour out a lifetime of sorrow.

For ten years he had lived in a house given to him by the Ruler of Fujeirah. 'I used to attend the Ruler's *majlis* every day. Those days were beautiful. The Fujeirans trusted the British. They knew that those of us from the TOS were honest and believed in and loved Fujeirah. We didn't stay to make money. We stayed because this was a cleaner life for us. But as time went on the Palestinians infiltrated the Ruler's court and would mutter to the Ruler that he should not trust the *kafirs*, the unbelievers. They do everything they can to belittle me. Nowadays, I'm never invited to the *majlis* at all.'

I had met a number of Englishmen like Abdullah in Saudi Arabia who had sincerely believed that by dedicating their unfulfilled lives to Arabia they would gain a new life and a new family that would be forever beholden to them. But however well they knew their Qur'an, however many times they had performed the Hajj to Mecca, they would always remain Europeans and would, as frantic nationalism increased to confront Western values and industry, become increasingly lonely and estranged.

From Fujeirah I drove along the coast to Khor Fakkan, passing on my left the minute Omani mountain enclave of Qidfa where produce was transported from faraway mainland Oman by helicopter. The coast is of beautiful beaches and dhows. Khor Fakkan, a pretty, semi-circular bay with an immense, clean beach, is an enclave of Ajman, a reflection again of the freezing of tribal movements when the British came and of the resultant muddled balkanisation of the emirates. There had just been a mini war at Dhaif because a man whose house was half in Fujeirah Emirate and half in Dubai Emirate had been forced to pay tax by the Emirate which he maintained that he was not in. Shots had been fired and a timid bank manager had tried to dissuade me from passing through but when I did I found nothing but a quiet village.

I stayed at the Holiday Inn which stands like a lighthouse at one corner of the beach. Like a ship it has little port holes instead of windows in the rooms. I woke up early the next morning to have a swim. I looked out at the sun spilling up over a big sea. I looked down at the beach and saw that its sands were moving like yellow ether. I blinked and doubted my eyesight. I looked again. When I refocused I saw that the beach was alive with crabs doing early morning side-sprints across the wet sand.

I had to tread warily across the beach through the little spaces the crabs, creatures which had with spiders been my childhood terror, vacated (I remember my grandmother flinging dead ones at me for fun). Once in the water I swam through the shallows to avoid any contact with the ogres.

After my swim I went to the Municipality which is run by pure Khor Fakkanians. I coined the word. Such coinings made the Fujeirans sound like inhabitants of a distant planet and Ras al-Khaimans like some sort of Arabian master race. The Khor Fakkanians, whose Municipality had rarely been visited by foreigners, flocked about me with excitement when I spoke Arabic. I asked for a map but they pleasantly ignored my request and insisted that I convert without more ado to Islam since I spoke the language of God.

Had I read the Qur'an? Yes, I had studied the Qur'an at university and I quoted some *ayas* from Surat al-Miriam to prove it. The officials in their spanking white *dishdashes* ran about the room with joy.

'But you are a Muslim, you are a Muslim. You have read the word of God. You are a Muslim.'

'I like Islam,' I replied, 'but I believe that Jesus is the son of God' (groans).

'But no, the Qur'an says that Jesus is a Prophet and we revere him as a Prophet. But God has no son. Is the Qur'an not God's spoken word? Can God lie?'

'No, but we Christians believe that much of the Qur'an is true but that it errs on the question of the status of Jesus' (groans, horror!).

A very clever man sitting in the corner tried to resolve my error and pointed out that Jesus may be considered the 'spirit' of God but in no way the son. Somewhere along the line I had been tripped up by my teachers. I asked for the map again. My friends looked quite shocked at the blasphemy of discussing maps at a moment like this and brought around a sixth cup of coffee instead. When the map finally arrived it was a huge scroll with every detail of every hill and cove and I realised that I couldn't really use it. But I had to accept it with pleasure and these delightful people spent ages binding it and wrapping it so that more time could be given to my conversation.

When I drove on along the coast towards the three Dibbahs which led into the mountainous Omani Musandan tip of the Emirates the mountains stretching out into the sea were ghostlike in a heat haze. The road ran up close to the mountains on the left and then recoiled around immense palm groves. I reached Dibbah Muhallab, an enclave of Fujeirah which formed the first branch of the three Dibbahs that wind around a bay similar to that at Khor Fakkan. I drove along narrow sand tracks between the clay and wattle buildings of the sleepy village which gave onto a silver sea full of fishing dhows.

As I approached the corniche my nostrils trembled with a disgusting smell. I soon saw why. The little fields in the village and the beach itself looked from a distance like sheets of silver. They were covered with tiny fish which were dried and spread over the palm groves as fertiliser.

Children in a perfect circle stood in the sea pulling a fishing net which spread out in a diaphanous triangle from a boat on which a fisherman was waving a placard like a conductor's stick. The children were chanting in unison '*Hula, hula*' ('Hey-ho, hey-ho!'). A group of Dibbans joined me and explained that they changed '*Hula, hula*' as they pulled the nets in and if the catch was big they would chant '*Hatha hut, hatha hut*' ('That's a whale, that's a whale').

I drove on along the corniche for a few hundred yards and when I asked for the correct road the people told me I was now in Dibbah Hassen, an enclave of Ajman. Although only a house divides enclave from enclave every local knows perfectly where each begins and ends.

I drove on another few hundred yards where the red-roofed houses gave way to *barasti* huts and the road led away behind the buildings and became track again. The tracks brought me back to the corniche where I took some more photographs of dhows, the same dhows I had been passing since my entry into the Dibbahs. Two neat policemen wearing British-style peaked caps and shorts and trotting down the track explained to me that I was now in Dibbah Bayah and therefore in Oman. Minutes later a bright new Mercedes drew up and an elegant man in impeccable Omani turban and Omani *dishdash* with its little twirl at the collar, stopped. 'Do you have ministry permission to take photographs?' he asked severely.

'In the UAE I'm allowed to?'

'Yes, but you're in Oman.'

I told him that I was taking pictures of the same dhows I had been photographing in the other Dibbahs and I drew out my notebook and asked him who he was.

'I'm the mayor of Bayah,' he replied grandly.

That shook me a little but I said, 'In that case can I quote you as saying that visitors are forbidden to take photographs in Oman?'

He back-tracked a little and repeated that I could take photographs if I had ministry permission.

'Where is the ministry?' I asked.

'The ministry's in Muscat,' he replied. Muscat was miles across the sea. The conversation was verging on farce. The two policemen, sensing trouble, wandered up, but the mayor, not knowing what to do with me and terrified of being quoted in my guide-book, tried to save face by saying in his impeccable Oxford English, 'Well, don't do it again, old chap,' and drove on.

From Fujeirah I returned to Abu Dhabi and from there to the Liwa Sands, one of the world's biggest dune seas and the start of the Empty Quarter which spreads out deep into southern Saudi Arabia. Before leaving Abu Dhabi my co-driver casually put on a blue film on his video. Ironically, it was the first I had seen. I have often remarked to Arabian friends that the blue films which are watched so casually by Arabian families are far more rarely seen by the corresponding classes in Britain. In any case it was a strange experience to watch writhing women and genitalia at 11.00 a.m. and then to be driving out in a Boy's Own gang for the huge dunes of an Arabian desert.

During these trips in my little Suzuki jeep I would make

precise kilometre readings for my guide-book. These would read thus: 'Tony, Sean and I watch blue film; pack up at 4.00 and drive out for Liwa. Down Arabian Gulf Street, reach new bridge at KM 32204, Musaffa refinery on right, dredging for pleasure lake on left, at KM 32207 turn right towards Musaffa at crossroads, petrol station on right, at roundabout Al-Ain straight on, 1 km after petrol station turn right for Tarif and pass Darmaki block tile factory and afforestation project.' The list read as a pure description of the emirates where factories and shops represent the principal landmarks of man-made enclaves in the sand.

The gas-gathering town of Habshan represents the end of the coastal built-up area of Abu Dhabi and the start of the journey into the desert proper. At dusk you see camels moving across the rippling flames of the gas flares as silhouettes. The town is a straight line of shops and apartments on both sides of the road and the ubiquitously creeping dunes are already spilling between the buildings. There was an unfinished row of villas with much elaborate arabesque, some supermarkets, and a smart little branch of the National Bank of Abu Dhabi with a brass name-plate. The people were almost all Indian. Brahmani cows ambled among the chairs of the pavement cafés beneath the pillars, dreamily seeking scraps. Habshan is the size of a small English village but you can buy anything from Earl Grey tea to tinned oysters in its supermarkets.

We reached Liwa Town at dusk. Liwa Town, locally known as Mayzari, consisted of a garage and a soap-box grocer's. The importance of Madina Liwa is that it lies at the end of the road and at the beginning of the web of tracks which wind their way through the dune seas of Liwa. Frauke Heard at the Emiri Documentation Centre in Abu Dhabi had advised us to drive through Liwa in convoy but we decided that she was remembering the olden days before the road to Mayzari had been built when she and her husband had taken important visitors over the peaks of the dunes. Having had cold drinks from the Baluchis who ran the grocery we took the right-hand track past the Radom army camp and took various turnings until we hit the dunes where we settled down to camp in sleeping bags.

When we awoke early next morning we found the tracks of a snake winding through the fine powder sands of the enormous yellow dunes about us. By eight the sand was too hot to stand on. We forged our ways on through the sandy tracks until we reached the compounds of white, wooden huts which are the core of a large afforestation project run by Pakistanis who explained casually that they were creating agriculturally self-supporting desert areas to which the UAE natives can return when the oil runs out.

Tiny trees were planted in neat rows, tidily contrasting with the great flesh-like dunes about us. The Pakistanis took us on a botanical tour of the plants. There was *Ziziphus jujubi* – in Arabic merely '*heh*', *Procupas junifrea* – in Arabic '*ghaf*' and in Urdu '*jand*', *Phoenex dactylifera*, otherwise the common palm tree.

From here we took a puzzle of tracks among dunes as big as mountains until we reached Al-Khis marked on the map. Al-Khis was a hut on the edge of a palm nursery and inhabited by three very lonely Pakistanis who greeted us with almost hysterical delight. They spoke no English but gave us tea and took us to a pool to swim. One of them told me with great mental clarity that he had had 'brain meningitis' and had completely lost his memory. He could not even remember people's names, he said. I assured him that I had never had 'brain meningitis' but had exactly the same problem.

Near the pool were some delightful dunes that rose to three levels, reaching about 600 feet at the top. I climbed up, burning my feet on the sand and constantly jumping from the hot patch that I had been on or else leaping onto a shadowed patch. It was like walking along the ridges of a soft, clean moon up there from where I gazed out onto an endless sea of canary yellow virgin dunes, with their bladed ridges trembling a little in an ether of wind-swept sand.

I discovered that if I slid down a dune it made loud booms – like a Hindu mantra. Soon all three of us were sliding down making these booms which we called cosmic farts. They echoed for miles. As we drove back to Mayzari at dusk magnificent, tall Baluchis wearing loose-wound turbans strolled along the tracks heading for their huts miles away. We squeezed one of them into the jeep and two on top of the bonnet and they shrieked with primitive laughter as we roared up and down the sides of the dunes.

14

A belle époque
in crumbling Cairo

Invited to dinner by Amy Matouk, the glamourous, jet-setting daughter of one of Cairo's sophisticated families, I entered the grand and dusty marble hall of her apartment building in prestigious Zamalek which is part of Gezira, the 'Island' between Ismail Pasha's *fin-de-siècle* Cairo and modern Muhandeseen, 'Engineer's City'. Zamalek contains the British-established Gezira Club, the villas of the affluent middle classes, and the city's most fashionable restaurants. I myself lived in Zamalek in a penthouse flat which overlooked the Nile in front and the Gezira Club at the back. It was the top floor of a 1920s apartment building called Dorchester House.

The lift had broken down and on a marble seat beneath a mirror sat an old lady and a handsome woman of a certain age. Raouf Mishriki, a tall, pleasant man with a walrus moustache, introduced them to me in French, the lingua franca of Egypt's old aristocracy. The younger woman turned to me politely and asked how I liked Cairo. I replied that I liked it very much. '*Ah, c'est foutue, c'est degeulasse, cette ville!*' she replied with contempt. Turning towards me with a look which reflected her bitterness she added, 'But of course you are too young to have known the 1950s. You cannot imagine how wonderful those days were. You cannot imagine how beautiful this city was. You cannot understand what they have done to it, these people,' she grimaced.

I looked at her with a little reciprocal contempt, musing on how these European tourists were unable to come to terms with the palsy of Third World cities. I guessed that she was a German tourist on a short Nile cruise. Responding to some inner doubt, however, I asked, 'Are *you* Egyptian?'

'Am I Egyptian? Am I Egyptian? he asks. Yes, indeed I am Egyptian. I was QUEEN of Egypt.'

I could have happily slipped under the marble floor. I swung in a complete mental circle and reminded myself of my oft-made resolution never in life to make judgments of people or events too quickly. I was talking to Queen Farida, King Farouk's once lovely first wife and the mother of his daughters Farial and Fawzia. It took me some moments to recover my composure, for if she didn't know what Egypt was like during that hedonistic era, then nobody did. She had been the gay heart of that world and I had often looked with fascination at the photographs of her splendid wedding to Farouk.

The fading palazzos, the outrageously affluent penthouse apartments with their priceless Ottoman furniture and English seventeenth-century paintings, the ground-floor apartments with Greek and Roman columns scattered among the palms of discreet gardens; these are the homes of Cairo's old aristocrats living on stories of their glittering memories and of the terrible days following the 1952 revolution and the mass sequestrations and imprisonments of the early 1960s. Many fled to Rome, Paris and London, returning when President Sadat ushered in a more liberal age with his open-door policy and his westward orientation.

Prince Hassan Hassan, the red-haired, white-skinned Cherkassi cousin of King Farouk, speaks English with an impeccable Oxford brogue and lives in a poor penthouse flat in Zamalek amid his paintings. A close friend of Amy's mother, Marguerite, who owned my Nile-side flat, Prince Hassan could be seen roaming the lawns of the Gezira Club almost every day. Lunching one day in the crumbling Rococo palazzo of Adel Sabet Bey and his frail and still somehow lovely 90-year-old mother, Prince Hassan would tell the stories of his family, of the royal intrigues and the terrible jealousies.

He told me of the day when his forebear Princess Nazli, the daughter of the Khedive Mohammed Tewfiq, was dining with her husband. A beautiful, pale-skinned Cherkassi girl was serving a dish to the prince and the tresses of her golden locks fell into the young man's sauce. 'Don't worry my sweetheart, my pet,' he said. 'It doesn't matter.' The virago princess gave her husband a stinging glance. On the following day a different slave served the prince. 'Do you want to gaze upon the face of your beloved, your "pet"?' asked the princess and so saying she lifted the silver cover and revealed the poor girl's head, her lovely hair scattered in the sauce. The poor prince leapt from the table and fled in terror. The story is also related in a manuscript of the royal family written by another member of the old set, Jean Papasian.

Jean Papasian, who calls himself John Papasian, with the stress on the second 'a', lives among his own abstract paintings which he dubs 'in motion perpetua' just off Kasr el-Nil Street in central Cairo. A handsome, theatrical man in his early 70s, Papasian would greet me in a billowing silk robe and offer me large glasses of potent *araq* when I visited him to research into a book on nineteenth-century Cairo. He told me in his flamboyant not-quite-Oxford English of the sensual days of his youth and of the young men he had known in London. Among them was my paternal uncle. 'Your uncle and I', said Papasian in his arty voice, 'were the bright young things of London in those days.'

Papasian is an Armenian and his father was piano-tuner to King Farouk. On the basis of piano lessons which he shared with King Farouk as a child he wrote a lurid book on the secret history of the Royal House of Egypt, but he showed me letters from British publishers explaining that the book was far too libellous to publish.

At a party given at the smart El Patio Restaurant in Zamalek I met an elegant middle-aged woman called Princess Najla whom I was told was Turkish. When I asked her whether she was descended from the last Ottoman sultan, Abdul Hamid, she grasped my hand and cried with affectionate astonishment, 'But how could you guess? He was my grandfather!' as if my guess was a one in a million chance. She was sitting with John Papasian, her close platonic friend whose ancestors had been massacred by the Turks either with Abdul Hamid's blessing or else with his secret connivance. I remember discussing Papasian with Princess Lodi Lotfallah in her palazzo in Alexandria's elite district of Boulkly. 'We all loved Papasian,' she said. 'He was such a handsome man. He knew all the princesses and the men felt safe to leave him with their women. That's why he knows so much about the secrets of the royal family.'

Of all Cairo's old aristocrats one of the best known is Adel Sabet Bey whose mother is the first cousin of King Farouk's domineering mother, Queen Nazli, and whose great-great grandfather was Sulaiman Pasha el-Faransawi (Sulaiman Pasha 'the Frenchman'), the French Colonel Sèvres who came with Napoleon Bonaparte and converted to Islam. Sulaiman Pasha is buried in a wrought-iron tomb built by the same Von Diebitch who designed the arches and pillars of the Gezira Palace, now the Marriott Hotel, built to house the beautiful French Empress Eugénie when she came to inaugurate the opening of the Suez Canal in 1869. The tomb stands derelict in the Masr al-Qadima quarter of Cairo beside the Christian, mainly Coptic, quarter of Babylon.

Adel's flaking palazzo stands beside the American Embassy in Garden City. Since various terrorist attacks on American embassies throughout the Middle East, the embassy had been heavily guarded and cars forbidden even to slow down outside it. Policemen with sub-machine guns stood outside Adel's little island of antiquity, which we all called Great Expectations, and languid officers munched their sandwiches in the police shooting-brake parked in front of his gates.

I first visited the house with the then *Guardian* correspondent, Kate Finch. We climbed the marble steps at dusk, entered the glass and wrought-iron door and came into the darkness of the hall on whose wall hung paintings of Cherif Pasha, Sulaiman Pasha's grandson, and sepia photographs of princesses, and which was furnished with Syrian chairs of mother-of-pearl and ivory. We called Adel's name through the gloamings but there was no reply so we felt our way through and into the second of the two interior drawing-rooms. In the corner a lamp glowed and beneath the lamp sat a frail and beautiful old lady, Adel's mother. She welcomed us warmly. 'Adel has not returned but please stay. He will be so sad if you go away.' She added, as if to explain herself but clearly without a trace of snobbery, 'You know, I am the cousin of Queen Nazli, King Farouk's mother.'

Adel was to become a close friend and was with me when, some months later, I was arrested for writing an article critical of

Cairo's urban planning and flung into a State Security dungeon. Adel knew about prison life and had spent eleven months in jail during the latter days of Nasser.

Adel became an integral part of the Glittering Triangle, as I named the triangle of 1920s buildings in which I and my friends lived on the Nile beside the Gezira Palace and the Gezira Club. There were some twenty of us – Jack Thomson, the BBC correspondent and his wife Kathryn Davies, the *Guardian* correspondent, who lived beside me in Park Lane; Liz Colton the *Newsweek* Bureau Chief and Anna Clopet her photographer who lived in a magnificent Nile-side flat that recalled an era from Somerset Maugham and where they gave continual parties at which you might meet every correspondent in the Middle East; an embassy friend Nick Bates and his wife Jane; and Hani and Rosemary Sabet. Hani was with me when one summer we were shot at with sub-machine guns on the beaches of Agami near Alexandria.

Adel with his white hair and perfect Oxford English was the epitome of the Victorian gentleman but he was a Germanophile. He had worked loyally with the British during the war and turned to Germany after the war had ended. He used to stress this point, since pro-Axis feelings were strong when Rommel's Afrika Korps was racing towards Alexandria in 1942 and a British defeat seemed imminent. That was the time of the Great Flap when the British community panicked, when there was a half-mile-long queue of British soldiers around Barclays Bank seeking to withdraw their funds and when Egyptian businessmen were suddenly heard conversing in bad German on the telephone lines. Luckily for the British Rommel was obliged to stop at El-Alamein because his troops were exhausted and his supply-lines over-extended.

Most of the old set went to French schools such as Cairo's Jesuit College and even those who didn't feel socially obliged to speak French at dinner-parties. French is as much the social lingua franca of Cairo and Alexandria's sophisticated drawing-rooms as it was in Tsarist Russia and on the beaches of Agami you will often only hear French spoken even among Egyptians who have a weak vocabulary in it.

Adel's faded drawing-room was always full of people:

transient professors from Oxford or Harvard; British correspondents; a red-haired American girl pop singer researching into Sufi *dhikrs* and demon-exorcising *zar* dances which she was to incorporate into 'Funk' songs in the United States. At Adel's dinner parties you barely knew what you were eating so dark was the dining-room. Guests dipped their spoons into huge pots full of black meats and white sauces asking each other in four languages what they were eating.

Adel was building a two-floor structure with a tree in its centre against the outside corner of his mansion in the midst of roaring, honking traffic. He planned to serve capuchino coffee and sell scents made from Egyptian essences which would be called Les Musts du Caire. One of the scents was to be called Shagar ad-Durr ('tree of pearls'), after the Turkish Mamluk wife of Al Salih Ayyub. On Ayyub's death she became queen and a wicked one, murdering her new husband Ayback in his bath when he tried to take a second wife. The Mamluks eventually dragged her out and she was beaten to death with the shoes of the young slave girls belonging to the favourite wife of Ayyub whom she had forced him to divorce. Dogs began to eat the corpse but according to the Egyptian writer Makrizi a man 'of the people' took pity on her and placed her body in a casket in the magnificant mausoleum already built for her near the Citadel.

Adel had planning permission to build his drugstore but one day the Deputy Governor of Cairo, passing by in a funeral cortège, asked his neighbours in horror what the erection was and demanded that it be knocked down without more ado. At the time of writing there has been a reprieve and the awkward structure is just one more half-built triangle in a city of half-finished buildings.

I returned to Cairo in November 1985 with my wife Elizabeth. We were taken in a roaring jeep by Raouf Mishriki to a huge picnic at Abu Sir, some ten kilometres off the road between the Pyramids at Giza and the Pyramids at Sakkara. Having passed through the fertile strip which is Egypt we came over rolling hills of sand until we arrived at the crumbling *mastaba* of Abu Sir whose obelisk has long disappeared. The *mastaba* and the pyramids of Abu Sir were erected by kings of the 5th Dynasty. Some thirty of us surrounded the huge white granite sacrificial altar of this sun temple and magnificent foods and wines were spread over it. Bees swarmed about the crumbling stone of the *mastaba* and bored tiny holes into it creating a honeycomb effect. At dusk we drove over the downs and came to the peak of one from where at sunset we gazed about an immense sterile desert landscape where we counted thirteen pyramids in a great magic circle about us, little abstract triangles which seemed to grow from the dry, scorched earth.

15

Shoot-out on the beach

We had dined well at Michael's, sipping a cool, white Gianaclis wine beneath an August full moon. Hani Sabet, a close Egyptian friend, was our host and my 19-year-old cousin Connemara and her equally pretty friend Emma were staying with me in Egypt on their first grand tour abroad. It was a beautiful night. We were all filled with the pleasure of being alive. Michael's is a pretty restaurant that stands among the villas of the rich in Alexandria's elite beach resort, Agami.

After dinner, we strolled to Hani's holiday villa nearby where we drank brandy with his mother and sister. Hani changed into a white *gelebiah*. As we drank, I suggested we go down to the beach for a midnight swim but Hani explained that it was forbidden to be on the beach at night as it was patrolled by soldiers on the lookout for boats smuggling drugs from Jounieh Port in Lebanon. We decided to go down to the beach all the same and sit and talk until dawn when we could swim.

The beach is a five-minute walk from Hani's villa. We sat against the garden wall of the spacious mansion of a government minister. Between us and the sea stood a Pepsi Cola kiosk which represented the holiday atmosphere of Cairo and Alexandria's French-speaking elite who crowded the beach by day in their Cardin and Dior bikinis. In the far distance we could see the little figures of soldiers like pin-men patrolling the shore-line. The moon filled the beach with a pale glow and the crests of the waves sparkled like phosphorus. It was a still night. Only the water hissing on the beach broke the silence. Hani wandered along the back of the beach with Connie whose exquisite face and waist-length hair glowed in the moonlight. I wondered whether they were amorous. I talked politely with Emma. Shortly after they returned our beach went crazy.

One of the black figures reached a point on the shoreline parallel with us. When he spotted us he screamed the most vile abuse. So doing, he ran some yards towards us, fell to his knee, raised his sub-machine gun and opened fire on us. Sparks poured from the gun and we heard the clatter of rounds against the wall behind us. We flung ourselves into the sand, trying to claw our ways beneath it. 'No, we must put our hands up,' I shouted to the others, remembering that that's what they do in films. Nobody, I felt, shoots people with their hands up. So there we sat, our hands held high like the victims of Goya's Bourbon firing squad in Spain.

By now, only seconds later, six soldiers, six thin black shapes, were racing towards us from six points along the shore, racing, dropping to their knees, opening up, leaping to their feet again and racing forward. It was like a firework display. My feeling throughout these deadly seconds was that of being in the midst of a 'feely' war film. I don't believe that any of us were frightened. We each felt that we were the spectators at our own deaths. I shouted 'Ihna siaheen inglizi-een' – 'We are English tourists'; 'Ihna asdiq'a' – 'We are friends.' It must have been fifteen seconds between the moment of the first shot and the moment when the soldiers surrounded us. We were all still alive and unwounded.

The men looked half tramps, half bandits. What went for uniforms were virtually rags. They wore woollen berets. Their little, Uzi-style sub-machine guns were clothed, too, in ragged wool. In their faces was utter hatred. Two of them grabbed Hani with a passionate intensity. They ignored the girls, who stood away from us. I, too, they tried to ignore. As they grabbed Hani, cursing, howling like wild animals, another one blazed his gun into the air beside me. I put my hands to my ears.

They raised their gun butts to strike Hani. I rushed up, pulling away the guns from hitting him and shouted, 'I'raf inana asdiq'a', 'Know that we are friends.' This seemed to provoke them to further fury as they shouted phrases to the effect of 'You f... bastards', 'You sons of bitches', 'Ummak', meaning 'F... your mother'. Every time I pulled the guns, like harsh little tentacles, from Hani, I felt the barrel of another gun poking into my ribs. I knew that some of the guns carried live bullets and others carried blanks; and I knew from schooldays that even blanks will kill at that range.

Then the men went completely wild, dragging Hani away from my grasp. I thought they were going to kill him. Later he admitted to me that he had just kicked one of them in the balls. They tried to drag him across the beach as far as the Pepsi Cola stand, evidently attempting to create the impression that he had been in the forbidden area of the middle of the beach. They would have used this as evidence that we were signalling the all-clear to smugglers' boats out at sea. We were later to gather that there had been a real gun battle with smugglers on one of the beaches some days earlier. Diplomats told me that they believed that there had been at least one death. I was to understand that we represented the established lookout group, men with two pretty European girls to give the soldiers the lie of conventionality.

At the moment that Hani was being dragged away – there was blood on his lip and spattered on my shirt from my attempt to wean the guns off him – he suddenly shouted 'Don't you know who I am? I am the son of Makram Obeid' (a former Deputy President who owned one of the beach's holiday villas). Makram Obeid was, indeed, a friend and Hani could make the story plausible. At that, the soldiers let go. The physical violence was over.

It was now 3.30 a.m. and we and the girls and soldiers sat in a circle to parley. Hani used his diplomatic skills to make his story believable. He pretended he was having an affair with one of the girls and didn't want his wife to know. He was willing, he explained nobly, not to report the soldiers for their conduct on condition that they whispered not one word about his dangerous liaison. As time went on the soldiers became human. The hideous little brute who had tried his hardest to break Hani's skull with his gun pulled off his beret and revealed the smiling, chubby little face of the 16-year-old *fellah*'s son that he was. He laughed at me, clapping his hands against his ears, and said 'The *ingleezi* was frightened of the bang. . . ha-ha!' I sneered. I was not going to play Hani's game of charmed diplomacy.

As dawn rose the soldiers were lolling about and laughing

like old friends, going over and over the story of that night's funny adventure, frightened now that they might be court-martialled for the incident. As the sun crept over the sea, they began to drift away. We struggled back to our villa, tired and bloody, with a story for our friends that we might never have been able to tell.

The Agha Khan's week-long conference on Urban Planning in Cairo some months later (Cairo – The Collapsing City, the cynics quipped) was a lavish affair. It was held in the Marriott Hotel in Zamalek. I came to know the organisers of the conference, the Agha Khan group who had come from Nairobi, Geneva and Paris for the extravaganza which was attended by leading academics from throughout the world. On the evening prior to the opening of the conference I helped to arrange a press party in one of the Marriott halls. I was an official guest accredited as a journalist to the conference. I was offered access to the Agha Khan's telex line to file my story to *The Economist* in London on the last day.

Having presented my report to the telex office I went into the Marriott's elegant gardens to talk with the Agha Khan's people as well as Adel Sabet and a writer on the Middle East, Malise Ruthven. Malise and I were to have lunch with Adel and his 91-year-old mother in their crumbling palazzo in Garden City.

As the three of us were leaving the hotel I went to the telex office to confirm that my message had been sent. 'No,' said the girl, 'they have stopped it.' Who was 'they'? I asked. 'The Deputy Front Desk Manager, Ashraf al-Banna,' said the girl.

I strode to the front desk and asked angrily for Ashraf al-Banna. Some moments later he appeared with three men, clearly policemen, and I was surrounded by a very hostile group. 'I stopped your telex because I don't like your political views,' said al-Banna chillingly. Quite a crowd had formed now, including girls from behind the desk who were eager to witness the arrest of the 'tourist'. I suggested that Adel and Malise leave since they could be of no help to me. Al-Banna, perhaps to impress the now very large crowd about me, said viciously, 'You are in very, very serious trouble.'

The police wanted my documents but I was carrying

nothing. They said that I must go to the police station. However, since I had been commissioned by the hotel to write a book about this former palace, I made for a door that led into a corridor where the office of the Marketing Manager, John Serbrock, was. Al-Banna was taken aback by this move. Serbrock was with a man from the *Sunday Times* and when they appeared the group quickly dispersed, the police withdrew some paces and al-Banna completely panicked, whispering to the police, 'He's a friend of the *Rais*' (the Manager).

Al-Banna was called into Serbrock's office and re-emerged, shaken. I was told that there was no further problem but that I should collect my passport from my flat next door. As I went out to do this one of the policemen ran after me to explain that, regrettably, my 'case' had been reported to the tourist police headquarters in Adly Street. There was really no problem. I should simply go to the police chief where I would enjoy 'a chat and a cup of tea'. 'Half an hour at the most,' said the policeman.

'Three hours at least,' I replied, 'I know Egypt.'

I returned to Serbrock. Without contacts in Egypt, indeed in much of the world, you're a dead duck. Serbrock told al-Banna to do all he could to switch off this syndrome. 'Do you know the story of the ant that turned into an elephant?' he said. Al-Banna was now running about like the March Hare trying to switch off a crisis that he had so energetically engineered. Then he disappeared, realising that it was too late. The policeman said, 'Just half an hour and a cup of tea; half an hour and a cup of tea.'

The hotel was teeming with contacts whom I could have used at this stage. Some, including Said Zulfiqar, the Agha Khan's sophisticated representative in Egypt, had direct access to the Presidency. But not wanting to embarrass my friends I decided to go with a police escort to the tourist police station and sort out what I believed would only be a 'little trouble'. The policeman refused to come with me, which was sinister, so I went with his very sympathetic assistant who kept repeating kindly '*Ma fish mushkila*' ('No problem').

At the tourist police station, the young, cynical policeman treated me with complete contempt, turning to his companion to say: 'This man speaks *wahesh* [muck] about Egypt.' The policeman began writing a five-page report in Arabic. He flipped through my telex and asked one question only; 'All this?' meaning, 'All these pages of "muck" about Egypt?' I explained in Arabic that the article was balanced and that taking phrases such as 'rotten wood' out of context, the tenor of the article was completely misunderstood. I had written that it was pleasing to see that Egypt's present, clean regime had allowed the rotten wood of negligent urban planning to be revealed.

I asked him how he could write a five-page report when he had not asked me a single other question. He ignored me as if I were the devil himself. After about an hour he stood up abruptly, handed his report to my police colleague and told him to take me 'somewhere'. 'Where am I going?' I asked. 'To the Mabahith Amn ad-Daula [State Security],' he said with Gestapo-like chill in his voice.

We returned to the street but the police driver had disappeared so we hailed a taxi. When we reached the State Security building at the back of the Ministry of the Interior in Garden City, the guards were reluctant to let a foreigner in. It was not the sort of place that Europeans went to. But a document was shown and we entered a courtyard and climbed to the second floor where I was ushered into a spacious office, heavily and vulgarly furnished. Behind an enormous desk sat an official who was watching a 1950s black and white film with Faten Hammama in the lead role. I asked him why I had been arrested. 'Because we must know everything,' he replied with emphasis on the 'everything'.

The phone rang and when he picked up the receiver he repeated the phrase 'Speaks *wahesh* about Egypt' which had been passed from the tourist policeman in the Marriott like a Chinese whisper. When I wanted to go the lavatory I was led down the corridor by two guards and when the man left his office for some moments a guard was stationed at the door to ensure that I did not run amuck. When the director returned he told me I had to wait for two hours until his director returned. Shortly after this he called in a *bawwab* and told him to take me somewhere to wait.

I imagined that I might be taken to a scruffy waiting-room but the *bawwab* presumably knew only one place to take his prisoners. He led me down into the courtyard, down some steps at the side of the building into a series of dark subterranean corridors where we had to squeeze past old papers and litter. As we passed the well of the building I heard the shrill squealing of rats. '*Far*' ('Mice'), I said, forgetting the word for 'rat', and my guide nodded in pleasant agreement.

At the end of the corridor we turned a corner. There, around a table, sat three dirty men. I found an old school chair and sat down in the corridor. The air smelt of dank urine. The men told me quite pleasantly to enter the cell in front of their table. I refused, explaining that I was quite happy on my chair which had now become my only symbol of liberty. The men became angry, insisting I enter the cell. I refused. They approached me, prepared to coerce me. Tired and hungry, I lost my temper and waved my chair at them.

At that moment an unshaven young man emerged from the cell and asked me nicely to come into his cell as he and his colleague would be glad of my company. I said that, in that case, I would be glad to join them and picked up my chair. But the trio of guards announced in once voice that that could not be. A chair was forbidden. There were nice blankets in the cell but chairs were utterly *mamnoo* (forbidden). I became angry again but my cell-mate said, 'Come, let's forget the chair. Come in and talk with us.' So reluctantly I put down my last link with freedom and followed him in.

The cell was about ten foot by eight. It was lit by a cracked neon light. There was a small barred window at the back. Hanging from each wall were big brass rings presumably to attach manacles. The walls were scrawled with Palestinian graffiti, 'Long live Arafat,' 'Long live Abu Iyad,' etc. The floor was scattered with dirty grey blankets and there were piles of fruit-peel in the corners. Under one of the blankets lay a big man with a sad, round, unshaven face.

Neither spoke English so we spoke entirely in Arabic. The young man was Egyptian and had studied agriculture in Vienna. He had been picked up by State Security in Khartoum and sent back for trial in Cairo. He didn't, he assured me, know why he had been arrested although I could hardly expect these men to trust their confidences to a foreigner and a potential spy. I guessed that he was a Muslim Brother since the Brotherhood or

Ikhwan were enjoying considerable prestige in Sudan at that time, with their leader Hassan Turabi acting virtually as President Nimeiri's right-hand man. Some months later in early 1985 Nimeiri was to crush the Ikhwan and arrest Turabi, shortly before his own demise in an army coup led by Swar ad-Dahab. 'This is the central State Security building in the whole Arab world,' my colleague told me with a mixture of warning and pride.

The Palestinian was pathetic and aloof. He clearly didn't trust me. When I asked why he had been arrested he simply replied, 'I'm a Palestinian –what else?' I gave the men cigarettes and they offered me an orange which I was reluctant to accept as they had no money and no food was served by the authorities. They explained that they had both been in the cell for three days and expected to be interrogated the following day. Habeas corpus applies in Egypt and prisoners must be brought before a magistrate within three days of their arrest.

'Is this the first time you've been interrogated?' asked the young man nicely. I explained that it was. I was a debutante. I asked how long I would be held. The young man said, 'Just a day or so, probably.' The Palestinian said ominously, 'You can never tell.' They asked me why I had been arrested. I replied that I had quoted speakers at the conference saying that Cairo's buildings were crumbling and that the streets were dirty. 'Oh, you shouldn't write things like that,' said the young man. 'You should write positive things about Egypt, not negative things.' I replied that I loved Egypt and that I was criticising it in the way I would criticise England. President Mubarak had often stressed that there was a free press in Egypt and the job of a journalist was not to make things look pretty but to tell the truth. But the young man looked incredulous. His sympathies clearly lay with Ashraf al-Banna, the tourist police chief, the State Security man, indeed the whole bureaucratic network through which I had passed that day.

I learnt much about Egypt in that prison cell. I think that had I been a criminal I would have enjoyed more sympathy than I did for criticising urban planning in Egypt, even if I was merely quoting from speeches given by people at the conference from the Prime Minister downwards.

I fell asleep under the neon light for an hour or so and when the guards opened the cell door I had been in it for four hours. I had begun to believe that I would remain in that cell for some days at least.

I was led down the corridors, up the steps, into the courtyard – it was night – and up to the second floor again. There I was ushered into a respectable office where an intelligent-looking man sat behind a desk. 'Please sit down,' he said as if I were coming for an interview.

'I refuse to answer any questions,' I said, 'I refuse to be interrogated until the British Ambassador comes here. I've been locked up for four hours in a horrible cell for writing an article and I demand an explanation.'

The man smiled with the utmost charm and said, 'Please, you are free to go now. There is the door. Please go, if you wish. However, my only request to you is that you be my "jest" and have a cup of tea with me. I simply want you to be my "jest" for a few minutes so that we can talk together.' I subdued a giggle at his attempt at avoiding the Egyptian 'g'.

Tea and cigarettes were brought. 'Do you write many articles about Egypt?' asked my interrogator for, despite the charm, this was an interrogation.

'Listen,' I replied, 'have you read the article I wrote on the conference?'

There is a skill in the tactics of Egypt's State Security. Perhaps intensive training by the KGB in the Nasser era and its many years of immense influence throughout the Arab world is responsible for this. The man handed me my article and said, 'Please publish it. We have a free press in Egypt.'

I asked, 'So why was I arrested?'

He replied, 'You were not arrested, we simply want to know who you are.'

So I explained who I was, who I worked for, where I lived. Indeed, I gave him so much information about myself that very little remained to be asked. I spoke to him in Arabic and even quoted a pre-Islamic poem to prove that I had studied Arabic classically. Before I left I asked him for his card. 'Please contact me if I can ever be of help to you,' he said. I promised him I would.

It was now ten o'clock at night. When I reached my flat two close friends, the *Newsweek* Bureau Chief, Liz Colton, and her photographer, Anna Clopet, were waiting for me in a car outside. I gathered from them that my plight had not been neglected. At that moment Adel Sabet emerged from the flat of Teddy Maggar next door. 'The Ambassador and Malise are scouring the streets looking for you,' said Adel with, I knew, considerable exaggeration.

Adel, Teddy and I went to the Agha Khan's press room at the Marriott where I was received with immense care and sympathy. When we dined, some twenty of us, that night I discovered from the journalists that my arrest had virtually coincided with that of two Britons, Shiner and Gill, accused of being sent to Egypt by the Libyans to assassinate Al-Bakkoush, a Prime Minister under the former King Idris. Egypt's State Security had uncovered the plot without revealing their discovery and produced a photograph of the bloody corpse of Al-Bakkoush. When Tripoli Radio heroically announced the success of the assassination, Al-Bakkoush was revealed, nervous but alive, to the journalists at a press conference. The photograph of the corpse had been faked.

16

No riots, please, we're British

When I visited Khartoum as a petroleum consultant in February 1984 the open spirit of this much-loved city had been shattered by the imposition of Islamic law and public executions and mutilations, by an impending civil war in the south, and by virtual economic collapse throughout Sudan.

Breakfast among the white, sunlit arches of the Britishers-only Sudan Club was where the stories of killings and kidnappings in the black, animist-Christian south began. But it was also the happiest time of day in this last vestige of Empire, the perfect setting for a Somerset Maugham novel.

The balconies of huge, high-ceilinged bedrooms with their slow turning fans look over clean-cut lawns and tumbling frangipani and bougainvillaea or upon an antique banyan tree sprawling out over its hundred roots. I would be awoken at 7.00 in the crisp and silent dawn by Ibrahim or Musa, as biblical as they sounded in bright, white *gelebiahs* and billowing turbans and glittering smiles on black, Nuer faces.

The magnificent former club was now the headquarters of the Sudan Socialist Union, the heart of President Nimeiri's regime. It was sequestrated in 1970 and the club moved to this pretty, nineteenth-century building in the heart of town. On Fridays British expatriates would gather on the lawn to watch a film or rehearse for *The Boyfriend*. But the banning of alcohol in late 1983 had struck at the club's heart and the riots of that week in February had reduced its clientele, apart from its regulars, to a trickle. Only on Fridays was everyone to be found lounging about the pool exchanging stories of the 'events'. Top oilmen with whom I and the journalists had fought to obtain interviews could be seen sprawled on deck chairs and trying to avoid eye contact with any of us.

The club's regulars formed one of those little tantalising groups that you find at the corners of empire. John Abazah was the handsome, middle-aged Egyptian whose pale face and British public-school accent gave him the air of an Oxford don. There was fat, smiley Ladi Marmol, the Czech pilot. Ladi had been visiting Khartoum regularly for three years to fight through the courts to regain his half-million-dollar hangar which had been sequestrated and given to a public sector company. Ladi was a pivot of information about the killings in the swamps and jungles of the south. There was Philip Wintour, the young Englishman, a Cambridge graduate who had started a boat-yard in Juba, the southern Equatorial capital. He knew every inch of the south and was the worst hit of all of us by the impending civil war and deadly strikes at foreign workers there.

There were the journalists who used the club as a quiet exile where they could share story and rumour alike. Carol Berger, the BBC and *Guardian* stringer, had had her flat raided two days earlier by thieves who put a knife to her throat. When they left, she found her stolen money flung on the floor of the next room. Some days later, via 'opposition sources', she discovered that they were security men. They wanted, it seemed, to encourage her to leave the country without having to expel her and risk publicity embarrassing to the government. She booked a flight out for three days later. There was Gill Lusk, the *Times* stringer who had a Sudanese boy-friend and was reluctant to inherit Carol's dangerous string and risk death threats and expulsion.

My oil service company wanted to build part of a marine terminal on the Red Sea coast near Port Sudan, the end of a pipeline from Bentiu in the south for which the Italian company Snamprojetti had recently won the contract from the US oil company Chevron. The Anya Nya 2 guerrillas in the south were making three demands to the government in Khartoum. The recent redivision of the south into three self-governing regions should be rescinded and the south should be unified again with its capital at Juba. No attempt should be made to impose Islamic law in the south which is at least nominally Christian. The pipeline, which the southerners saw as an attempt by the Arab and once slave-trading north to export southern oil in exchange for hard currency which would only benefit the north, should be cancelled. Instead, a refinery should be built in Bentiu and the oil shipped north by boat or truck.

Some weeks before my visit three Chevron employees at the Rub' Kona compound near Bentiu had been murdered by guerrillas, ruthless men as the word Anya Nya implies. (Anya Nya means a poison made from snake venom and the mildewed bark of a tree.) On the day that I arrived it was reported that seven employees of CCI, a French company cutting a canal through Jonglei, had been kidnapped and taken probably to Ethiopia. The Jonglei Canal project aimed to drain the swamps of the Sudd, roughly the size of England, and to increase the flow of the Nile north. Many Sudanese believe that the project would mainly benefit the Egyptians by increasing the flow of water into the Aswan High Dam.

Two days after my arrival an Australian pilot had flown to Jonglei and been murdered in his bed the night he arrived. Ladi had been his friend and had helped him refuel. Ladi was almost crying over breakfast. 'Won day you seet dreenking cowfee in ze club with a frent and ze nex day heez ded.'

I drove early the following day through still, cool Khartoum to the 'Extension' quarter where the Chevron offices are, passing a wood-veranda'ed building with a big notice reading 'Venereal diseases clinic'. I could see pretty Sudanese women in diaphanous *tobes* wandering about the hemp beds of the open, first-floor verandas.

Chevron was heavily guarded. According to rumour a man had been seen wandering the Riyadh area carrying a sub-machine gun and looking for Chevron family homes. 'We're pulling out of the south,' Chevron's man told me. 'It's too dangerous to operate any more.'

Back at the club news was filtering through of a guerrilla attack on four huge passenger barges strung together on the White Nile. Out of 1,000 passengers, 300 were said to have been killed. An hour later the rumours were confirmed by Carol on the BBC. The local Arabic press maintained that a paraffin stove had set fire but that nobody had been killed. Within days it became clear that up to 1,000 people had died.

My company's agent's agent (the agent was the Sudanese Director of Dubai Municipality) was the Chairman of Friendship Hall, a dapper, retired general called Mr Fakhi who excelled in the kind of nonsense public relations that exasperates and eventually reduces to a frustrated silence the inquisitive reporter.

Toad Hall, as I couldn't resist calling it, is a huge white building built by the Chinese for the 1973 Organisation of African Unity Conference. Impeccably clean but almost completely empty, the hall is a warren of well-equipped theatres and conference halls.

The general sent a car around for me. I was led through the immense main hall glimmering with factory-built chandeliers and down a long corridor into a big reception room. In the reception room stood a long board-room table and a row of chairs whose legs were hidden with white, frilly skirtings. At the end of the room was a massive, empty desk and behind the desk sat a slim man of a certain age wearing a khaki pyjama suit.

The general leapt up smiling from behind his desk. 'Mr Mostyn, what a pleasure! I have been told to look after all your interests. Wherever you wish to go I shall arrange for you to go. Whoever you wish to see I shall arrange for you to see. My car is at your disposal. Please regard my Hall as your home.' The general ordered me *kirkaday* and brought out fat albums of photographs of his father, Kaimakam Yuzpashi al-Fikr, receiving the OBE for saving a British police commandant from a furious Khartoum mob in 1953. 'Sadly, the commandant subsequently died of his wounds,' said the general.

I devoted half an hour to greetings and album gazing, then I casually mentioned that I felt that the instability in the south might jeopardise my company's plans.

'But, no. No, there is no problem at all,' said the general. 'Everything is entirely under control. In two weeks the rains will come and the jungle trenches will fill with water and the guerrillas will be unable to operate.'

'But surely the army will be unable to operate and the guerrillas will flourish.'

'Yes, yes. No, no. It is all being solved. There are no guerrillas. They are all Ethiopians and Libyans. It's a Communist plot. The government made the mistake of not sending in the army at once after the November attack.'

'Oh, so there is a problem. The army cannot contain the guerrillas and foreign companies are pulling out because their employees cannot be guaranteed protection from attack.'

'Please, Mr Mostyn, have some more *kirkaday*. Everything is fine. Everything is excellent. Please let my servant show you around the Hall.'

I visited the French oil company Total who were operating betwen Juba and the southren town of Bor near the Ethiopian border. 'We fly a white flag from our compound,' said pleasant Monsieur Touranshed. 'We are in touch with local chiefs. We have told the southerners loud and clear that we have their inteıests at heart. We are apolitical. But we are very, very frightened.' Until the previous November kidnappings of Chevron employees, Chevron had apparently felt safe despite warnings from the CCI company at Jonglei that they were not. When the CCI employees, including a pregnant woman, were kidnapped, nobody felt safe any more.

When I returned to the Hall the general said, 'You see Mr Mostyn, everything is all right now, huge battalions of troops [he spread his arms out wide to demonstrate the mass] have been sent down to the south. The trouble is over, Chevron will be returning to Bentiu quite soon.' According to my more reliable sources southern soldiers were going over to the Anya Nya in droves while Muslim northerners were terrified of duty in the south. The Anya Nya regarded anywhere in which northern soldiers were involved as fair game. 'The solution,' said the general from behind his empty desk, 'is quite straightforward. Send down the troops and smash the guerrillas.'

'But during seventeen years of civil war this policy failed and it was Nimeiri's peace dialogue with the Addis Ababa Conference that led to the concordat which brought peace.'

'That was different,' said the general. 'That was a war between southerners and northerners. This time it is Ethiopians and Libyans disguised as southerners attacking northerners.' Ah, so that was it!

I was invited to lunch by the British Ambassador, Dick Fyjis-Walker, a well-preserved man with a big walrus moustache, and his beautiful, accomplished young German wife, Gabie. When I reached the Residence, a large square 1960s building with aluminium slats which a Sudanese visitor had compared with a transistor radio, crowds of students were milling at the end of the street in the university campus area. The Fyjis-Walkers' loving Ethiopian nanny Giragesh led me into the garden where their child Matthew was playing. The marchers were approaching and shouting slogans to applause. Soon I smelt the smell of an acrid bonfire and began coughing and crying as the tear-gas seethed over the garden wall.

Matthew sobbed and we withdrew into the house. We piled into the Land Rover and drove out of Khartoum to a beautiful lush garden at Manshia on the banks of the Nile. Surrounded by dusty land and rubbish hanging in limp saplings, this garden with its luxuriant orchards, perfect lawns and tumbling bougainvillaea was a veritable Muslim Paradise. It shone with light and colour. Blood red flowers of bougainvillaea were freshly bright and trembled in the breeze. Across the river were wide dusty banks and clay and wattle villages and Sudanese in shorts held their white *gelebiahs* billowing like air-stockings in the wind.

We sat on the lawn discussing the rumours. Apparently the Sudanese staff at the Chevron Bentiu compound had been forewarned by the Anya Nya of the attack but had not dared tell their Western employers. The local Sudanese villagers had crept away as if by magic on the night before the attack. The riots at the university, I gathered, were unconnected at that stage with troubles in the south. The security forces had arrested and beaten up a student on the campus.

When we returned to Khartoum the streets were blocked off by mobs and burning towers. Black smoke billowed from the Burri power station exciting much rumour although it appeared to be a coincidental burning-off of dirty diesel fuel. We made a loop around the city and approached the Embassy Residence where burnt-out tyres were scattered in the street. At the Residence the Defence Attaché was looking in consternation for his wife. He couldn't give me a lift to the Sudan Club because he was going in the other direction, he said, as he drove off, it seemed, towards the club.

In the evening I returned to the Residence with Philip Wintour from the club to make sure all was well. There had been an electricity cut and there were no lights. We approached a mob at the end of the street to get information. Students were setting fire to a barricade they had built. 'Why are you doing this?' we asked.

'Because the *jihaz al-am* [security forces] invaded the campus and kidnapped two of our brothers. One is still in hospital.'

It transpired that for the first time ever the Muslim Brotherhood fundamentalists had been defeated by a left-wing coalition in the science and engineering faculty elections. We knocked on the door of the Residence and an angry-looking ambassador appeared with a torch, eventually smiling a little and thanking us for our trouble when he saw that we had not come to burn down the Residence.

When I returned to the Hall the following morning, the general was seated beside an old imam who was teaching him verses from the Qur'an. When I had last visited him he had been with a slick Lebanese businessman who could build fifteen-storey buildings in two months, the sort of buildings that I reminded myself to avoid. The general had printed invitations for me to invite my friends, above all the ambassador, to a dinner party at his house. I seemed to have carte blanche to invite whom I liked and I took three invitations to the British Embassy. But nobody from the embassy, the ambassador included, came. Wherever I went I had my cards and a big square printed map of the general's house.

On the following day there were riots all over Khartoum. There'll be a coup today or tomorrow, buzzed the club. My driver was terrified. We drove to the national oil company, GPC, but most of the roads were barred off. We drove to the centre of the town to confirm my booking at Egypt Air but columns of riot police with round wooden shields were marching down the stone-strewn central thoroughfare, Sharia Jumhuriah, and shop-keepers were desperately pulling down their shutters. We reached the club before the demonstrators and my driver drove off again with a roar of panic.

Inside the club expatriates in bikinis were lounging in the sun. I stood outside the gate with two black servants as we waited for the chanting mob to reach our street. 'This is the end of injustice and Islamic law,' said one of the young black servants, a student

from Gedaref, 'now we're going to have a revolution.' The
marchers were mostly black southerners and when they reached
the corner of our street and saw my white face the girls leading
them pointed my way to suggest passing the club. Thinking they
intended to ransack the club I entered quietly but they marched
past with a roar of 'Death to Nimeiri' and I gathered that they
simply wanted to show foreigners what they wanted.

I went to send a telex from the Greek-run Acropole Hotel.
The street was electric and the demonstrators could be heard
approaching again. The Greeks, mostly Sudan-born, looked
miserable. When the march filled the street again there were
slogans of 'Death to Nimeiri. End Islamic law. Food prices
down.' A southerner behind a pillar said, 'It's good, isn't it?
We're Christians, we don't want Islamic law. Nimeiri must go.
He only cares for the north.' I asked him whether the
demonstrators were anti-foreigner and he grasped me by the
shoulder and said, 'No, we like foreigners. We want them to
understand what we are asking for.'

I had dinner with an old friend, the bookseller Panos
Aristides, a Sudan-born Greek. 'I have seen this coming for
many years,' he said. 'Two years ago I sent my books down by
lorry to Juba. The rebels hijacked the lorry near Tolga on the
White Nile. They took out the driver and the other northerners
and shot them.' Panos is a big friendly man with an inner tension
that shows in badly bitten finger nails. He is one of the key
figures in the 1,200-strong Greek community who, Sudan-born,
love the country despite all. He resented the sixteen mainland
Greeks who taught at the big Greek school beside the embassy.
'They tell the children that they are nothing; that they are not
real Greeks but African Greeks, and the children come away with
an inferiority complex.'

On the seat of his car as we drove to the Greek Club for
dinner was a jar of what I thought was urine. 'Strong tea,' said
Panos as I sniffed the now wickedly illegal whisky. The Greek
Club, for its very Third World drabness, contrasted with the
bright little Sudan Club. It seemed to justify the indictment of
mainland Greeks that their Sudanese cousins had gone native. We
sat at a solitary table in a huge empty dining hall scattered with
cheap, decaying chairs. An irksome fly buzzed about the plastic

tablecloth almost as an accomplice of the old toothless waiter who told us almost everything was 'off, dear'.

Over *mezze* and steak Panos explained that the West must support Nimeiri. 'He's unpopular at the moment but he has encouraged Western business and allowed us to repatriate profits and he has encouraged all religious denominations to practise freely. It was Nimeiri who brought peace to the south. He has never been afraid to change his mind when necessary. After him there could be one hell of a deluge.'

The dinner with the general was a sad affair. He had lit up his green dome so that the guests could find their way: 'You see Riyadh is a new area and nobody knows their way around so I built a dome so that everyone could find my house.' One guest arrived two hours late because the local people told him the dome was a mosque, an impression generally held in the neighbourhood. It was a big house with a pleasant walled garden. An oblong of chairs were laid out and at the end was a bar from where the turbaned waiters served Coca Cola and water. Few of my invitees came but the general was waiting for only one, the ambassador.

'I left the invitation at the embassy,' I had told the general, 'so I don't know whether he can accept.'

'Oh, he will come,' replied the general. 'He is English. If he could not come he would send his apologies.' All evening the general glanced at the gate but the ambassador did not come and when time had passed and it was certain he would not come the general sat away from us sadly as we sipped our tonic waters to the murmur of mosquitoes.

Index